State & Local
Government

PETER LANG
New York • Washington, D.C./Baltimore • Boston
Bern • Frankfurt am Main • Berlin • Vienna • Paris

Michael Engel

State & Local Government

FUNDAMENTALS & PERSPECTIVES

PETER LANG
New York • Washington, D.C./Baltimore • Boston
Bern • Frankfurt am Main • Berlin • Vienna • Paris

Library of Congress Cataloging-in-Publication Data

Engel, Michael.
State and local government: fundamentals
and perspectives / Michael Engel.
p. cm.
1. State governments—United States.
2. Local government—United States. I. Title.
JK2408.E525   320.8'0973—dc21   98-14867
ISBN 0-8204-4111-2

Die Deutsche Bibliothek-CIP-Einheitsaufnahme

Engel, Michael:
State and local government: fundamentals and perspectives / Michael Engel.
–New York; Washington, D.C./Baltimore; Boston; Bern;
Frankfurt am Main; Berlin; Vienna; Paris: Lang.
ISBN 0-8204-4111-2

Cover design by James F. Brisson

The paper in this book meets the guidelines for permanence and durability
of the Committee on Production Guidelines for Book Longevity
of the Council of Library Resources.

© 1999 Peter Lang Publishing, Inc., New York

Printed in the United States of America

For Jackie, Sara, and Emily

Table of Contents

Introduction

The study of politics yields information that is crucial for making intelligent choices about how we live. The way our society organizes itself to deal with social and economic conflict forms the context within which individuals determine their own directions. Politics on the state and local levels in particular involves matters directly affecting the quality of our lives.

Unfortunately, many students do not agree. They, like many of their elders, feel that politics in general does not concern them and the supposed unsavory nature of politics and government is best left unexamined, perhaps because it cannot be changed. Studying politics often appears as boring memorization of facts about government, and in any case state and local politics seems to lack the significance and drama of national politics. This text intends to show the error of these points of view, which are based on an overly limited concept of politics, a vastly underestimated concept of the responsibilities of state and local governments, and a view of political science as mere data gathering.

The Nature of Politics and the Role of Government

Not only do political scientists disagree on a definition of politics, but many do not even try to define it. Generally, politics is seen as a particular social process or more narrowly, as a form of behavior. According to the former definition, it is the resolution of conflict, the activity of government, or the authoritative allocation of values (deciding whose political wants will be satisfied). According to the latter definition, politics is what politicians do every day to create consensus, or the exercise of power by those who have it.

Underlying this text is a broader definition of politics as a process of conflict over how society is to organize the allocation of what people need in order to live. The basic needs are food, clothing, and shelter; a longer list might include additional necessities such as health care, education, jobs, and community life. The conflict is universal and unceasing, and therefore politics involves everyone. A person who claims to be "apolitical" makes a conscious or unconscious decision to allow other people to determine what her or his life will be like. Abandoning involvement and interest in politics amounts to abandoning responsibility for oneself and others. This definition of politics reflects a distinct point of view, as do all the others, and thus each definition should be evaluated by the reader in terms of her or his own view of both the world and the nature of politics.

The primary but by no means exclusive institution of political decision making is government, however established, which is the major focus of the study of politics. In American politics more attention is reserved for national government, which makes crucial economic and military decisions, than for state and local governments, which are often unjustly ignored. State and local governments run the public schools and colleges, administer a variety of welfare services, conduct most of the criminal justice system, provide public health and safety services, decide how communities will be designed and organized, and in large measure structure the process by which we choose political leaders. The expansion of state and local governments has been proportionately greater than that of the federal government in recent years. Most importantly, state and local politics is at least in theory more accessible than national politics to direct participation. The possibility and practicality of experimentation and innovation on the state and local levels are also greater.

In short, states and localities constitute a significant political arena. In being concerned with getting an education, finding a job, and residing in a livable community, we have to understand and be involved with state and local politics.

Studying State and Local Politics

The primary purpose of learning about politics ought to be the development of a personal point of view on political matters, with the ultimate aim of participating in the political decision making that affects us. Neither memorizing facts nor merely hearing one particular political perspective to the exclusion of others will accomplish this. An individual must be able to evaluate the world of politics in terms of different possible explanations of how it operates.

Just as there are different forms of government, there are different ways of understanding how governments act and the reasons for their actions. Those ways are known as "theories"—and theories are essentially educated guesses about how parts of a system fit together and relate to each other. This text will consider two theoretical frameworks: "consensus" and "conflict."

Governments make political decisions, which reflect one or more points of view on how political issues should be considered—these are "ideologies," that is, political value systems. The political conflict arising from opposing ideologies shapes state and local public policies. In order to affect the outcome, a person must take sides. This text will examine three such ideologies: conservative, liberal, and socialist.

The Plan of the Text

The book begins by establishing the theoretical and structural context: describing the theories and applying them to the federal system. Chapters 3 to 8 apply these theories to the overall structure of state and local government and their specific components and analyze the expression of political action within communities and through the democratic process. Following a discussion of the three ideologies (Chapter 9), the text describes the major issues in states and localities and enumerates ideological alternatives in four policy areas: public finance (Chapter 10), economic development (Chapter 11), welfare (Chapter 12), and education (Chapter 13).

The goals of this text are to enable the reader to: (1) be familiar with the structure of state and local government, the democratic process, and state and local political issues; (2) observe how state and local government and politics work in terms of the theories and draw the appropriate conclusions; (3) develop a more or less consistent personal point of view on major state and local policy issues and be prepared to debate and defend it; and (4) be motivated to participate thoughtfully in state and local politics at the appropriate level.

Chapter 1: Theoretical Approaches

Most people prefer to learn facts rather than theories. Facts are certainties that supposedly make up "science" and are easy to deal with, since they are not open to question. Theories, on the other hand, are thought of as airy inventions of the mind with no relation to the "real world." Perhaps then that is why most texts in social science, including state and local politics, focus on facts and discuss theories marginally, if at all. In view of this, the use of theory as a starting point requires an explanation.

Why Theory?

Contrary to the stereotype, theories are an indispensable means of explaining the world. A theory is an attempt to describe relationships among facts, to create a whole out of parts, and to provide a context for understanding and evaluating those parts. Social scientists agree that theory is important but differ on how to develop and use it. The dominant approach to social science sees theory as the end result of collecting facts, which means, in practice, specializing in a relatively narrow field of research and amassing substantial amounts of data based on "objective" experimentation and observation. Theorizing on the grand scale, from this point of view, falls outside the realm of science and is best left to philosophers; that is why textbooks are filled with facts and professional journals are made up of mathematical and statistical studies of esoteric subjects.

An alternative approach sees the collection and evaluation of facts as useful only in the context of testing a given theory. In other words, a social scientist must start with some general idea of how things may fit together—a guess, perhaps—and choose to analyze those facts which may lead to a confirmation or a rejection of the theory. This provides a means of sorting through a mass of data in pursuit of a particular goal by allowing people to ask the right questions before they try to collect the answers.

The analysis of state and local politics in this text is based on the alternative approach because the goal here, as previously mentioned, is to provide readers with the means for developing their own points of view. A collection of facts alone will not do this. The appropriate tool is theory applied to the evaluation of facts and vice versa, and a choice of theories will further ensure that this approach is not limited.

Theories in State and Local Politics

Most contemporary studies of American politics, including state and local politics, fall within the boundaries of either of two theoretical frameworks, which we shall call "consensus" and "conflict." They will be used in this text to evaluate the institutions and processes of state and local politics.

Theories of society generally start from assumptions about what holds a society together and what pulls it apart. "Consensus" theories assume that a workable, stable society is based on a set of social, economic, and political values shared by most of its members. This means that there are no irreconcilable or permanently polarizing conflicts among its people, and that the institutions of society are oriented toward maintaining social stability by preserving and strengthening a consensus on values. The role of government in particular is to facilitate this process by promoting public policies based on compromise among groups with competing demands. If the government and other societal institutions are doing their jobs properly, the result should be a society which remains stable by accommodating as much as possible the basic needs and wants of most of its people. Obviously, this process does not always work smoothly, and in some cases it does not work at all. The United States and other economically developed "westernized" societies are considered to be "functional" systems because their basic institutions generally work to maintain a value consensus and social stability. "Dysfunctional" social systems, such as exist in many less developed nations, degenerate or are destroyed as a result of either institutional inflexibility or unsuitability, or persistent and severe internal conflict. From this point of view, our system can therefore provide a model of economic and political development for less fortunate countries. American government is not perfect, but it provides a means for improvement through incremental change, which is all our society requires.

"Conflict" theories reject all of these assumptions. They claim instead that long-term social stability is an illusion, and that societies constantly change, often radically, as conflicts over basic values are fought out in the political arena. Every society is in one way or another split between people who possess wealth and power and those who do not. The conflicts between them are built into the social structure and can ultimately be reconciled only by the victory of one side or the other. From this point of view, politics in the long run is a "zero-sum game"— if the rich and powerful win, the poor and powerless lose, and vice-versa. Any consensus on social values in this context is therefore an illusion. This fundamental struggle, however, may not be all that apparent or uncomplicated. In most societies it is connected with and compounded (and in certain cases obscured) by racial, ethnic, gender, and other group conflicts. Nor is the difference between the "haves" and "have nots" necessarily explicit or clear-cut, especially in societies which, like the United States, appear to have a substantial middle class. Nonetheless, conflict theorists argue that, appearances notwithstanding, these contests arise in all societies and are played out in the political arena. The purpose of government is to resolve them in the interests of those who hold power in the society. Its particular method of doing so and the solutions it comes up with depend on who is in charge and what the balance of power is within the society. Normal societies are therefore in an endless state of transition, sometimes gradual and peaceful but more often sudden and even violent. What consensus theorists see as unity, compromise, and stability appears to conflict theorists as repression, co-optation, and stagnation. From that perspective, the United States is long overdue for radical political change.

Each of these frameworks is represented by more specific theoretical applications in the various social sciences. In political science, the most important of these are pluralist, elite, and Marxist theories.

Pluralism is consensus theory applied to political science. It assumes that capitalism and liberal democracy are among the values consciously and voluntarily shared by most Americans and that a system of dispersed political power, limited government, and incremental political change keeps the society going by resolving competition among interest groups.

Elite theory seems to share some of the characteristics of both conflict and consensus theories, but its essential assumptions are consistent with the former. While agreeing with consensus theorists that societies are held together by a shared value system, it argues that those values are imposed by a powerful elite on the masses through control of government, the media, schools, and other major social and economic institutions. Like the Marxists, elite theorists maintain that the interests of the elite and of the masses are in sharp conflict, but repression and manipulation by the elite keep the masses in line. Political change on behalf of the interests of the masses is therefore hard to achieve. Elite theory focuses on the mechanisms of power that maintain the position of the ruling class.

A classic conflict theory is Marxism, which sees all societies as divided by conflict among social classes whose interests are inherently opposed as a result of how the capitalist system operates. There is no system of shared values. Social stability is not a long-term condition; it is a way station between larger or smaller social transformations constantly generated by class conflict. Marxist theory is concerned with these mechanisms of conflict and change which it both hopes and assumes will lead to a socialist society.

Historical Background

Each theory in political science has its own history. Pluralism originated in the early part of this century. Until then, most political analysis in America was strictly institutional, focusing exclusively on the constitutional and legal structure of government. This narrow approach failed to satisfy some scholars, who began to argue that politics was really an outgrowth of group conflicts in society. From this beginning in what was called "group theory," pluralism developed into a general theory of American politics, which by the 1950s had become the dominant theory—a position it still holds. Pluralist theory provides both the starting point for most political research done in the United States and the framework for most textbooks in American politics.

Elite theory has its origins in Europe around 1900 in the writings of Gaetano Mosca, Vilifredo Pareto, and Robert Michels, who analyzed politics in terms of the relationships between elites and masses. The first thorough attempt to analyze American politics along the lines of elite theory was C. Wright Mills's *The Power Elite*, published in 1956. This book created a great deal of controversy, especially since it came out during a period in American history when challenging orthodox theories, such as pluralism, was unpopular. Subsequent elaborations of elite theory have generally used Mills's work as a starting point. Much of the research in American politics, as do many textbooks, focuses on the pluralist-elitist debate over the nature of power in American society.

Marxism, of course, has its origins in the writings of Karl Marx. Most of his voluminous writings involve analysis of the workings of the capitalist economy. Many important political and social issues, such as the nature of social classes and the role of the state under capitalism, were not fully discussed by Marx himself. Elaboration on these topics and others, including what a socialist system would be like, was left to subsequent writers and thinkers, who often came into conflict with each other over interpretations of Marxist theory. Until recently, the expansion of Marxist theory in the United States has been severely hindered by periodic attempts to suppress socialist or communist ideas as well as by the public belief that there is an automatic connection between Marxism and the former Soviet Union. Paradoxically, many now argue that the collapse of the Soviet system demonstrates that Marxist theory is now obsolete or irrelevant. Most American Marxists, however, have always rejected both the Soviet version of Marxism and the Soviet form of government and thus claim that these events require a re-examination of classical Marxism but do not disprove it. They have also begun to expand Marxist analysis beyond issues of social class divisions to include concerns about race and gender. The future of Marxist theory is in question, but it still provides a useful alternative perspective in political science.

Applying Political Theories

The differences between consensus and conflict theories can most clearly be illustrated by their answers to certain fundamental political questions:

1. What are the most important political divisions and what kind of conflict do such divisions produce?
2. What characterizes political change and development?
3. What role does government play in the society?
4. What is the nature of the political process?
5. What political goals are desirable for the future?

Cleavage and Conflict

Consensus theorists conceive of politics in America as a process of competition among interest groups—voluntary organizations whose purpose is to promote a particular political or economic goal. That competition goes on within the framework of agreement on basic societal values and the "rules of the game." Many Americans belong to one or more such groups, and most others at least identify with a group. Interest groups thus constitute the primary means by which Americans attempt to influence government. There is no permanent polarization among these groups in terms of social class, gender, race and ethnicity, or region. They arrange themselves in different combinations with different political positions depending on the particular issue involved. Moreover, individual membership in one group often overlaps with membership in another. Therefore the cleavages among all these groups are crosscutting and constantly shifting. No one group or set of groups is in a sufficiently powerful position in the long run to get everything it wants, and no group need be entirely excluded from the political process. Consensus theorists do differ among themselves as to just how much influence each group has; many acknowledge that business groups have a predominant and perhaps disproportionate influence. The result is that political conflict in the United States is rarely intense, since the stakes are limited. In order to build coalitions to maximize influence, groups must negotiate, bargain, and compromise, thus avoiding sharp and enduring differences. Groups have to accept the consensual rules of the game to be effective politically. The process thus works to maintain the stable operation of the political system.

Conflict theorists believe that American politics—indeed, politics in every society—can be characterized by sharp and irreconcilable conflicts among distinct sectors of the society. They differ, however, on the question of which conflicts are the most significant. According to elite theorists, the basic cleavage in American politics is between a power elite on the one hand and the mass public on the other. C. Wright Mills defined the power elite as "composed of men whose positions enable them to transcend the ordinary environments of men and women; they are in positions to make decisions having major consequences. . . . They rule the big corporations. They run the machinery of the state and claim its prerogatives. They direct the military establishment. . . . Insofar as national events are decided the Power Elite are those who decide them" (1956, 3, 18). Michael Parenti describes the United States as a "plutocracy": "Almost all the social institutions existing in society . . . are under pluto-cratic control, ruled by nonelected, self-selected, self-perpetuating groups of affluent corporate representatives answerable to no one but them-selves" (1988, 36).

These theorists differ as to the structure of the power elite. Thomas R. Dye, for example, identifies 7,314 "elite positions" as the institutional basis of the U.S. power elite (1983, 14). G. William Domhoff talks of the power elite as the "leadership group or operating arm of the ruling class" (1978, 13). In any case, though, this elite is overwhelmingly white and male. On the other side, they agree, there is a fragmented and pow-erless mass public, rendered politically impotent because it is dominated, manipulated, and repressed by the power elite. Between these extremes there exists a middle level of power, groups and institutions such as small property owners, labor unions, and political parties which cannot become part of the elite but have not yet been suppressed into the mass. This overall national picture is duplicated on the state and local levels.

From this perspective it is often more accurate to speak of domina-tion rather than conflict as characterizing the day-to-day political rela-tionship between the power elite and the mass public. Through its finan-cial control of the political process, its ownership of the media, and its control of the educational system, the power elite is generally successful in shaping the political expressions of the masses. Elite theorists agree that American society, indeed all societies, can be divided into the rulers and the ruled. The power of the rulers flows from their institutional po-sitions, and they are little influenced by those over whom they hold power.

Marxists base their analysis of politics on the concept of social class. There is, however, no single Marxist definition of class. Since Marx never thoroughly explained the concept, there has been some dispute among Marxists as to its precise meaning. On the most general level, however, Marxists understand class as a group of people who over time share a similar position in terms of relative economic power, in particular the extent of productive resources they own and control. As a result, each class has a common history, a similar set of values and life experi-ences, a particular kind of internal social relationship, and a particular relationship to the other classes. If people are also aware of being part of a class ("class-conscious"), which may not always be the case, they may begin to share common political interests and act together as a political unit, leading to the possibility of revolutionary change.

There are at least four significant classes in capitalist society: (1) a capitalist class, which owns and controls the society's "means of production"; (2) a middle class of independent professionals, small businesspeople, and farmers; (3) a working class composed of wage earners of all kinds; and (4) a lower class consisting of those discarded by the capitalist system—the very poor, the homeless, and people forced to live off petty crime. Marx believed that the economic and political interests of the different classes, especially capitalists and workers, are inherently and permanently in conflict. He asserted that capitalists' profits are derived from the "surplus value" produced by workers, that is, the difference between the value of what they produce (not the same thing as the market price, according to Marx) and the wages paid to them. Higher profits thus depend on increasing surplus value by reducing the workers' standard of living or making them work harder for less money. Political conflict naturally erupts as a consequence. The conflict may vary in intensity, depending on circumstances of time or place, but Marx argued that ultimately all political disputes are rooted in the conflict between capitalists and workers. He believed that ultimately the conflict would be resolved by a socialist revolution organized by the working class; it therefore becomes the task of Marxists to further that historic goal.

It should be added that American and European Marxists have largely abandoned such revolutionary strategies, opting to work for socialism through peaceful and democratic means. They have also generally discarded Marx's predictions of an inevitable historical transition to communism and have attempted to broaden his analysis to recognize that class conflict interacts with racial and gender conflict, especially in the United States. Most Marxists now believe that divisions based on gender and race as well as social class must be taken into account in order to formulate an accurate analysis of American society and a viable strategy for political change.

Political Change and Development

The approach of each theory to the issue of political change and development is directly related to its perspectives on the extent of political conflict among Americans and how it is expressed. Consensus theory rests on the assumption that American society survives on the basis of consensus on essential social and political values. Robert Dahl (1981, 42) says that "the early tendency toward a widely shared set of beliefs seems to have persisted throughout American history." He cites survey research indicating widespread support for democracy as a form of government, belief in the Constitution and in appropriate legal methods of change, an unwillingness to transform existing economic institutions, and a faith in the possibilities of personal achievement. There are of course differences in the depth and distribution of consensus over time, but overall support for the existing system remains strong. Combined with the crosscutting cleavages of political conflict, this consensus normally precludes a need or desire for radical change. To put it simply, most Americans, whatever their complaints about government, like their system pretty much the way it is. Intense conflict and agitation for change arise in the United States every thirty or forty years, but they have up to now been part of the normal pattern of politics. As Dahl puts it, "The system encourages incremental changes; it discourages comprehensive change. It facilitates the negotiation of moderate conflict" (1981, 219). This is one of its strengths, according to consensus theory. With the important exception of the Civil War, the American political system has kept its balance and stability by resolving conflict through slow, piecemeal policy changes. It follows that those interest groups willing to abide by the rules of the game have a reasonable chance to gain specific, limited benefits from the political system.

Conflict theorists differ among themselves on the extent to which radical political change is possible (although they all agree it is desirable) and the methods by which it can be achieved. Those who argue that the United States is under the control of a power elite believe that it has generally been able to keep the masses in line and is likely to continue to do so. A genuine democracy is an impossible dream. Insofar as dissent is expressed, the elite is usually able to co-opt or repress it. Thus political change and development within the existing system can be explained in terms of its usefulness in maintaining the power of the ruling class. This means that reform legislation is often planned by the elite itself and is not implemented unless it is consistent with the interests of the elite. Political change therefore does not really have much impact in the sense of improving the lives of the masses or redistributing benefits to them. No group organizing for political change will progress unless it accommodates itself to the likelihood that there will always be a ruling class. It must be emphasized that this does not mean that elite theorists favor rule by an elite; it is just that they see no realistic alternative.

Marxists argue that in fact the U.S. government often has been forced by organized movements of working-class people, women, and minority groups to make unwanted concessions. The level and the extent of those concessions depend on several factors: the unity of the capitalist class, its hold on public opinion, the makeup of the government at any particular time, and the political capacity of the working class to organize for its own interests (Fainstein and Fainstein 1978, 125–146). To the extent that the first is weak and the last is strong—which is infrequent—significant gains for the working class are possible. The opposite is more often the case, and capitalists are generally able to resist pressure for change. The contours of the class struggle determine the shape and direction of political change.

The Role of Government

The most crucial question is the role of government, since the purpose of this text is to provide alternative explanations for the workings of state and local governments.

The consensus theory of government rests on an analysis of its structure and social function. Pluralists argue that government in the United States, like the society over which it presides, is itself a collection of groups. Each branch of government (executive, legislative, judicial) is responsive to a different constituency. Each level of government (national, state, local) has a different geographical jurisdiction. Within each branch and each level there exists a multiplicity of interrelated departments, agencies, committees, courts, and the like. Rather than having one government, we have thousands of governments (over 85,000, to be precise) which—owing to their institutional rivalries and their relative lack of coordination—provide a neutral machinery for the impartial arbitration of group conflicts. Thus no interest group is always favored by government, and all interest groups have multiple, although not entirely equal, opportunities for influence.

Conflict theorists challenge the assertion that the state is politically neutral and accessible to all groups. Some analysts claim that the direction is set by the decision-making power of top governmental elites; Dye (1983, 14), for example, identifies 284 elite positions within the "governmental sector" of the national elite. These analysts emphasize the social class background and shared ideology of most decision makers as the basis for domination of the government by the ruling class. It follows that nonelite groups are likely to be deliberately excluded from access to decision making. Insofar as the purpose of government is to maintain the existing distribution of wealth and power, it will at the very least resist attempts to challenge that intent. Government officials thus have a stake in granting access to some groups and denying it to others. As G. William Domhoff (1990, 185) puts it,

> There are conflicts within the fragmented American state, but they primarily concern conflicts among segments of the ruling class . . . Middle-class reformers and working-class leaders often create pressure for change, especially on domestic issues, but they usually sign up on the side of one ruling-class segment or another. Farmers had their moments in the now-distant past, and trade unions had their innings in the 1930s. . . . However, most evidence suggests that the American ruling class has had more influence over its government in the twentieth century than any counterparts in other advanced European capitalist nations. . . . The most celebrated pluralist nation may be the least pluralist of the major democracies when it comes to political power on major issues.

Other conflict theorists see the government as somewhat more open to political change. Most Marxists would agree with Edward Greenberg (1979, 42), who states that "government policy is never a simple reflection of class interests, but the result of a complex class struggle which has both interclass and intraclass components. . . . The state is not merely a class instrument, though many of its activities can be so explained, but rather the product of class struggle." The Marxist economist Paul Sweezy claims that within a constitutional system "the ruling class operates within a definite framework, more or less restricted according to circumstances, which it can ignore only at the peril of losing its power altogether" (Gillam 1971, 48). From this point of view governments in America, although committed structurally and ideologically to defending capitalist interests as a whole, operate within limits that may require them to discipline parts of the capitalist class or to make genuine concessions to the working class, depending upon political circumstances. By the same token, both the capitalist class and the government are dominated by white males, who pursue racist and sexist policies to protect their own economic and political interests. Yet in the past thirty years, they have been forced to yield some of their power and privilege to minorities and women. The guiding principle may be capitalist ideology and interests but government can be pushed in anticapitalist directions if the working class, women, and racial minorities are sufficiently unified, organized, and politically active.

The Political Process in States and Localities

All of this can be combined into two composite pictures of state and local politics. In the view of consensus theorists, it is an ongoing process of negotiation, bargaining, and compromise that operates as interest groups try to advance their goals by gaining favorable government policies. Decision makers try to accommodate these demands, subject to the constitutional rules of the game and the particular configuration of constituency pressures. The result is incremental political change, which in the long run satisfies enough of the demands to maintain political stability. This precludes the need for radical change, since the system functions as democratically as can be expected. Many consensus theorists therefore study the behavior of interest groups, voters, and political institutions to understand how the overall balance of the system is maintained.

Conflict theorists see state and local politics as an endless struggle between those who have wealth and power and those who do not. They are, however, not in agreement about how the struggle turns out. To elite theorists, the political process is one of domination and manipulation of the mass public, resulting in state and local policies which favor elite privilege and power at the expense of everyone else. Genuine political change is unlikely; what appears to be significant political change is symbolic or illusory. These theorists therefore focus on the relationships between powerful individuals in elite positions in and out of government and examine how the behavior of state and local political institutions reflects the direction set by the elite. Political processes are analyzed in terms of their function of keeping the masses quiet.

Marxists, on the other hand, look at state and local politics as a process of class struggle, compounded by racial and gender conflict. There is an unending contest among classes to achieve their political and economic goals. The expression of that struggle varies in quality and intensity in each area over time, and is related to what is taking place nationwide. State and local governments, often fragmented and relatively weak, are staffed by individuals, disproportionately white, male, and middle- or upper-class, who largely share the same overall political and economic perspective and who work toward capitalist goals. Their success depends on the balance of power among social classes, which usually favors capitalist interests. Marxists thus focus on the impact of class, race, and gender conflict on state and local political institutions and processes, with particular emphasis on the nature of political change.

Table 1.1: A Comparison of Consensus and Conflict Theories

Questions	Consensus (Pluralist)	Conflict
What are the key sources of political conflict?	Competition among interest groups.	(Elite) Conflicts between elites and masses, and among competing elites. (Marxist) Conflicts among and within social classes.
What are the key sources of political stability?	Consensus on values and "rules of the game"; "cross-cutting cleavages" among interest groups.	Ruling class repression, co-optation, and control of instruments of political so-cialization (media, schools, etc.).
Who or what determines state action?	Citizens and groups in soci-ety organized through in-terest groups and political parties.	(Elite) Ruling class/power elite interests. (Marxist) Class/race/gender struggles and the constraints of capitalist democracy.
Is the state biased in favor of certain inter-ests?	The state is a neutral arena within which group com-petition occurs; the state acts as an "umpire."	(Elite) The state is an in-strument of the ruling class to control the masses. (Marxist) The state is sys-tematically biased in favor of capitalist class interests.
How is state policy made?	Negotiation, bargaining, and compromise among competing interest groups and government officials.	(Elite) Consensus within the ruling class. (Marxist) Consensus within the capitalist class limited by potential opposition from the working class.
What is the content of state policy?	Reflects the relative balance of interest group influence and public opinion.	(Elite) Reflects the interests of the power elite. (Marxist) Reflects the bal-ance of class forces in politi-cal and economic struggles.

Political Goals

Thus far we have dealt exclusively with what are called the "empirical" aspects of these political theories, that is, descriptions of the political process as it now operates. Each theory also has a "normative" aspect—a prescription for the future related to the empirical theory.

Consensus theorists are primarily concerned with maintaining overall political stability. Most are generally satisfied that existing political institutions and processes achieve that goal. But an increasing number see deterioration in the performance of the system. Robert Dahl (1982) lists the primary defects in "pluralist democracy" as excessive political inequality, exclusive concern with private interests rather than public goods, avoidance of certain crucial political issues, and an excess of public functions under private control. The root cause of these defects is too much economic inequality, which strengthens the hand of wealthier groups, creating a dangerous imbalance in the pluralist system. The solution, says Dahl, is incremental change toward greater equality, especially a limit on corporate power. Most consensus theorists would not go as far as Dahl but share his opinion that American political institutions must function equitably and efficiently to maintain public support. Many have recently expressed concern about the expense of political campaigns, along with a decline of "civility" and the rise of sharp ideological conflict in governing institutions. They believe, however, that these problems can be remedied by incremental reforms, and that major changes in the political system are unnecessary.

Conflict theorists of all kinds are in agreement that the existing system is unjust and requires drastic changes to make it more democratic and egalitarian. There is disagreement, however, as to just what kinds of strategies are needed to make these changes happen and whether such changes are even possible.

For the most part elite theorists believe that political realism dictates overall acceptance of elite rule, however unsatisfactory it may be. Their interpretation of history leads them to believe that all social institutions inevitably gravitate toward elite control, no matter how democratic their origins or intentions. There are nevertheless two pathways toward making elites more accountable. One is protest, even to the extent of violent disruption. The ruling class is concerned with maintaining order, so a threat of disorder may be sufficient to throw the rulers off balance and gain some concessions. A less risky path is trying to join the elite or trying to marshal enough resources to make deals with it. In either case, although a more responsible ruling class may be desirable, this is not easy to accomplish.

In the long run, Marxists favor the establishment of socialism (see Chapter 9) and an end to the power of the capitalist class. In a political environment such as ours, revolutionary methods are considered by most Marxists to be ineffective and self-defeating. Rather, the task is to increase the political organizing capabilities of the working class by building effective coalitions among groups who suffer social and economic disadvantages under capitalism. These groups could work together to fight for programs benefiting the poor, racial minorities, women, and working people in general. Ultimately, the goal would be to establish a political party which works for democratic socialism.

How Do We Choose Among Theories?

Verification of a theory requires formulating a hypothesis—a specific statement which can be tested to see if the theory holds up. This can be done by framing such statements in quantitative terms to allow for statistical analysis, and in fact most political scientists use this kind of methodology. But statistical methods, however useful they might be, are not indispensable. If we are asking the right questions and are willing to keep an open mind in examining all the data, there is no single set of methodological rules that we must follow. We can be perfectly scientific in testing theories by using reason and logic to see if theory and data are consistent; if not, we discard the theory and test another one. In short, we can test the theories by looking at the "real world" of politics and deciding which of them best explain what we see. We must remember that a theory must be treated not as an absolute truth but as a working assumption, that is, an explanation which makes sense until we find a better one. Each chapter in this text begins with a set of general hypotheses in the form of summaries of the theoretical approaches to the subject at hand. Relevant facts and research findings are then presented to allow the reader to reach tentative conclusions. And tentative they must be, because the scientific method demands a continued openness to challenge our own and others' most firmly held theories.

Chapter 2: The Federal System

The United States is characterized by considerable regional differences in wealth, population, economic development, history, and culture. It therefore makes sense to structure the American political system so as to allow a degree of regional and local autonomy. A federal system is one means of accomplishing this.

Federalism is a system in which authority is divided between a central government and regional governments. Authority may be mutually exclusive or shared (concurrent), but each level of government is an entity in its own right. A confederation joins autonomous regional governments under a weak central authority. Unitary systems, in contrast, concentrate all authority in a central government, which may then choose to delegate parts of it to regional or local governments. Examples of federalism include the United States, Canada, Germany, and Australia; Britain and France are unitary systems. From 1781 to 1789 the United States was governed as a confederation under the Articles of Confederation.

A federal system attempts to establish a balance between centralized and decentralized governments to promote both national unity and regional autonomy. If there is a national consensus on certain political goals, the central government should have the power to achieve them. Yet regional governments should have sufficient independence to assert their particular interests within the system and to deal with issues specific to their jurisdictions. The two levels of government should then be capable of resolving the conflicts that arise. The main question to be addressed in this chapter is whether the U.S. federal system measures up to this standard.

Federalism and Diversity

The particular kinds of regional differences that prevail in the United States pose special problems for our federal system.

The various racial and ethnic groups that make up the population are unevenly distributed. Blacks are concentrated in the South and in northern cities. Mexican-Americans live predominantly in the Southwest, Cuban refugees have found a haven in Florida, and Puerto Ricans have moved to New York City and other urban centers. The most recent wave of immigrants has been Asians, who have settled in many locations throughout the country. Although Americans of Irish, Italian, and Polish ancestry are generally widespread, certain other ethnic groups are more concentrated in particular areas: Scandinavians in the upper Midwest, French Canadians and Portuguese in New England, Jews in major cities, and so on. Some states, such as Hawaii, New Mexico, and Louisiana, have a racial or ethnic cultural style that is distinct from all other states. How does federalism affect the political position of minority groups? Is that position enhanced or undermined by geographic dispersion or by local concentration?

Urban development is an uneven process. Certain states are highly urbanized, whereas others are largely rural. Different problems arise as a result. Likewise, diverse economic bases in each region produce conflicting political interests. A modern federal system must be capable of organizing urban and economic development in a nationally coherent way without unduly abusing the rights and interests of particular regions. Does our system accomplish this? Is it sufficiently balanced to effect appropriate compromises between city and country, factory and farm, producer and consumer?

The differences in wealth among the regions of the nation produce different capacities for taxation and spending, resulting in different means for providing publicly funded services. There has been increasing concern over inequities in the quality of education, accessibility to health care, welfare programs, and housing, yet the federal government cannot assume the responsibility of unilaterally redistributing the nation's wealth. Does our federal system promote a balance in this regard?

Each region has its own particular set of historical and cultural traditions, largely based on what types of people settled there and when they arrived. Brief descriptions of these variations would sound like stereotypes; yet they do exist and must also be taken into account in a federal system. No central government can be totally sensitive to all regional variations, yet national policy making requires at least an understanding of them. Sufficient leeway must exist to enable regions to handle some of their problems as they see fit without contradicting national goals, or at least to implement national policy in a manner consistent with regional needs and traditions. Is this possible under our federal system?

This chapter cannot answer individually all the questions posed here. Most of the specific issues will be dealt with as we proceed in the text. The ultimate issue is the conflict between the national interest in achieving a certain degree of equity and consistency in policy, and regional interests in protecting their own advantages and maintaining their special character. The evaluation of how the federal system affects this conflict will be the focus of our analysis.

Federalism and the Constitution

The Constitution of the United States was developed to replace the Articles of Confederation, which provided the framework of the new U.S. government after the Revolution ended in 1781. The Articles established a weak unicameral Congress to which each state legislature sent representatives. Each state had one vote; at least nine states had to agree on any action taken by Congress. There was no executive. As a result, there was no effective national government, and states had many of the powers of independent nations. This presented significant problems for economic development and national defense. Those who favored greater centralization made several attempts to revise the Articles. Finally, fifty-five delegates from twelve states (mostly landowners, lawyers, and businessmen) gathered in Philadelphia in May 1787. Almost immediately the agenda became the establishment of a whole new system of government, although the convention lacked any such authorization. After a summer of intense discussion and debate, thirty-nine of the delegates signed the new Constitution on September 17. References to the states are made throughout the Constitution, but certain sections deal with them specifically (no mention at all is made of local government).

Article I, Section 10 strips the states of many of the powers they had under the Articles:

1. No State shall enter into any treaty, alliance, or confederation; grant letter of marque and reprisal; emit bills of credit; make anything but gold and silver coin a tender in payment of debts; pass any bill of attainder, ex post facto law, or law impairing the obligation of contracts, or grant any title of nobility.

2. No State shall, without the consent of the Congress, lay any imposts or duties on imports or exports, except what may be absolutely necessary for executing its inspection laws. . . .

3. No State shall, without the consent of the Congress, lay any duty of tonnage, keep troops, or ships of war in the peace, enter into any agreement or compact with another State, or with a foreign power, or engage in war, unless actually invaded, or in such imminent danger as will not admit of delay.

Article III, Section 2 establishes the jurisdiction of the U.S. Supreme Court involving

controversies to which the United States shall be a party; to controversies between two or more States; between a State and citizens of another State; between citizens of different States; between citizens of the same State claiming land under grants of different States; and between a State, or the citizens thereof, and foreign States, citizens, or subjects.

Article IV deals in its entirety with the states:

Section 1:

Full faith and credit shall be given in each State to the public acts, records, and judicial proceedings of every other State. And the Congress may by general laws prescribe the manner in which such acts, records and proceedings shall be proved, and the effect thereof.

Section 2:

1. The citizens of each State shall be entitled to all privileges and immunities of citizens in the several States.

2. A person charged in any State with treason, felony, or other crime, who shall flee from justice, and be found in another State, shall on demand of the executive authority of the State from which he fled, be delivered up to be removed to the State having jurisdiction of the crime.

3. No person held to service or labor in one State under the laws thereof, escaping into another, shall, in consequence of any law or regulation therein, be discharged from such service or labor, but shall be delivered up on claim of the party to whom such service or labor may be due.

Section 3:

1. New States may be admitted by the Congress into this Union; but no new State shall be formed or erected within the jurisdiction of any other State; nor any State be formed by the junction of two or more States, or parts of States, without the consent of the legislatures of the States concerned as well as Congress.

2. The Congress shall have the power to dispose of and make all needful rules

and regulations respecting the territory or other property belonging to the United States; and nothing in this Constitution shall be so construed as to prejudice any claims of the United States or of any particular State.

Section 4.

The United States shall guarantee to every State in this Union a republican form of government, and shall protect each of them against invasion; and on application of the legislature, or of the executive, when the legislature cannot be convened, against domestic violence.

The new Constitution thus limited and restricted the powers of the states in order to set up a strong national government with extensive economic, military, and foreign policy powers. Yet at the same time, the states retained a measure of sovereignty along with certain protections against arbitrary federal action.

Ratification of the Constitution required the assent of nine states. But practically speaking, approval had to be nearly unanimous if the new nation was to function. There was significant opposition in many quarters, and in a few state constitutional conventions the margin of victory was close. By 1789 all but Rhode Island had ratified it, and with the inauguration of George Washington as first president in April of that year, the new governmental system was in operation. In 1791, as a result of promises made during the campaign for ratification, the Bill of Rights was added, consisting of ten amendments. The last of these declares that "the powers not delegated to the United States by the Constitution, nor prohibited by it to the states, are reserved to the states respectively, or to the people."

The Federalist Papers

What was the political purpose of the design of the federal system? This question is answered in the collection of eighty-four essays known as *The Federalist Papers*. The most important of these are numbers 10 and 51, written by James Madison.

Madison was a major figure at the Constitutional Convention. Not only did he record the debates, but his participation in them reflects his position as a representative of the ideological middle ground. His beliefs were typical of the majority of the men at the convention. When the Constitution came up for ratification in New York, Madison, Alexander

Hamilton, and John Jay anonymously published a series of essays in local newspapers in its defense. *Federalist Papers* numbers 10 and 51 are
complex but concise statements of the political thinking that led to the
drafting of the Constitution, and they offer insight into the meaning of
federalism in the minds of the Founding Fathers.

Number 10 argues that the purpose of the Constitution is to "break
and control the violence of faction." Faction is defined as any group of
citizens, of any size, which promotes a program "adverse . . . to the permanent and aggregate interests of the community." An end to political
liberty would, of course, end factions, but Madison rejects this idea. We
could also attempt to "give to every citizen the same opinions, the same
passions, the same interests." This cannot be done, however, for two
reasons: one is the basic "passion" of self-interest, which prevents people
from thinking in a community-minded way; the other is "the diversity in
the faculty of men from which the rights of property originate," the protection of which "is the first object of government." In other words,
government must protect property rights as a means of preserving a system which properly rewards with wealth those people whose "faculties"
are superior to other people's.

This necessarily results in "a division of the society into different
interests and parties," that is, factions. Madison adds that "the most
common and durable source of faction has been the various and unequal
distribution of property. Those who hold and those who are without
property have ever formed distinct interests in society." This means that
the causes of faction cannot be eliminated, but the effects can be controlled. Madison was particularly concerned with factions composed of
the majority of the people, that is, those with little or no wealth, for they
might be the ones most tempted to attack property rights. He saw "republican" (representative) government, rather than direct democracy, as
the solution. First of all, it would "refine and enlarge the public views by
passing them through a medium of a chosen body of citizens"; second, it
would include "a greater number of citizens and extent of territory" under the same government. This would structurally "make it less probable
that a majority of the whole will have a common motive to invade the
rights of other citizens." The rationale behind the federal system is expressed near the end of the essay:

> The influence of factious leaders may kindle a flame within their particular
> states but will be unable to spread a general conflagration through the other
> states. A religious sect may degenerate into a political faction in a part of the

confederacy but the variety of sects dispersed over the entire face of it must se-
cure the national councils against any danger from that source: a rage for paper
money, for an abolition of debts, or an equal division of property, or for any
other improper or wicked project, will be less apt to pervade the whole body of
the union than a particular member of it.

In *Federalist* number 51 Madison elaborated on this theme and applied it to the federal system:

> Different interests necessarily exist in different classes of citizens. If a majority
> be united by a common interest, the rights of the minority will be insecure. . .
> [The federal system] will render an unjust combination of a majority of the
> whole very improbable, if not impracticable. . . . Whilst all authority [in the
> federal system]will be derived from and dependent on the society, the society
> itself will be broken into so many parts, interests, and classes of citizens that
> the rights of individuals, or of the minority, will be in little danger from inter-
> ested combinations of the majority.

Why Federalism?

Consensus theorists argue that the intended purpose of federalism
was a political system that dispersed power and moderated conflict. This
required a structure that carefully balanced federal and state power. Establishing a powerful central government while at the same time guaranteeing the existence of states as autonomous entities with powers of their
own would set up competing centers of power to check and balance each
other.

A pluralist reading of *The Federalist Papers* thus deemphasizes its
hostility to majority rule and focuses instead on the goal of controlling
the "violence of faction" as a whole. Madison's statement on breaking
up the society into many parts to protect individual rights is seen as a
defense of regional and local diversity against an overwhelming national
majority. His points about the "influence of factious leaders" can be read
as a justification for permitting states to experiment with new policies
without involving the entire country. From the pluralist perspective the
founders' version of federalism was

> the authentic American contribution to democratic thought and republican gov-
> ernment. . . . It emphasizes a partnership of individuals, groups, and govern-
> ments in the pursuit of justice, cooperative relationships that make the partner-
> ship real, and negotiation among the partners as the basis for sharing power. . . .
> Contractual noncentralization—the structural dispersion of power among many

centers whose legitimate authority is constitutionally guaranteed—is the key to widespread and entrenched diffusion of power that remains the principal character of and argument for federal democracy (Elazar 1984, 17).

Conflict theorists, on the other hand, believe that Madison's writings clearly demonstrate that the federal system was designed as part of an antimajoritarian plan to concentrate power in the hands of the political and economic elite. In 1913 the historian Charles A. Beard published *An Economic Interpretation of the Constitution of the United States*. The book started a controversy which has lasted to the present day. Beard claimed that the framers of the Constitution represented a particular set of interests, namely, "personalty"—financial capital. The framers felt that their financial interests were endangered by what they saw as political instability under the Articles of Confederation. Thus they undertook more or less secretly to devise a centralized government more in keeping with their commercial needs. The result was a constitution which in its overall structure and specific provisions reflects the goals of an economic elite. Beard argued that the struggle over ratification was intense and that it divided the participants according to the type of property they owned: mercantile interests on the federalist side, landed interests on the antifederalist side. The Constitution passed narrowly in some important states and, Beard claimed, fraudulently in a number of others.

On the basis of this analysis and others like it, elite theorists conclude that the purpose of the Constitution was to benefit the ruling class by weakening the forces of democracy that had been unleashed by the Revolution. Its method, as reflected in *The Federalist Papers*, was to minimize public participation in government and protect the property interests of the "minority faction" by dividing the majority with a federal system. At best, federalism may provide leeway for state political and economic elites to dominate their own jurisdictions, leaving the national elite to concentrate on the "big picture." Indeed, the Constitution removed most of the economic and military powers possessed by the states under the Articles of Confederation and vested most of them in Congress. The states are left with "residual" powers, that is, those not important enough to concern the national power elite. From this perspective federalism in the United States is a sophisticated way of protecting the property rights of the power elite.

Marxists conclude that Madison's outlook is consistent with a class analysis, but from the perspective of his class, the upper class. Madison's description of economic inequality as "the most durable source of fac-

tion" was not far from what Karl Marx would write in *The Communist Manifesto* sixty years later: "The history of all hitherto existing society is the history of class struggle." The difference is that Madison was concerned with protecting individual property rights, whereas Marx wanted to end them. If protecting property rights means maintaining the dominance of the upper class in society, then the lower classes must be rendered politically weak; the founders' solution was "divide and conquer." From a Marxist perspective the federal system was thus created to fragment and weaken the majority faction in order, as Madison said, to guarantee that "a rage for paper money, for an abolition of debts, for an equal division of property, or for any other improper or wicked project, will be less apt to pervade the whole body of the union than a particular member of it." The Constitution established a government that is centralized enough to allow the ruling class to tend to its own military and economic affairs, but also sufficiently decentralized and fragmented to make national working-class political unity difficult if not impossible by breaking the society into numerous "parts, interests, and classes."

The Politics of Federalism

The theories also differ in how they assess the impact of federalism on the resolution of political conflict.

Consensus theorists claim that, with the notable exception of events leading to the Civil War, federalism in the United States has worked admirably to sort out federal from state issues and facilitate action by the appropriate level of government.

Although the federal system placed African-Americans at the mercy of segregationist state governments until the 1960s, the national government finally stepped in when it became apparent that their plight was a national concern. The federal system rightly places most of the responsibility for local economic development on the states, yet this has not precluded substantial federal aid. States and localities decide for themselves which tax-supported services they want to provide, while the federal government makes it possible through grants-in-aid to have certain minimum standards in place everywhere. The pluralist argument is that the federal system is sufficiently flexible to balance autonomy and equity throughout the nation.

Above all, federalism recognizes the inherent differences among the

fifty states and grants the appropriate political leeway. Pluralists presume that the United States has a variety of definable "political cultures." Political culture is the practice of politics and government in a particular area as shaped by its social values and behavioral styles. Political scientist Daniel J. Elazar has gone so far as to categorize the states in these terms: "Traditionalistic" political cultures, emphasizing social order and reduced public participation, are found in the South. States across the northern tier and along the West Coast are "moralistic" in their predisposition toward greater participation and "good government". "Individualistic" political cultures, mostly among industrial states, foster an approach to politics which encourages self-interest and personal gain (1984, chap. 5).

Our federal system supposedly acts to integrate these diverse political cultures into an overall national consensus on basic political values. The federal system may not always work smoothly, but in the long run it maintains political stability by making such a balance possible. Federalism is institutionalized pluralism; it safeguards diversity and autonomy without eliminating consistency and unity in the nation as a whole.

Conflict theorists share a more critical perspective. They argue that the ultimate purpose of the existing U.S. federal system—although not necessarily of federalism itself—is to protect the ruling class against the effects of majority rule, as the founders intended. The fragmentation of government isolates the rich from the poor. The burdens imposed by racial problems, economic underdevelopment, fiscal crises, and environmental decline are largely borne by the states and localities most directly affected and least able to cope. This insulates the upper class from social responsibility. In their view, for example, civil rights legislation finally became a reality in the 1960s in spite of the federal system, not because of it. State and local financing of public education results in disastrous inequities favoring the wealthy communities that can afford good schools. Environmental regulation has been hindered by the fragmentation of authority resulting from the federal system. This is not to say that states and localities should not have the authority to make political choices; in fact, conflict theorists tend to favor a democratically decentralized government. Rather, they argue that the current setup actually deprives state and local governments of the resources necessary to finance those choices—and increasingly makes them the object of policy mandates from the federal government which they are expected to finance without federal help. Political unity is sacrificed to diversity be-

cause the latter protects the existing distribution of wealth.

Indeed, the whole point of federalism, from this perspective, is to exacerbate social and political divisions to preclude the possibility of unified national political action by the working and middle classes. What consensus theorists interpret as the moderation of conflict by the federal system is seen by conflict theorists as a diversion and suppression of conflict. Issues of racial, fiscal, or economic inequality are translated by the federal system into purely regional or local concerns instead of national problems. This tends to isolate the affected populations from one another, thus strengthening the overall position of the ruling class.

Conflict theorists differ among themselves in estimating the potential for changing all this. Some see federalism as just another card in a stacked deck favoring the ruling class. Others see a possibility for establishing movements for political change in state and local governments and building from there.

Of course, the politics of federalism cannot be completely understood in terms of its constitutional origins or in terms of conjectures about its impact on conflict resolution. We must address the question of how it has developed and changed.

The Development of Federal Government

The formal constitutional arrangements of American federalism have not changed much, but the contemporary reality of federal-state intergovernmental relations bears little resemblance to what existed two centuries ago.

First and foremost, American government on all levels has assumed vast responsibilities in all areas of our lives. In its grants of powers to the federal government the Constitution was open-ended enough to allow for expansion, yet none of the founding fathers could have envisioned the enormous changes to come. Eighteenth-century American governments were quite limited in their impact on citizens; they existed essentially to protect the country militarily and establish certain minimal ground rules for a private enterprise economy. Federal, state, and local governments in the United States now spend over $3 trillion annually and employ 18 million people to maintain a huge military establishment, regulate all facets of the economy, and provide a vast array of services.

Within this overall development, the federal government has as-

sumed the predominant role. The Civil War resolved a seventy-year dispute about the legal and constitutional supremacy of the federal government over the states; the New Deal propelled the federal government into new economic and social service responsibilities. The trend toward "big government" and national predominance with an interdependent relationship between federal and state governments began in the 1930s and reached its peak forty years later. The Reagan administration, which took office in 1981, halted and began to reverse that trend.

There are two issues to be considered here: why these changes have occurred and whom they benefit. Once again, the three theories offer different analyses. Evaluation of these perspectives requires a survey of the historical development of federalism. Political scientists differ in how they treat the history of federalism, but perhaps the most useful approach is to break it into four historical periods: (1) Revolution to Civil War (1789–1861); (2) Civil War to Great Depression (1865–1933); (3) post–New Deal (1933–1981); and (4) the present day (since 1981). Each period represents a different set of issues and conflicts in the development of the federal system.

Revolution to Civil War

The most contentious issue during this period was the supremacy of the national government versus the sovereignty of the states. The main arena for the resolution of this conflict was the U.S. Supreme Court.

In the early days of the new nation, some states assumed the right to prevent the execution of federal laws they deemed unconstitutional. In 1798 Congress passed the Alien and Sedition Acts, restricting the rights of aliens to citizenship and punishing public criticism of the government; the latter provision clearly contradicted the Bill of Rights. The intention was to repress Jeffersonian attacks on President John Adams's Federalist administration. In response, the legislatures of Kentucky and Virginia passed resolutions, respectively drawn up by Thomas Jefferson and James Madison, arguing that states could decide for themselves whether federal laws were constitutional and therefore should be obeyed. This particular confrontation was resolved by the election of Jefferson as president in 1800 and subsequent repeal of the acts by Congress.

In 1803 the Pennsylvania legislature attempted to block the execution of a decision by a lower federal court. The case, *United States v. Peters*, reached the Supreme Court in 1808. Chief Justice John Marshall, deciding that Pennsylvania had acted illegally, declared that "if the leg-

islatures of the several states may at will annul the judgments of the courts of the United States . . . the Constitution itself becomes a solemn mockery." A similar case arose when the Virginia Court of Appeals refused to obey the Supreme Court's mandate reversing its ruling on a property ownership case. In 1816 the Supreme Court, ruling in *Martin v. Hunter's Lessee*, declared that the Constitution was established "not by the states in their sovereign capacities, but emphatically, as the Preamble of the Constitution declares, by the People of the United States," and reaffirmed its mandate to Virginia.

The ultimate test arose in 1819 in the case of *McCulloch v. Maryland*. The U.S. government had chartered the Bank of the United States to operate as a national bank, a decision arousing a good deal of opposition. Maryland had imposed a tax on the banknotes issued by the Bank's Baltimore branch. The issue was one of competing sovereignties: Did the U.S. government have a constitutional right to establish the bank, and if so, to what extent could the states interfere with its operation? Again, Marshall affirmed the doctrine of national supremacy within a context of implied powers. In the language of Article I, Section 8, Congress had the right to enact laws "necessary and proper" to execute its powers. This, Marshall said, included the Bank. "Let the end be legitimate, let it be within the scope of the Constitution, and all means which are appropriate, which are plainly adapted to that end, which are not prohibited, but consist with the letter and the spirit of the Constitution, are constitutional." Moreover, he added, "The states have no power by taxation or otherwise to retard, impede, burden or in any manner control the operation of constitutional laws." Once and for all, the Supreme Court made a clear statement in favor of the supremacy of the national government.

The court was not the only arena of conflict. There was considerable political debate during the 1820s concerning the role of the federal government in economic development. "Nationalist" politicians, such as Henry Clay, later a Whig party leader, favored federal action for "internal improvements," a program of aid for road and canal building which never became law. The Clay faction also favored the Bank of the United States. The states' rights position was reflected in President Andrew Jackson's opposition to the Bank, which ultimately resulted in its destruction. An example of the extreme states' rights point of view occurred in 1832, when the South Carolina legislature declared that a recently passed federal tariff did not apply to that state. This doctrine of "nullification" had been advanced four years earlier by Vice President

John C. Calhoun. His theory was based on the concept that the federal union was a compact of states rather than of individuals. This particular confrontation ended with a show of force from President Jackson, whose states' rights position did not extend to nullification.

Starting in the 1830s, the Whig and Democratic Parties generally, although not consistently, opposed each other on these issues, with the Whigs taking the nationalist view. The Democratic perspective was exemplified in 1854 by the message of President Franklin Pierce accompanying his veto of legislation designed to aid states in caring for the indigent insane: "I cannot find any authority in the Constitution for making the federal government the great almoner of public charity throughout the United States. It would in the end be prejudicial rather than beneficial to the noble offices of charity to have the charge of them transferred from the states to the federal government" (Hale and Palley 1981, 7).

It was on the issue of slavery, however, that the question of federal supremacy came to a head: To what extent did Congress have a right to legislate on the subject? Was slavery the exclusive province of state authority? In 1820 Missouri had been admitted by Congress as a slave state as part of a compromise which forbade slavery in future states carved out of the Louisiana Territory north of 36 degrees latitude. The Kansas-Nebraska Act of 1854 modified this significantly, but the Supreme Court had the last word. In 1857, it ruled on the case of a slave, Dred Scott, who had been brought into a free state by his owner and who was now suing for his freedom. In *Dred Scott v. Sandford* the court declared that the states did indeed have exclusive power over slavery, that the federal government could not control slavery in the territories, and that the Missouri Compromise was invalid. This decision helped make impossible any further compromises in the conflict over states' rights and slavery, hastening the beginning of the Civil War.

The Republican Party was founded in 1854 on a platform hostile to the spread of slavery; in 1860 the election of its presidential candidate, Abraham Lincoln, prompted the secession of eleven southern states to form the Confederate States of America. The Civil War began in April 1861; the victory of Union forces over the Confederacy in 1865 settled once and for all the issue of whether the United States was a nation or simply a collection of states.

Civil War to Great Depression

With the issue of federal supremacy resolved, the federal government, after a brief interlude of activism on civil rights, assumed a largely inactive role in national affairs during the period when the United States transformed itself from an agricultural into an industrial society.

For a decade after the Civil War the federal government became directly involved in "Reconstruction" in the South, that is, enforcing the civil rights of the newly freed slaves. With this purpose in mind, the Fourteenth Amendment to the Constitution was passed in 1868. Its first section provided that "no state shall make or enforce any law which shall abridge the privileges or immunities of citizens of the United States; nor shall any State deprive any person of life, liberty, or property, without due process of law; nor deny to any person within its jurisdiction the equal protection of the laws."

Until the end of Reconstruction in 1877, states' rights in the South took a backseat to the power of the national government, which made efforts to guarantee the political and civil rights of black citizens. In the decades following Reconstruction, however, white-dominated state administrations in the South imposed laws mandating racial segregation and robbed blacks of their voting rights. This was encouraged by a number of Supreme Court rulings that interpreted the Fourteenth Amendment in such a way as to limit the jurisdiction of the federal authorities. In 1896, in the case of *Plessy v. Ferguson*, the court ruled that state-mandated segregation of public facilities—in this case, railroad cars in Louisiana—was not inconsistent with the Fourteenth Amendment. This put a constitutional seal of approval on similar laws throughout the South. It was not until the 1960s that the federal government stepped in again to enforce civil rights.

It was also during this time that the federal government began a few limited cash grant-in-aid programs to the states. Prior to the end of the Civil War, federal aid programs were limited to land grants, as in the Morrill Act of 1862, which provided federal lands that could be sold to fund higher education. The first actual program, passed in 1879, granted cash to states for a specific purpose in exchange for the acceptance of certain minimum standards; in this case, for financing teaching materials for the blind. This was followed in 1887 by grants for state agricultural experiment stations, and in 1888 by grants for veterans' homes. The first fairly large-scale program was the Federal Highway Act of 1916, in which states received federal contributions in the form of matching grants for road construction. The formula for the aid was based on the size, population, and rural route mileage of the particular state. In 1917 and 1920 Congress passed grant-in-aid programs for vocational education and rehabilitation.

Overall, this period produced little growth in government and no great change in intergovernmental relations. In the area of civil rights, the government stepped back from its initial involvement in Reconstruction. In the area of economic development, notwithstanding the social turmoil resulting from industrialization, the government held to the position of laissez-faire: the economy could run by itself, and the limited regulation deemed necessary could be handled by the states. Even the states were limited by the Supreme Court in the extent of their regulatory powers. When the Great Depression hit in 1929, federalism had not changed much since the Civil War.

The New Deal and After

The revolutionary changes really began with the Depression, which created massive new problems and new demands for government action. In 1933, with a quarter of the labor force unemployed and the economy on the brink of total collapse, President Franklin D. Roosevelt took office and began to push through Congress a series of emergency measures which drastically expanded the responsibility of the federal government and changed the nature of intergovernmental relations. The Agricultural Adjustment Act and the National Industrial Recovery Act gave the federal government wide powers of economic planning. Legislation in the areas of banking, securities, housing finance, and labor relations expanded its regulatory functions. The Federal Emergency Relief Act authorized $500 million in payments to the unemployed. The Civil Works Administration (CWA) and the Civilian Conservation Corps (CCC) were set up to provide emergency employment. Later employment relief programs, notably the Works Progress Administration (WPA), functioned in cooperation with local governments.

The first part of this "New Deal" agenda was followed by a second phase, which institutionalized the new federal system in a number of large-scale grant-in-aid programs. In exchange for developing programs consistent with federal regulations, the states would receive a federal grant reimbursing part of the cost of the programs. In 1935 the Social Security Act was passed, including a grant-in-aid welfare system for the aged, the blind, and dependent children. Two years later the nation's first public housing program was passed, establishing a relationship among all three levels of government in that policy area. The New Deal thus set precedents for a new system of cooperative federalism in which federal, state, and local governments shared the responsibility for a wide range of functions.

The Supreme Court at first struck a blow at the New Deal by declaring both the National Industrial Recovery Act and the Agricultural Adjustment Act unconstitutional. Starting in 1937, however, after some personnel changes and political pressure stemming from Roosevelt's proposal to add more justices, the court ruled in favor of unemployment insurance and the National Labor Relations Act. Succeeding cases continued to broaden the respective powers of the federal and state governments in regulating working conditions, including hours and wages, and in controlling the economy.

In the next twenty-five years the basic New Deal approach was further developed and applied to new policy areas. The emphasis was on conditional or categorical grant-in-aid programs to state governments— money given for definite programs according to an established formula or for a specific project. The most notable of these included the Hill-Burton Act for hospital construction (1946), urban renewal (1949), Aid to the Disabled (1950), aid to areas affected by federal facilities (1950), interstate highway construction (1956), and the National Defense Education Act (1958). By 1960 there were 140 federal grant programs; all but fifteen had been implemented since 1930.

President Lyndon B. Johnson's "Great Society" expanded considerably on the precedents set by the New Deal and brought the federal government back into the arena of civil rights. More than 200 new programs were added between 1964 and 1969, including the Elementary and Secondary Education Act, providing federal aid to schools in poverty areas; and Medicaid, which paid medical costs for poor people. Localities, especially urban areas, increasingly became the direct recipients of federal money, often bypassing the states. The War on Poverty and the Model Cities Program both aimed at alleviating urban problems and represented a new "targeted" approach to the allocation of federal funds. Block grants, represented by the Partnership for Health Act of 1966 and the Omnibus Crime Control and Safe Streets Act of 1968, were developed as a means of granting money to states and localities for certain general purposes rather than for specific federally developed programs. Throughout all this, of course, the states were expanding their own responsibilities, partly in response to all the federal incentives. Many states began to increase their subsidies to local governments, especially for education. The growth of federal power did not mean an eclipse of state power; they grew together, with the federal government the senior partner in a cooperative arrangement. Indeed, state and local expenditures tripled between 1957 and 1970 and would triple again by 1980.

The Johnson administration also implemented new federal efforts to guarantee the rights of black citizens in the states. In 1954, the Supreme Court had unanimously declared in *Brown v. Board of Education* that state laws mandating segregated schools were unconstitutional, thus reversing its decision in *Plessy v. Ferguson* sixty years earlier. This helped inspire an already growing civil rights movement whose purpose was to end racial segregation and the disenfranchisement of southern blacks. The struggles of that movement elicited a response from the federal government. The Civil Rights Act of 1964 outlawed segregation in public accommodations; the Voting Rights Act of 1965 authorized the use of federal officials to register voters in states which had a record of discrimination against blacks who attempted to register to vote. The federal government thus completed the job it had set out to do 100 years earlier, during Reconstruction.

President Richard Nixon, who took office in 1969, attempted to reverse the direction of the Great Society through cutbacks in many federal programs, especially those connected with the War on Poverty. His major thrust in the direction of what he called "New Federalism" was General Revenue Sharing. Passed by Congress in 1972, this program returned federal revenues to state and local governments with no strings attached. The dollar amounts were never large, but the principle was important in signaling a change in intergovernmental relations toward more state and local responsibility. Notwithstanding this shift the federal role continued to expand, albeit more slowly. One hundred forty grant programs were added during the 1970s, and the extent of federal regulatory authority expanded greatly. As environmental quality became a national concern, the federal government increased its involvement in that area. By 1980 there were over 500 categorical grant and five block grant programs disbursing over $80 billion, with another $7 billion in revenue sharing. Federal aid equaled over 25 percent of total state and local financial outlays. At this point, the extent of federal responsibility to state and local governments had reached its peak.

Federalism Since 1981

Ronald Reagan won the presidential race of 1980. A strong conservative, he believed that state and local governments ought to assume most of the responsibility for their own problems. He campaigned explicitly on a platform of reducing the size of "big government"; after his inauguration he proceeded to deliver on that promise. In 1981 he pushed through a Democratic Congress a budget proposal which eliminated sixty federal aid programs and consolidated seventy-seven categorical grant programs into nine block grants. At the same time, federal funding for intergovernmental programs of all kinds was cut. Eligibility for welfare programs funded by grants-in-aid was tightened, and spending restraints on the Medicaid program were imposed. Substantial cuts were made in grant programs such as child nutrition, energy conservation, wastewater treatment, urban development, and social services. In a similar vein, the Reagan administration reduced the federal role in enforcing civil rights laws by appointing individuals opposed to the concept of federal involvement to head the agencies responsible for enforcement. Reagan charted a clear course away from federal predominance in intergovernmental relations.

In 1982 he sought a more far-reaching change, which he called (as Nixon had) "New Federalism." In exchange for the state's assumption of certain welfare programs, the federal government would assume responsibility for Medicaid, while abandoning sixty other grant programs which the states could choose to take over using revenue-sharing money. Although this failed to pass, by 1984 the number of federal grant programs had declined from 539 to just over 400. State revenue sharing had ended in 1980; in 1986 the portion going to local governments was also terminated.

By the end of Ronald Reagan's second term in 1989, states and localities had become far less able to depend on the generosity of the federal government. His administration had set into motion a process of "devolution": a shift of financial and administrative responsibility for government programs downward to the state and local governments. This process continued despite the fact that states and localities were increasingly subject to requirements from Washington to implement costly programs at their own expense, especially in the important area of environmental protection. Such "unfunded mandates," on top of cutbacks in federal assistance and deteriorating economic conditions, significantly worsened the financial position of states and localities in the 1990s. Even though a law was passed in 1995 prohibiting such mandates, it had sufficient exceptions and loopholes to raise questions about whether the practice would indeed come to a halt.

In 1994, the Republicans took control of Congress and launched a "Contract with America" that called for an even more severely reduced federal role in social and economic policy, once again raising the issue of state and local capabilities. Under the leadership of Newt Gingrich (Republican, Georgia), Speaker of the House of Representatives, the Republicans proposed to dismantle the guarantees of federal aid provided by categorical grants, replacing them with block grants. The most prominent target of this strategy was the welfare program. The result would be to give states greater leeway in designing their own programs, but without assurance that a constant proportion of the cost would be borne by the federal government. Many governors, especially Republicans, welcomed this change. Although President Bill Clinton vetoed parts of the Contract with America on the basis of his objections to certain specific provisions and funding cutbacks, he signed the Republican welfare bill into law in 1996. Clearly, at least the short-term political direction of fiscal federalism appears to be toward a reduction of the federal role in financing social programs. This constitutes a significant reversal of the direction set by the New Deal and the Great Society .

Viewpoints on the Development of Federalism

Consensus theorists evaluate the development of federalism in terms of how well it has worked to maintain the stability of the U.S. political system. Conflict theorists are more concerned with its impact on the distribution of wealth and power.

Consensus Theory

According to consensus theory, the government has to accommodate a variety of political demands to ensure its continued authority. The most pressing demands come from public opinion, which after the New Deal began to expect more of government. In addition, urbanization, industrialization, and the resulting regional interdependence have forced the "nationalization" of government. Finally, the proliferation of government services has produced new bureaucracies that constantly fight for survival and expansion. Hence the overall trend, at least until the 1970s, was toward an activist government and a larger federal role. Changes in that trend since then, consensus theorists argue, largely repre-

Table 2.1: Federal Grants-in-Aid Summary: 1970 to 1996

YEAR	TOTAL GRANTS (million dollars)	GRANTS AS PERCENT OF STATE-LOCAL GOVT. OUTLAYS
1970	24,065	19.0
1975	49,791	23.5
1980	91,385	26.3
1985	105,852	21.3
1990	135,325	18.7
1995	224,991	22.2

Source: U. S. Dept. of Commerce, *Statistical Abstract of the United States 1997*, p. 302.

Table 2.2: Federal Aid to State and Local Governments, Selected Programs: 1970 to 1996 (In millions of dollars for fiscal year shown)

PROGRAM	1970	1980	1990	1995
Total	24,065	91,385	135,325	224,991
Natural Resources and Environment	411	5,363	3,745	4,148
Highways	4,395	9,208	14,171	19,475
Urban Mass Transit	104	3,129	3,730	4,353
Community and Regional Development	1,780	6,486	4,965	7,230
Education, Employment, Training, Social Services	6,417	21,862	23,359	34,125
Medicaid	2,727	13,957	41,103	89,070
Family Support Payments	4,142	6,888	12,246	17,133
Housing Assistance	436	3,435	9,516	18,416
General Government	479	8,616	2,309	2,172
Administration of Justice	42	529	574	1,222
Agriculture	604	569	1,285	780

Source: U. S. Dept. of Commerce, *Statistical Abstract of the United States 1997*, p. 302

Table 2.3: Fiscal Dependency of Lower Levels on Higher Levels of Government, 1957-1990. (Intergovernmental revenue as a percentage of general revenue from own sources)

YEAR	State from Federal	Local from Federal	Local from State
1957	21.3	1.9	41.0
1975	37.3	12.9	60.5
1980	36.6	16.3	62.5
1985	30.7	10.1	53.9
1990	30.3	5.7	53.6

Source: Harold Stanley and Richard G. Niemi, *Vital Statistics on American Politics*, Washington, DC: Congressional Quarterly, 1994, p. 324.

sent changes in public opinion; the Reagan presidency and the Republican congressional victory in 1994 are said to reflect a more conservative electorate. Cutbacks in spending are a political response to taxpayers' increasing resentment of "big government."

The critical issue for consensus theorists is whether the structure of federalism has adapted appropriately to changes in the political and economic environment. Exploring this issue requires, first of all, a framework for analysis, that is, a description and classification of the forms of federalism found in American political history. Second, these forms have to be evaluated in terms of their impact on the stability of the American political system.

"Dual federalism," which predominated until the New Deal, was a system in which central and regional governments operated more or less independently while competing for governing power. Pluralists agree that this structure was consistent with the limited responsibilities of government during that time. The New Deal changed all this, ultimately creating a new arrangement known as "cooperative federalism" in which national and state governments began to work together to achieve common goals. The grant-in-aid was a symbol of this new collegial relationship. At least until the 1970s the expansion of federal power within this system did not necessarily mean the decline of state and local governments. Despite the changes, cooperative federalism could maintain a functional balance of power and responsibility.

Consensus theorists are divided, however, on the political significance of more recent developments in federalism. According to Daniel Elazar, the trend during the period between 1965 and 1980 was "unambiguously centralizing. . . . Federal intervention into state and local affairs reached its apogee and then began to collapse of its own weight" (1990, 12). Similarly, David Walker (1981, chap.7) argued that the federal system as of 1980 was "overloaded" with federal participation and as a result had been transformed from cooperative federalism into "co-optive," "dysfunctional" federalism. Increasing federal regulation was the hallmark of this period. In 1970, the amendments to the Clean Air Act required states to meet specific standards of air quality. In 1974, highway grants-in-aid were tied to adoption of the 55-mph speed limit; ten years later, a similar connection was made with setting the drinking age at twenty-one. In 1983, cities were required to spend billions of dollars to build wastewater treatment plants; since 1990, the Clean Water Act has had a similar impact. To many pluralists, this was "regulatory federalism" gone berserk. A more sympathetic view of this development, however, is offered by Reagan and Sanzone (1981, 78), who characterize it as "permissive federalism": a sharing of power between governments in which the states' share rests on the permission of the national government. This, they claim, is good "because it can strengthen the national government by permitting firm national definitions of policy objectives and program approaches at the same time that it can make all the room needed for appropriate state and local inputs."

The Reagan administration's sharp turn away from increasing federal involvement forced pluralists once again to assess the status of federalism and its impact on the political system. Some analysts offer a positive evaluation; Elazar (1990, 21), for example, argues that what he calls Reagan's "neodualism" provides "a serious opportunity to strengthen the basic noncentralization of the American system in new ways." Richard Nathan and Fred Doolittle (1987, 362) conclude that the most important change in federalism brought about by Reagan's policies was positive and unanticipated: these policies "activated state governments and enhanced their role in the nation's governmental system" by forcing the states to fill the gaps left by reductions in federal grants. Others offer a more balanced assessment:

> Many of the changes since 1980 are welcome ones [such as] the somewhat smaller federal domestic agenda. . . . These in turn suggest far less systemic overload, more balance, and a degree of vitality in our federalism that has as-

tonished many observers. Yet the continuities with the past are just as significant and some are not promising. . . . Localities and states continue to be incapable of asserting by any means an authoritative role in national governmental
actions affecting their jurisdictional and operational integrity. This does not
bode well for the future of American federalism (Walker 1989, 10).

An increasingly influential approach to evaluating American politics,
which is consistent with a pluralist approach, is known as "public
choice" theory. Taking its cue from economics, it uses the "free market"
as its framework of analysis. Politics is seen as a process in which individuals compete with one another to maximize their individual benefits.
A properly functioning political system is one that facilitates choice and
competition. From that perspective, Thomas R. Dye sees increasing federal involvement through grants-in-aid as a "baneful" attempt "to sub-
stitute the policy preferences of a national elite for the preferences of
multiple state and local elites," hence limiting freedom of choice for
"consumers" of government services. Federalism, he argues, is "an expression of contrasting social values: hierarchy, collectivism, redistribution, and equality of results versus individualism, competition, efficiency, and equality of opportunity. . . . The preservation of federalism
depends on a resurgence of national interest in economic development
and equality of opportunity." He therefore sees the need for restoration of
what he calls "competitive federalism" (1990, 107, 199).

Conflict Theory

Elite theorists and Marxists go beyond structural analysis to focus on
how federalism affects political and economic outcomes. This involves
making value judgments on policy—judgments that most pluralists find
unacceptable since they prefer to treat politics as a "value-free science."

Elite theorists see the shift to greater federal power and responsibility
after the New Deal as primarily a response to the needs and pressures of
the economic elite to defuse social discontent and maintain social control
over the masses. Michael Parenti (1980, 67) argues that during the latter
part of the nineteenth century, "when the [federal] government inter-
vened in the economy it was almost invariably on the side of the strong
against the weak." William Domhoff (1970, chap. 6) states that the
major social reforms of the late nineteenth and early twentieth centuries
were shaped by the power elite, not by competing interest groups or
classes. He notes that the National Civic Federation—a "leading organization of the power elite"—and similar groups had a strong influence

in supporting programs such as workmen's compensation, regulatory agencies, social security, and labor legislation. They did so in the interest of limiting the movement toward socialism. The New Deal transformed American federalism, and from the point of view of elite theory, it did so in the interests of the rich and powerful. As Barton J. Bernstein (1969, 282) puts it, "In acting to protect the institution of private property, and in advancing the interests of the corporate capitalists, the New Deal assisted the middle and upper sectors of society. . . . Seldom did it bestow much of substance upon the lower classes." In their widely read book *Regulating the Poor*, Richard Cloward and Frances Fox Piven argued that the expansion of welfare during the Great Society was a means of quieting the violent inner-city protests of the 1960s.

A Marxist analysis of federalism also focuses on its policy impact, but this analysis differs from the rather one-dimensional perspective of elite theory. Marxists see a number of contradictory forces at work in the development of federalism, which benefit different classes at different times. James O'Connor (1972, 90) argues that "monopoly capital requires more top-down administration and budgetary planning"; hence centralization has created a "gradual erosion of the traditional federal system in the United States." At the same time, however, Marxists also recognize that the New Deal and the Great Society were positive political responses to organized social movements demanding greater social and economic equality. In large part, federal social programs and civil rights measures did in fact promote that equality at some cost to the ruling class. Capitalists thus welcomed Ronald Reagan's attacks on those programs, which had a disproportionately negative effect on poor people, women, and minority groups. Thus the development of federal government can cut both ways because it is an outgrowth of conflicts within and among social classes.

For example, the disputes over federal power before the Civil War reflected profound inter- and intraclass differences over the direction of the economic system. Although reformists and trade unions made gains in the states, the ruling class, through the Supreme Court, nullified those gains. The near-collapse of the economy during the Depression divided capitalists over the merits of activist federal government; at least initially most of them recognized the need for the New Deal, even if the working class made gains as well. After World War II, as long as the economy kept growing, working-class demands could be accommodated; economic difficulties after 1970 and the destruction of the social movements

of the 1960s made it easier for the Reagan administration to take back
the benefits that had been gained. Plotkin and Scheuerman (1994, 89)
argue that in the 1990s "the mix of federalism, capitalism, and stagnation
puts business in the catbird seat, giving capital more power to impose its
own terms of investment on local communities and states."

A Marxist analysis of federalism, in any case, is firmly based on a set
of values favoring the working class. Robertson and Judd introduce their
study of how governmental structure influences public policy by declaring their adherence to particular positions on the issues:

> We believe that the relative absence of social policies that can mitigate
> disastrous life circumstances is unjustifiable. We also assert the poli-
> cies that underwrite more material inequality . . . constitute bad policy.
> And we believe that with respect to fundamental human needs . . . uni-
> versal and nationally consistent programs are superior to fragmented
> and variable policies. (1989, 21)

In line with this, most conflict theorists are sharply critical of the
trend toward a reduction of the responsibilities of the federal government
to minorities and the poor. Left to themselves, the state governments
historically have done little to promote egalitarian public policies. As
Forrest Chisman (1995, 601) describes it, "The disadvantaged are almost
by definition politically weak. They discovered long ago that their best
strategy is to concentrate on trying to affect policy at the federal level
rather than dissipate their energies trying to influence fifty separate
states." Indeed, the states have every incentive to balance their budgets
on the backs of those who have the least power: "States compete with
one another to attract business investment. In this competition, keeping
down taxes and improving services targeted at companies and their middle class employees score points; improving services to the poor does
not." Civil rights for African-Americans and government assistance to
the poor thus have come mainly as a result of federal initiatives. Conflict
theorists argue that if the current trend toward devolution of responsibility to state and local governments continues, economic and racial inequality will certainly increase.

Conclusion

Federalism is a means of structuring a nation's government to resolve the conflicts that arise between the need for a central government which can achieve national goals and the need for units of government which can represent and accommodate regional interests. In the United States this has taken the form of an allocation of powers between federal and state governments as established in the Constitution and elaborated by subsequent historical developments. Given the considerable diversity in this country, how has the federal government functioned in this regard?

The answer of consensus theory is that it has generally functioned well, although in recent years it has been threatened by an overload of federal power. Its original design was based on a concern with balancing and thus limiting the power of government, and the history of federalism indicates that it has worked to accommodate the pressures of public opinion and social change. Consensus theorists differ among themselves as to what constitutes the proper balance between federal and state governments, but none would quarrel with the assertion that the mechanism itself promotes the goals of integrating regional concerns with the national interest and facilitating overall political consensus and stability.

Conflict theorists, on the other hand, believe that the founders established federalism as a means of weakening the "majority faction" and protecting the interests of the ruling class. In that sense, the structure permits assertion of regional political interests only for the purposes of quarantining radical political movements within the confines of a few states or allowing regional elites to dominate their own jurisdictions. The national government steps in only when organized political pressure is too great for states to accommodate or when conflicts among regional elites become irreconcilable. In either case the government acts for the purpose of limiting the downward redistribution of wealth and power. Although the working class benefited from expanded federal government powers after the New Deal, ultimately a "balance" is preserved to protect the interests of the capitalist system and its dominant class. Thus federal social programs were cut back or eliminated after 1980 as the ruling class tired of paying the price and became more politically assertive against a weak and divided working class.

The future of federalism can thus only be assessed from one or the other point of view. Consensus theorists see inevitable pressures arising from societal changes, presenting new challenges for building consensus. The system can generally be expected to respond accordingly if not perfectly. Conflict theorists see new problems of social control arising with which elites will have to cope, using the mechanisms of the federal system. The likelihood is for greater centralization of political control along with a decentralization of financial responsibility for services, allowing the ruling class to maintain power without having to pay the bills. From this point of view, the political question is just how much conflict will be generated over the growing inequalities created by this strategy.

Chapter 3:
The Structure of State and Local Government

Fragmentation and decentralization are the most notable structural characteristics of state and local government in the United States. The structure of state government is based on the separation of powers, which assigns different and mutually exclusive functions to each branch of government (allowing for some overlaps) and renders each accountable to a different constituency. The executive, legislative, and judicial branches of state government are separately elected or appointed by different sets of voters or officials and operate to limit each other's power. The result is a complex system of "checks and balances." Writing in *The Federalist* number 51, James Madison asserted that separation of powers was "essential to the preservation of liberty. . . . The great security against a gradual concentration of the several powers in the same department, consists in giving to those who administer each department the necessary constitutional means and personal motives to resist encroachment of the others. . . . Ambition must be made to counteract ambition."

Local government is highly decentralized. It is conventional to begin a discussion of local government in the United States with the observation that there are 85,000 such governments across the country. Governing authority is divided into a maze of overlapping jurisdictions including counties, municipalities, school districts, and special districts.

The United States is distinctive in terms of state and local government structure. Most nations with a federal system have national and state or provincial parliamentary systems in which the executive and legislative branches are interdependent. The head of the former (prime minister or premier) is chosen by and from the latter and stays in office only as long as he or she is able to command majority support in the legislature. Thus, there is no separation of powers and there are no formal checks and balances; the government is designed to function as a policy-making unit, with the executive and legislative branches pursuing the same agenda. The ultimate limit on its power comes from the electorate, not from the structure itself.

The question to be answered, then, is how fragmentation and decentralization affect political accountability and effectiveness, and whose interests are served by the existing arrangement. This requires a general survey of state and local government structure, beginning with a look at state constitutions and the legal basis for local government.

State Government

State Constitutions

The development of state constitutions broadly reflects the political currents in U.S. history: revolution, the struggle for democratization, the Civil War and its repercussions, progressivism, and the expansion of government since the New Deal.

The first state constitutions took shape during the American Revolution and were understandably brief, incomplete, and hastily put together. Many were revised immediately afterward. Only the Massachusetts Constitution of 1780, the oldest now in force in the United States, was drafted by a convention and ratified by the voters.

The state constitutions adopted before 1820 severely limited executive power. Many governors were elected annually, some by the legislature, and in many cases they had no veto power; most authority was given to the legislature. This was a reaction to the autocratic powers of royal governors during the colonial period. This tendency was generally reversed by amendment or revision as time went on and it became apparent that a more balanced system was needed.

Between 1820 and 1860 new states joined the union with constitutions which granted universal white male suffrage; older states followed suit by eliminating their original property qualifications. Limits on legislative power increased and more offices, including judges, were made elective. This democratization was a result of the political pressures of the Jacksonian era, as citizens pushed for greater involvement in government.

During the period between the Civil War and 1920 state constitutions developed in three different directions. Following the war the southern states had to revise their constitutions in line with the requirements of Reconstruction. After Reconstruction ended in 1877, many states reversed direction, reimposing racial segregation and disenfranchising black voters by revising the Reconstruction documents. In the North, constitutions were revised and amended to provide for new state government functions needed in an industrializing society. Many interest groups, seeking to bypass the legislature, had their own political privileges written into constitutions. Thus executive functions multiplied in the form of hundreds of new boards and commissions. Finally, around 1910, the impact of the Progressive movement resulted in new constitutional provisions for, among other things, direct primaries; public control of the judiciary; popular initiative, referendum, and recall; and nonpartisan elections. In many cases the result was a long and detailed constitution, sometimes running to several hundred pages, which placed significant restrictions on the ability of the state government to do its job. This situation, although modified, continues today and is one of the major criticisms aimed at state constitutions.

The period between the two world wars saw little in the way of constitutional change. Activity increased after 1945 and reached its peak around 1970, partly because of the expansion of government on all levels during this time and the subsequent need for constitutional adjustments. The most immediate impetus was provided by Supreme Court rulings in the early 1960s requiring the states to reapportion their legislative districts. Amendments and revisions focused largely on legislative reapportionment, judicial reorganization, expanded gubernatorial power, "home rule" for localities, and especially state and local finance.

At this point the states use four methods to revise or amend their constitutions: legislative proposal (the most frequently used method), popular initiative, constitutional convention, or constitutional commission. In all the states the legislature may propose amendments or revisions which must generally be approved by popular vote. Seventeen states allow voters to initiate constitutional amendments. This requires submitting to the secretary of state a petition signed by a prescribed number of registered voters. The proposed amendment is subsequently submitted to the electorate for approval (see Chapter 5). This method is not generally used and when it is used, it often fails of passage. It can, however, produce dramatic change; the most notable example is California's tax-limitation proposal, known as Proposition 13, which passed in 1978.

All state legislatures may in practice call constitutional conventions; forty-one state constitutions provide for them specifically. This requires approval by the voters. Conventions may be limited to certain topics or unlimited. Some states have provisions for periodic or automatic submission of a proposal for a convention. Many states have also set up constitutional commissions to propose changes. These may be, and often are, only study commissions with advisory powers to the legislature. So far their major impact has been indirect, in submitting proposals for legislative consideration.

Although state constitutions in themselves do not reveal much about the nature of state politics, they do set up the basic structural framework for the resolution of political conflict—the rules of the game. This leads to a closer look at the structure of the individual branches as mandated by the constitutions that established systems based on separation of powers.

The Executive Branch of State Government

The separation of powers has created a situation in which the executive branch of state government can function only by overcoming both its own internal divisions and the fragmentation of state government as a whole. The major formal responsibility of the executive branch is the day-to-day administration of the governing process. It "executes" the laws of the state by putting programs into action. Nationwide, over three million people are on its payrolls.

The nominal head of the executive branch in all states is the governor, who must exert political leadership within the structural limits of the office. Those limits have evolved in the direction of expanding gubernatorial powers. The initial custom of short gubernatorial terms and legislative selection ultimately gave way to longer terms and popular election. Almost all states have a four-year term for the governor, although most states set some limits on reelection. The governor's formal powers generally include the right to propose programs to the legislature, to formulate an annual budget, and in most states to veto bills passed by the legislature on an item-by-item basis. The chief executive can thus act to set the legislative agenda and block its actions, but there is no mutual accountability or impetus for cooperation in the manner of the parliamentary system. In a sense, the separation of powers operates within the executive branch. In the majority of states it is headed by a half dozen or more separately elected officials.

All but eight states have a lieutenant governor, and half of the lieutenant governors are elected separately from the governor. The office essentially exists only to provide a replacement in case of the governor's death, disability, or absence. In about half the states the lieutenant governor serves as president of the state senate, usually but not always a figurehead position.

Most states have a secretary of state, who keeps the state's official records and documents and performs a variety of other administrative and clerical duties. In most cases the office is politically unimportant, but in some states it can be a source of political power through patronage and the awarding of state contracts.

The attorney general is the most "political" position next to that of the governor. This officer serves as a legal adviser to the state's officials, acts as chief prosecutor, and represents the state in court. To these ends the attorney general usually has a staff and a considerable amount of independence. The office can be and has been used as a springboard to the governorship.

The treasurer has the responsibility of safekeeping and disbursing state money. The extent of the treasurer's power is usually limited by statute, but decisions about how and where to invest state funds may be subject to some discretion by that official; hence the office has a certain significance in some states.

All states have one or more officials who are responsible for determining the validity and legality of state expenditures before or after the fact. The former function is known as "preaudit," the latter as "postaudit." These audits are variously performed by controllers (or comptrollers) or auditors, who are usually elected. Auditors and controllers thus have an important "oversight" role in monitoring the financial affairs of the administration. The postaudit function is particularly important, and in almost all states this position is independent of the governor by election or appointment.

The Book of the States, a biennially published reference work for state officials, lists four dozen different categories of administrative officials working in the executive branch of state governments. Only a few states allow the governor alone to select many agency heads. In most states, the governor's appointment power is limited. For example, Virginia requires approval of most gubernatorial appointments by both houses of the legislature; Connecticut allows for approval by either house. Most states simply require senate approval. Some states take appointment power entirely out of the governor's hands, as in Maine, where the legislature chooses the secretary of state, auditor, treasurer, and attorney general. South Carolina excludes the governor almost entirely and depends heavily on appointments by boards and commissions. There are also significant differences in the extent to which voters are involved in choosing executive officials. North Dakota relies on a "long ballot" (eleven officials are chosen by popular vote), while voters in Tennessee elect only the governor and the public utilities commissioner (Council of State Governments 1996, 35 ff.)

Thus the distribution of power within the executive branch as a whole works to limit the power of the governor, who must usually deal with other officials in the executive branch as independent centers of power accountable to popular or legislative constituencies. This situation is, of course, compounded when the governor's political party does not hold all the offices. Structural fragmentation of the executive branch provides the context for gubernatorial politics, described in Chapter 6.

The Legislative Branch of State Government

According to James Madison, the most likely instrument for expressing the political will of a "majority faction" would be the legislative branch. To avoid unlimited majority rule, separation of power becomes necessary within that branch itself:

> In republican government, the legislative authority necessarily predominates. The remedy for this inconvenience is to divide the legislature into different branches and to render them by different modes of election and different principles of action, as little connected with each other as the nature of their common functions and their common dependence on the society will admit. (*Federalist* number 51)

State legislatures have at least these six basic formal responsibilities, in approximate order of importance:

1. Power to pass legislation and set the direction of state public policy.

2. Power of investigation into matters which may require legislative action.

3. Overseeing the functions of administrative agencies through the legislative process and other procedures.

4. Power to amend or revise the state constitution.

5. Involvement in the ratification process for amendments to the U.S. Constitution.

6. Appointment or confirmation of judicial and administrative officers, as well as their impeachment.

All the legislatures, except that of Nebraska, are bicameral, consisting of an upper house, called the senate, and a lower house, known in forty-two states as the house of representatives (it is called the assembly in California, New York, Nevada, and Wisconsin; the general assembly in New Jersey; and the house of delegates in Virginia, West Virginia, and Maryland). Nebraska's unicameral legislature consists of forty-nine "senators" who are elected on nonpartisan ballots. Membership in state senates varies from twenty in Alaska to 67 in Minnesota; the average is forty. In the lower houses it ranges from 40, again in Alaska, to 203 in Pennsylvania and 400 in New Hampshire. The average is 110. In thirty-eight states, senators serve for four-year terms; members of the lower house serve for two years, except in Alabama, Louisiana, Maryland, and Mississippi, where they serve for four years (Council of State Governments 1996, 63, 68).

Public dissatisfaction with state legislatures has led citizens in some states to use the initiative process to impose limits on the number of terms a legislator can serve. California, Colorado, and Oklahoma were the first to do so, in 1990. In 1992, the U.S. Supreme Court ruled that such measures were constitutional. By 1997, twenty-one states had imposed such limits; specific provisions vary. Some states have voted lifetime limits, generally six to eight years, while others specify that legislators may serve only a specific number of years out of a given period of time, for example, six years out of twelve. Most of these states attempted to impose limits on terms in the U.S. Congress, but this was ruled unconstitutional by the U.S. Supreme Court.

Some thirty-five states provide for the legislature to meet every year, usually starting in January. About half of these set no limit on the length of sessions; the California legislature, for example, is legally in continuous session for the entire two-year period between elections. Of the remainder, which technically allow only biennial sessions, most provide loopholes. Only about a dozen states seriously restrict the length of legislative sessions.   The Texas legislature, for instance, has five or six months every other year to do its job, although it uses special sessions to prolong its meetings.   Until recently, the trend was away from such limits, given the volume of business to be transacted by most state governments; however, in some states questions have been raised whether legislative procrastination has made its sessions too long.

About two-thirds of the members of state lower houses and 85 percent of state senators are elected from single-member districts; the remainder come from districts which elect more than one representative. Determining the size and shape of legislative districts is the responsibility of the legislature itself, subject to gubernatorial approval.   Reapportionment usually follows the completion of the decennial U.S. census of population, and it can be particularly contentious when there is divided party control of state government.

The population of legislative districts was the subject of an especially intense political conflict until the early 1960s.   Until then most states did not apportion all districts to have equal numbers of citizens. Many used counties as a basis for representation, at least in one house, and others established maximum or minimum numbers of representatives for cities or towns regardless of population.   Some senate districts were fixed by the state constitution.   Although most constitutions required reapportionment of both houses at least every ten years, many states had failed to do so for as long as fifty or sixty years.   The Vermont House of Representatives, for example, had its apportionment constitutionally fixed to that provided for in 1793.

This, of course, resulted in drastic differences in the size of districts. The single Los Angeles County senate district contained over six million people, whereas a rural county district elsewhere in California had fewer than 15,000.   Each was represented by one senator.   This meant extreme overrepresentation of rural areas; yet most state courts, as well as the United States Supreme Court, refused to take action on what they considered a "political question."

By the 1960s, however, the Supreme Court was ready to take a more activist role.   In 1962, in a case dealing with the Tennessee legislature (*Baker v. Carr*), the Court reversed an earlier decision and gave lower federal courts jurisdiction to consider suits dealing with malapportionment, using the Fourteenth Amendment as justification.   Two years later the Court itself established the principle of "one person, one vote" in the case of *Reynolds v. Sims*, which required both houses to be apportioned according to population. It rejected the analogy between state senates representing counties and the U.S. Senate representing states as a rationale for unequal apportionment. Within a few years most states had complied; the overall benefit accrued to suburban districts.

The shape of districts is still subject to some legislative discretion, however. "Gerrymandering"—drawing district lines in odd configurations to suit the party in power—is still a common practice in most states and is usually used to construct "safe" districts for one party or the other. It has also been used, however, to construct districts containing significant minority group populations, so that they can be represented in the legislature.

The nature of legislative structure and representation thus reflects the philosophy of the separation of powers. By varying sizes, terms of office, and electoral constituencies between each of two equally powerful branches, states have reduced, although certainly not eliminated, the capacity of legislatures to assume policy leadership on behalf of a majority faction.

The Judicial Branch of State Government

The ultimate example of structural fragmentation is the judiciary as it is constructed in most states. A judicial system should indeed be independent of other branches of state government, but it can be argued that the extent of fragmentation seems to go beyond what is necessary.

State judicial systems have two basic responsibilities: the adjudication of cases in criminal or civil law, and judicial review. Criminal cases are brought by the government against individuals accused of infractions of state laws. The responsibility of the court is to determine guilt or innocence and, if an individual is guilty, prescribe punishment.

Civil cases involve a plaintiff bringing suit against a defendant over property, contracts, family matters, or torts (wrongful acts against the plaintiff). State and county governments may be plaintiffs but not defendants without their consent (although municipalities can be both). The job of the courts in civil cases is to adjudicate the dispute and prescribe lawful remedies.

Among the most important responsibilities of the state's highest court is judicial review, which is the power to decide whether a specific law is consistent with the state constitution. Laws that are not deemed consistent are thus invalidated. With the exception of a few states where nonbinding advisory opinions are permitted on request of the governor or legislature, such decisions must wait until a relevant case is appealed to the highest court.

It is impossible to characterize a "typical" state court system. There are two general types of courts: trial courts, which have original jurisdiction over criminal and civil cases, and appeals courts, which consider appeals from those dissatisfied with the decision of the trial courts. The trial courts consider the evidence and render a verdict; the appeals courts determine whether the law has been correctly applied.

Trial courts are distinguished by different jurisdictions. Justice courts, presided over by a justice of the peace, provide one-person (and often nonprofessional) justice in minor criminal and civil matters. Special courts, usually found in urban areas, have particular functions such as traffic, family, probate, housing, or small claims, among others. Other county and municipal courts have broader criminal or civil functions within the particular jurisdictions implied by their titles.

Above these minor courts are the general trial courts, usually known as circuit, superior, or district courts. These generally have unlimited jurisdiction over civil and criminal cases. They usually handle the more serious offenses or suits and often involve jury trials. Each state has a different combination of trial courts, more or less centralized or consolidated. Some states have numerous courts with different jurisdictions that are highly independent of each other. Others have fewer courts with clearer lines of authority.

There are two levels of appeals courts. Most states have some kind of "intermediate" appellate court with the responsibility for the first screening on appeal of lower court decisions. All states have a "court of last resort," generally known as the supreme court. A chief justice provides over a court of five to nine justices who decide cases they accept for appeal by a majority vote. This court has the responsibility for judicial review, and is the end of the road for the state appeals system—though the U.S. Supreme Court is the ultimate appeals court.

There are at least five basic methods of selecting judges in the states: partisan elections, nonpartisan elections, legislative selection, and appointment by the governor alone or subject to either legislative or voter approval. In the last case, many states have "retention elections" in which voters cast "yes" or "no" votes on appointed judges who run on their records, a system known as the "merit plan." The wide variation in selection methods reflects sharp conflicts over the issue of controlling the courts and how best to maintain separation of judicial powers from the other branches. Advocates of popular control favor elections; opponents of political party machines favor nonpartisanship; legal professionals and politicians interested in patronage might favor appointments. None of these methods has consistently achieved the goals of advocates. The attempt to create an independent judiciary on the state level that is still accountable has resulted in a complex and confusing array of court systems among the states.

Theoretical Perspectives on State Government

By and large, consensus and conflict theorists evaluate the separation of powers much as they do federalism. The former accept the idea that separation of powers was intended to prevent concentration of power in a few hands. Most maintain that this has worked and has also contributed to the democratization of the state political system. Like federalism, separation of powers not only protects us from arbitrary authority, whether from the majority or the minority, but gives citizens multiple opportunities for political influence as well. If the legislature is unmoved by political pressure on civil rights, for example, perhaps the courts can provide satisfaction for a group organized around that goal. When legislatures refused to reapportion themselves, the courts stepped in. If the executive branch fails to implement a program properly, the legislature may intervene on behalf of complaining citizens in its capacity as overseer of the administration. A fragmented bureaucracy accountable to different constituencies and independent of the governor will be better able to respond to a variety of pressure groups.

Most importantly, separation of powers eventually forces groups in and out of government to negotiate, bargain, and compromise on their differences in order to achieve their goals. Bills must pass both houses of the legislature and be signed by the governor to become law; ultimately they may face judicial review. Consensus theorists believe that, as a result, arbitrary and ill-considered measures on the whole will have less chance of adoption. Because each branch of government represents a different constituency within the state, the tendency will be for public policy to represent trade-offs among the branches. A balance is therefore established between statewide and local interests.

Some, however, see another side to this. Separation of powers, taken to an extreme, may obstruct effective policy making by creating a condition popularly referred to as "gridlock." A noted pluralist theorist, V. O. Key (1956, 61), took the position that separation of powers could be "an

Good b/c does not allow for cance. y pwr

obstacle to popular decision," especially if branches were controlled by opposing parties. In 1993, for example, only seventeen states gave one party the governorship and a legislative majority; "divided government" prevailed in all the others (Stanley and Niemi 1994, 143). Key states that if "at times of widespread public exasperation . . . one set of politicians cannot be simultaneously thrown out of both executive and legislative posts without a virtual popular uprising, something short of popular government in the conventional sense of the term exists." Similarly, Charles Lindblom (1980, 59) notes that the "libertarian rules" of the separation of powers "complicate policy-making in many ways. . . .It differs from and conflicts with the intention to provide instruments for popular control over policy-making."

attorney general vs governor

Similar problems arise within the branches of government. "Fragmentation of executive branch leadership complicates the politics between the actors involved," notes Thad Beyle (1997, 99–100). He cites numerous examples of battles between the governor and other executive officers over issues ranging from administrative regulations to budgetary matters, and even over the question of who is in charge of state government when the governor is out of state. Fragmentation also "restricts what governors can accomplish in high priority areas such as education . . . because other elected officials with responsibility in the education policy area may have different views about what should be done."

Conflict theorists would agree with Key and Lindblom, but would add that blocking majority rule was the whole point of separation of powers. The purpose was to fragment the working class, diminishing its opportunity to assume control of the entire political system at one time. If state power requires the election of a governor and several other executives as well as two legislative branches with different constituencies and terms of office, only a well-organized and overwhelming majority faction could succeed. What appears to most pluralists as a boon to democracy is, to conflict theorists, an obstacle to its accomplishment.

elit

From the perspective of elite theory in particular, separation of powers deliberately provides a "veto power" to entrenched minority factions. It allows powerful individuals or interest groups to block change by controlling a few key legislative positions, judicial seats, or executive agencies. Thus an elite can maintain its domination of state government by using its limited numbers in strategic places, thereby frustrating majority rule.

Marxists see another side to this: Separation of powers also prevents

Marxists black change unless class organizes

the ruling class from imposing its own policies by majority vote. It may control enough votes in the legislature or enough positions in the executive branch to block change, but probably not enough to make its own changes. In the nineteenth century, when limited state governments served capitalist interests by allowing them to do what they wanted, this was not important. In the twentieth century, even capitalists want and need a certain amount of activist government; yet the separation of powers works to prevent this. Thus both capitalist and working-class interests may be to some extent frustrated by the separation of powers. Yet overall, the system probably has a more serious limiting effect on the latter.

Clearly, then, state governmental structure has an important impact on policy making; the theoretical perspectives offer sharply different evaluations of separation of powers in that regard. For a more complete picture, however, it is necessary to examine the structure of local government as well.

Local Government

Although the U.S. Constitution explicitly provides for state governments, local government is unmentioned. There is no formal constitutional basis for the existence of local governments; they are entirely the creation of the states. As such, their structure and jurisdiction depends entirely on decisions made by the state governments and therefore varies widely across the country. There are five basic types of local government in the United States; each state has its own particular way of combining them (Nathan and Nathan 1979, 2–6):

1. Municipality: A concentration of population in a limited area which has been characterized by the state as a "municipal corporation," a chartered and incorporated legal entity with prescribed boundaries and governmental structure. Municipalities may be called cities, towns, townships, (except in states with organized towns or townships; see below), villages, or boroughs. There are some 19,000 municipalities with over 150 million residents.

2. Town or township: An organized local government which may or may not be chartered, generally in a suburban or rural area, existing in

twenty states. There are 17,000 organized towns and townships with over 50 million residents. In New England, New York, New Jersey, Pennsylvania, Michigan, and Wisconsin, these units have the responsibilities of municipalities in other states and sometimes encompass smaller "village" governments.

3. County: A political subdivision of the state, existing everywhere although only nominally in Connecticut and Rhode Island, generally responsible for administration of selected state functions. In many cases it delivers services otherwise provided by municipal or town governments. There are 3,000 counties in the nation, encompassing or coterminous with other forms of local government.

4. Special district: A unit of local government, overlapping other units, which is established by the state to perform certain specialized functions within its jurisdiction. There are almost 30,000 special districts, half of them in nine states.

5. School district: A form of special district which is responsible for the administration of public elementary and secondary schools. There are over 15,000 school districts in forty-five states.

Municipalities

Municipal Charters. A municipality is established by the state through an act of incorporation—the legislative grant of a charter specifying civic boundaries, governmental structure, and the extent of municipal authority. Charters are often highly complex, detailed documents which in larger cities run to several hundred pages.

States have developed four different systems of chartering municipalities. The oldest is the special act charter, individually designed for the particular community. Used regularly only in a few southern states, it involves state legislative approval of individual charters and therefore embroils the legislature in the details of governance for each community. Most states have adopted the general act charter, which establishes a uniform charter for each type of municipality, usually according to population size. This still requires municipalities to seek special legislative permission for any changes, and it is much the same as a special act charter for the largest cities, which are in a class by themselves. Both methods are rather inflexible; this has given rise to a third system: optional charters, which communities may choose from a selection offered by the state. The least rigid system is the home rule charter, which the locality drafts for itself within the limits of state law and presents to the legislature for approval. The municipality is then empowered to make a limited number of structural changes and political innovations on its own.

States have over time combined these systems, so in any one state municipalities may have different types of charters. Most states have some kind of optional charter plan as well as home rule guaranteed by the constitution or by legislation; only a few allow no home rule. In any case, even under home rule the right of a municipality to make a particular decision may end up being resolved in the state courts.

Forms of Municipal Government. There are three basic types of municipal government in the United States: (1) mayor-council, (2) council-manager, and (3) commission. The oldest and the most prevalent form is the first, in which the mayor is elected as chief executive officer of the municipality, usually for a term of two or four years, along with a city council of anywhere from two to fifty members. City charters may provide for a strong or weak mayor. Strong mayors, found mostly in large cities, have veto power over bills passed by the council or actual voting rights on the council. Strong mayors have the means to control the administration by appointing or removing department heads and formulating the municipal budget. In a weak mayor system, council approval may be needed to hire and fire administrators, or they may be separately elected by the voters. Budgetary power may be in the hands of a city council committee or a council-appointed official.

The city council has the legislative power in municipal government. The extent to which it takes the initiative depends largely on the legal authority and political leadership of the mayor. The stronger the executive branch, the more likely the council is to be working on the mayor's agenda rather than its own.

Council members are elected either at large (in about two-thirds of all municipalities), by ward, or by a combination of both. A council member at large is elected from a single list of candidates offered to all voters in the municipality. A ward system divides the municipality into districts, each electing a council representative. The ward system tends to favor representation of geographically concentrated minority groups.

About two-thirds of all cities, especially in the West, conduct all municipal elections on a nonpartisan basis.

A municipality under a council-manager system elects what is usually a fairly small council, which then hires a professionally trained city manager to perform the administrative work under its policy direction. The manager serves until dismissed by the council. This system developed in the early part of the twentieth century as an attempt to professionalize municipal government. The assumption behind it is that administrative work on a local level can and should be conducted in a businesslike manner without the potentially corrupting influence of partisan politics. In practice, however, some city managers are highly political, taking stands on policy issues and attempting to influence their bosses on the city council. Others assume a more passive role, but in any case the manager's job of implementing policy inevitably involves politics in the sense of dealing with conflicts among and within city departments and dealing with the demands of residents.

The council–manager system is most prevalent in medium-sized, middle- or upper-class communities, especially in New England, the southern Atlantic coast states, and the Pacific coast states. There is often a "mayor" in a council-manager municipality, but he or she is essentially a figurehead, often selected by the city council, and has no significant authority.

The commission system calls for the election of several commissioners, each functioning as the head of one part of the city administration; collectively the commissioners serve as a policy-making body. This system originated in Galveston, Texas, in 1900 as an emergency response to a natural disaster and attracted a flurry of interest between 1915 and 1920. Most commission cities ultimately changed over to the council-manager system, which seemed to accomplish the same goals without the disadvantages of fragmented leadership and poor accountability. Currently, no more than 3 percent of all municipalities are governed this way.

Counties, Towns, and Townships

The importance of counties, towns, and townships as units of government varies from region to region. Counties were initially established as administrative subdivisions of the state. Even today, their structure and functions are determined entirely by the state government, although a few have home rule. In rural areas they have provided a limited range of services, such as law enforcement and highway maintenance. At present, counties have little or no importance in New England, but are increasingly significant elsewhere. In suburban areas they have become a convenient means of coordinating the provision of services among constituent municipalities, including libraries, recreation, public health, and welfare, in addition to those previously mentioned. Several urban counties are coterminous or nearly so with major cities (New York City, Philadelphia, Boston), and as a result some have been consolidated. In other cases, as in Virginia, cities have been separated from counties.

Most counties are governed by a board of commissioners or board of supervisors which has both legislative and administrative powers, similar to the municipal commission plan, and which is elected at large by the county's voters. A smaller number of counties have, instead, a board of township supervisors, which is elected from the county's townships and whose members also hold township office. A few more urbanized counties have moved toward establishment of a single executive office, such as a county supervisor or executive.

Eleven of the twenty states with town or township governments are known as "strong township" states, where most of the towns are similar in structure and authority to municipalities. This is especially true in New England, where towns are the prevalent basic unit of local government. Many of the smaller towns have a "town meeting" form of government, where citizens themselves or in some cases representatives elected by the citizens, regularly gather to vote on local policy issues. The executive branch is composed of a three- or five-member board of selectmen, often assisted by an appointed administrator. The remaining nine states, located mostly in the Midwest, are "rural township" states, where 10,000 township governments perform a very limited set of functions. Most of them have no full-time employees. They were originally intended to duplicate the New England towns, but they ultimately failed to do so.

Special Districts and School Districts

Special districts and school districts were set up as a means of delivering services to a particular region. These districts may be coterminous with one or more municipalities or counties; school districts in particular may constitute subdivisions of counties or cities. Both often have some kind of administrative and financial relationship to the other units of local government as well as to the state.

Special districts are usually run by an elected or appointed board or commission. Most are established to perform a single function such as fire protection, water supply and drainage, soil conservation, or public housing. Some 1,000 multiple-function districts provide water and sewerage for large areas. The largest districts, in terms of revenue and expenditure, have been established for the purpose of transportation. Transit authorities in major cities and the Port Authority of New York and New Jersey are examples. The latter operates a vast network of ports, terminal facilities, bridges, tunnels, airports, and railroads in the New York City metropolitan area.

School districts are specifically responsible for the administration of the public schools. Each school district is run by a school board; most of these boards are popularly elected. The board appoints a superintendent of schools to perform the day-to-day administrative work. The power of school boards varies from state to state; in actuality most of them limit themselves to overall issues of finance and administration.

Responsibilities of Local Governments

Each of the fifty states has its own particular pattern of allocating responsibility for providing services among its local governments. Even within each state several units of local government may share the same responsibility in the same region. In very general terms, however, the state government is the sole or predominant provider of public higher education, state highways, and, with notable exceptions like New York and California (where the counties assume that role), public welfare. Public health and hospitals are usually the responsibilities of the state, although counties and municipalities have a major role in many states. The municipalities have the primary responsibility for administering and financing the services that most directly affect citizens on a day-to-day basis: elementary and secondary education, public safety, public works, sanitation, libraries, local roads and streets, water supply, and recreation, among others. Land use planning, as defined by zoning regulations, and economic development are also mainly local responsibilities. All states have some form of state aid to local governments to help fund these services, as well as regulations that limit local options in providing services and mandates that require provision of certain services. Overall, it is safe to say that governmental decentralization and fragmentation have created a patchwork arrangement of organizing the services that make community life possible. This is why it is often difficult and frustrating for the average citizen to know whom to praise or blame, as the case may be, for the quality of local public services.

Theoretical Perspectives on Local Government

The existence of 85,000 local governments sharing administrative and financial responsibility for a wide variety of services raises the important question of whether such extensive decentralization is in the public interest. Three-fourths of the nation's people live in nearly 300 regions considered by the federal government to be Metropolitan Statistical Areas (MSAs). These are centers of concentrated population (i.e., a major city or cities) together with adjacent communities socially and economically integrated with those centers. These MSAs are serviced by over 25,000 separate governments. Would the development of a "metropolitan government," or any other kind of centralized administration, therefore be desirable?

From the 1920s to the 1960s fragmentation of local government was a heated issue for urban reformers, who—with some success—pushed for greater metropolitan centralization. A few urban areas have approved city-county consolidation plans (Baton Rouge, Louisiana; Miami, Florida; Nashville, Tennessee; Jacksonville, Florida; and Indianapolis, Indiana), but the concept of a governing unit matching metropolitan areas has not caught on. Instead, county governments, whose boundaries do not necessarily make sense geographically or economically, have in many states assumed greater responsibility for a variety of services. Many communities, in fact, have attempted to secede from larger units of government. Recent examples include the New York City borough of Staten Island, which resented its use as a prime location for the city's garbage; and a campaign in the 1980s by some African-American activists to carve out of Boston a predominantly black city, to be known as "Mandela." It is therefore useful to ask what is gained or lost by the presence of so many local governments.

Consensus Theory and "Public Choice." There are two sets of arguments that support the current structure of local government, and both are related to consensus theory. One argument is that strong, independent local governments afford protection against the undemocratic tendencies of centralization. The other, which has become increasingly popular among political scientists in recent years, is that a multiplicity of local governments provides the necessary menu of choices for "consumers" of their services. The latter argument is known as "public choice" theory.

An example of the anticentralist argument is provided by Frank Bryan and John McClaughry (1989, 84 ff), who argue that "giantism is corrupting our political institutions." They propose "the creation of governments of human scale" in which direct democratic participation is possible. To that end they offer their home state of Vermont as a laboratory to test their system of "shires," new and powerful units of government combining existing towns and governed by regular meetings of the citizens.

Far more prevalent in the local government literature is a framework that applies free-market economics to the political system. One of the first statements was the "Tiebout Model," named after its originator, which conceptualizes local governments as providers of public goods, much as corporations market commodities in the economic system. Thus the more sellers there are in the market, the more choices are available to consumers and the more likely individuals are to be able to express their preferences for particular goods and services.

Of course, one cannot buy a particular set of local government services the same way one purchases a commodity. There are different methods of expressing choices in the political system: voting for political leaders who support particular programs, articulating grievances to local government officials, organizing new political subdivisions within older ones, or moving from one community to another (Ostrom, Ostrom, and Bish 1988, 91–95).

From this point of view, competition among numerous governments is beneficial to the consumer of public services, the taxpayer, who can demand change or move out if dissatisfied. This kind of competitive free market would create at least in theory a variety of local governments with differing types and extents of services according to the prevailing consumer demand. As Nelson Wikstrom puts it,

> On balance, a decentralized metropolitan political system is not simply defensible, but preferable to one of a more unified nature. The public choice scholars of urban government are correct in their contention that the presence of a large number of general purpose governments in the metropolis, each with its own package of private goods and public services, and all in competition with one another, allows the citizen-consumer to look around and move around to maximize her or his pattern of priorities. We have learned that in terms of metropolitan governmental structure, bigger is not necessarily better. (1978, 7)

Conflict Theory. These conclusions are sharply challenged by a number of scholars. As Robertson and Judd (1989, 279) put it, "The p̲o̲ ̲ṷ̲c̲a̲l̲ fragmentation of governments in urban areas underwrites and intensifies racial and social class segregation and operates as a redistribution mechanism that benefits affluent individuals and groups." This is done by incorporating new municipalities to avoid annexation to central cities, and by imposing zoning regulations favoring single-family homes with large plots of land, which together have the effect of keeping racial minorities and working-class people out of a community. Many states, especially in New England and the Middle Atlantic, have laws that make annexation nearly impossible, creating what David Rusk (1994, 7) calls "inelastic cities," which are "trapped within existing city limits. . . . Even at the center of seemingly prosperous regions, inelastic cities are failing." Gregory Weiher (1991, 166 ff) argues that such formal measures are complemented by less visible factors: "Political boundaries support the recruitment that is the complement to exclusion in urban sorting. They are significant themselves as a system of information, a frame of reference which provides cues to persons making locational decisions." In other words, blacks and Hispanics know where they are not welcome, and whites choose their residences accordingly. It is true that early in this century, economic elites were the strongest supporters of metropolitan federation plans. Jon Teaford notes that such proposals generally came from the managerial classes, who believed that "government was a business and the essence of successful business was economy and efficiency" (1979, 110–113). Yet they failed to achieve their objectives, largely because most upper- and middle-class people preferred to avoid any connection at all with impoverished urban areas and their problems.

This resulted in a proliferation of suburbs, especially in the Northeast, which had the effect of socially and economically isolating the "dependent city," as Paul Kantor describes it. Localities depend heavily on a tax base provided by business investment and expansion. Large, "multilocational" businesses are in a position to play off competing governments against each other, leaving cities in a poor market position and making them "dependent" on outside aid (Kantor 1988, 170–176). President Reagan's policy of reducing federal assistance and forcing communities to support themselves thus created even greater inequalities between rich and poor communities. The wealthy suburbs thus come out on top

because they escape society's most severe social problems. Poverty is more heavily concentrated in the cities, and political independence allows suburbanites to escape the financial burdens of supporting welfare programs, public hospitals, special school programs, public hospitals, special school programs, increased police expenditures, and other services which cannot be totally provided by poor residents. Fiscal disparities further aggravate the problems of the poor, since provision of public services is more costly in the city. (Judd 1979, 178)

Suburbanites are thus able to avoid responsibility for urban problems. As Plotkin and Scheuerman put it (1994, 124), "The exclusionary logic of Fortress Suburbia was the most powerful force in twentieth-century local government. . . . In the fractured metropolis, where classes and races may legally live apart, no public framework exists requiring majority rule to resolve clashing interests. In this neat world of separate and unequal interests, conflicting political ambitions need never collide, much less counteract one another."

Conclusion

The framework of separated powers was based on a philosophy of limited government. Whichever theoretical perspective one accepts as a reason for this, the establishment of a system whose component parts are internally divided and mutually competitive may make sense only if not much is expected or desired of state government. Given the increased responsibility it has acquired recently, there is a serious question as to whether separation of powers merely contributes to "gridlock" and subsequent governmental ineffectiveness. Likewise, no matter how one may evaluate the existence of 85,000 separate local governments that finance and administer public services, there are also questions about how this facilitates or hinders the existence of livable communities. Whatever our conclusions, this structure of state and local government has a major impact on the political decision-making process, and it is unlikely to change in any substantial way in the near future.

Chapter 4: Voting, Parties, and Elections

At the very least, democracy means that citizens choose their political leaders from among opposing candidates in regular elections. This implies that most citizens should be willing to participate, that there are real choices to be made, and that these choices make a difference in the policies that are implemented by government. There are, however, serious questions about whether these conditions are fulfilled in state and local politics in the United States or, for that matter, in the American political system as a whole. The democratic political process may not be functioning as it should, and this raises doubts about how democratic the system really is.

Voter participation in U.S. elections is low relative to other democratic nations and continues to decline. It is especially low on the state and local level. The political parties appear to be less and less effective in nominating candidates for office and presenting alternative programs. Elections are costly contests among politicians who rely on media "image" rather than reasoned discussion of issues. From the perspective of consensus theory, these are more or less serious flaws in a system that still is reasonably effective. To conflict theorists, these phenomena are both a cause and an effect of an alienated, disenfranchised mass public, and evidence of a decaying and unrepresentative political system. To reach any conclusions, it is necessary to examine voting, parties, and elections on the state and local level in some detail.

Voting

The outstanding characteristic of American voting behavior is low participation, especially in state and local elections. In 1994, there were 190 million Americans of voting age; 62 percent were registered to vote, and only 45 percent reported having voted in the elections for Congress and state officials held that year (U.S. Department of Commerce 1997,

Table 4.1: Average Voter Turnout, United States and Other Nations, 1980-1989 (Percent)

Nation	Rate	Nation	Rate
Belgium	94	Israel	79
Austria	92	Greece	78
Australia	90	Finland	74
New Zealand	89	Great Britain	74
Sweden	88	Ireland	73
West Germany	87	Canada	72
Denmark	86	France	70
Italy	84	Japan	68
Netherlands	84	*United States*	*53*
Norway	83	Switzerland	49

Source: Ruy Texeira, *The Disappearing American Voter,*
Washington, DC: Brookings, 1992, p. 8.

288). And this proportion is probably overstated, because survey respondents usually claim to be voters even if they are not. This represents a steady decline since 1970, when 68 percent were registered and 55 percent claimed to have voted. Voter turnout for elections involving only local offices or for primary elections, which determine who will be the candidate of a particular party, is generally much lower, usually in the range of 20 to 30 percent of eligible voters. This contrasts sharply with turnouts in other nations, which generally range well over 70 percent.

Historically, voter turnout in both presidential and "off-year" elections reached a peak in the late nineteenth century, when the proportion of eligible voters participating reached 70 to 80 percent or more. This percentage fell off rapidly by the 1920s, increased somewhat thereafter, and began to fall off once again in the 1970s.

History of Suffrage

The preceding statistics are particularly surprising given the fact that the achievement of universal suffrage took two centuries of struggle. In the United States determination of voting qualifications was left to the states by the Constitution. The original thirteen states in 1789 all restricted voting rights to white males over twenty-one who either owned property or paid taxes. Vermont (1791) and Kentucky (1792) were the first states to enter the union with no such qualifications for voters. Other new states followed suit, but such requirements continued until after 1850 in a number of other states. Women, slaves, and many free blacks were entirely excluded. Nevertheless, this represented a significant advance over almost every other nation in the world, where voting rights were far more limited or entirely nonexistent.

The Fifteenth Amendment to the Constitution, passed after the Civil War, was intended to prohibit the exclusion of the newly freed slaves from voting. Nonetheless, through various subterfuges, that right was gradually stripped away in the South in the decades following the end of Reconstruction in 1877. Registration was made more difficult by literacy tests that were unevenly applied. Potential black voters, for example, were asked to interpret sections of the state constitution and were almost always "failed" by white officials. Ten states adopted the poll tax, which although nominal was often cumulative, thus placing a burden on both poor whites and blacks. Primary elections were officially restricted to whites through the legal device of declaring political parties private associations. In the one-party Democratic South this effectively eliminated any role for blacks in making a real choice. The "white primary" was ruled unconstitutional by the U.S. Supreme Court in 1944. Blacks who tried to overcome these obstacles were intimidated economically, personally, or by outright terrorism. Thus by the first decades of this century, southern blacks were once again barred from voting.

The struggle for women's suffrage began in the first half of the nineteenth century, and some states permitted women to vote in limited circumstances, such as school elections. In 1890 Wyoming became the first state in the union to let women vote in all elections. As the movement gained strength, a number of other states followed suit, and in 1920 the Nineteenth Amendment gave women the right to vote in all elections. Black women in the South were still effectively excluded by state actions, however.

The civil rights movement of the 1950s and early 1960s broke the logjam in the South. In 1965 Congress passed the Voting Rights Act, which put the federal government in charge of guaranteeing blacks' right to vote. Poll taxes were eliminated by the Twenty-Fourth Amendment in 1964. Within a few years, universal suffrage for all citizens over twenty-one was a reality, and in 1971 the Twenty-Sixth Amendment lowered the voting age to eighteen. Almost 200 years after the Declaration of Independence, all Americans except felons and the mentally incompetent had the right to vote both legally and in fact, with the only requirement being advance registration.

Voter registration laws were developed in the early 1900s as a means of eliminating fraud. These laws included registration in person, residency requirements, and periodic purging of voter lists. During the 1960s the registration laws were significantly liberalized. As of 1990, twenty-six states allowed registration by mail, no state imposed more than a thirty-day residency requirement (eighteen states had none at all), and the majority allowed voters to stay on the rolls four years or more without voting. In 1993, the federal government passed the so-called "motor voter" law, which further liberalized registration. This law enables voters to register at certain government offices (including motor vehicle registries) and requires all states to allow registration by mail. In addition, as of 1996, seventeen states mailed ballots to all registered voters for certain local elections (and three states did so for statewide elections), a dozen allowed unrestricted absentee voting, and seven permitted voters to vote in person at a local government office twenty to forty days before election day (Busch 1997, 11 ff).

Only in the United States, however, is registration entirely an individual responsibility; in most other countries registration is automatic or organized by the government. In Canada, for example, provincial governments help pay for door-to-door registration of voters by the political parties. In several nations voting is actually compulsory. Italian citizens carry identity cards (as do most individuals in European countries), which are stamped "Did Not Vote" if they failed to do so.

It should also be noted that election day in the United States falls on a Tuesday and is not a legal holiday anywhere. Polls in some states do not open until 8 A.M.; some close at 6 P.M. Local elections often have even more limited hours. Thus full-time workers encounter a good deal of inconvenience. In a number of European countries, elections are held on weekends and sometimes last for two days. All of this raises the question of whether the process of registration and voting prevents many people from participating.

Voting Participation

Four factors are most directly related to voter turnout nationally and within the states: age, education, income, and occupation, as shown in Table 4.2. Less than 20 percent of those aged eighteen to twenty turned

TABLE 4.2: Reported Voting and Registration, November 1990

	PERCENT REGISTERED	PERCENT VOTING
TOTAL POPULATION	62.2	45.0
AGE 18–20	35.4	18.4
21–24	43.3	22.0
25–34	52.0	33.8
35–44	65.5	48.4
45–54	69.8	53.2
55–64	73.5	58.9
65–74	78.3	64.1
75 and over	73.7	54.5
EDUCATION		
0–4 years	29.5	16.5
5–7 years	41.1	25.7
8 years	53.3	34.8
9–11 years	47.9	30.9
High School graduates	60.0	42.2
Some college	68.7	50.0
College graduates	74.5	59.0
Postgraduate	81.5	67.8
OCCUPATION		
Professional	77.9	62.3
Managerial	73.3	56.5
Technical/sales/clerical	66.5	48.1
Farming	58.4	43.2
Service	52.0	34.3
Craft	53.0	35.7
Machine Operators	48.5	30.7
Laborers	42.8	26.1
INCOME		
Under $5,000	50.7	32.2
$5,000–10,000	48.3	30.9
$10,000–15,000	54.8	37.7
$15,000–20,000	56.8	38.8
$20,000–25,000	58.0	41.3
$25,000–35,000	63.9	46.4
$35,000–50,000	68.3	51.0
$50,000 and over	76.4	59.2

Source: U.S. Bureau of the Census, *Current Population Reports.*

out in the elections of 1990 as compared with two-thirds of those aged sixty-five to seventy-four. Those employed in higher-status occupations and earning higher incomes have a turnout rate twice that of the poor and of blue-collar workers. Almost 70 percent of individuals with postgraduate education vote; while 70 percent of high school dropouts do not vote. In short, voters are older, wealthier, and better educated than nonvoters.

Thus not only do fewer voters turn out in the United States than in other nations, those who do, tend to be better off. This obviously says something about the relationship of U.S. citizens to their political system. As might be expected, analysts differ in their explanations.

The views of consensus theorists on this question have changed over the years. Most studies published before the 1960s tended to attribute nonparticipation to the particular social and psychological characteristics of the citizens themselves: failure to understand differences in issues, lack of a sense of "political efficacy," apathy, and the like. Some analysts took this a step further: If such people did not vote, so much the better, because their uninformed participation could destabilize all levels of the political system. Their apathy was considered by these theorists to be "functional," that is, it kept the system going. Too much participation might be destructive, since their commitment to democratic values might not be particularly deep. To some observers, the political upheavals of the 1960s demonstrated this all too clearly.

Contemporary consensus theorists have modified this approach. The continuing decline in voting has raised the question of whether political stability is endangered by too little participation. Some analysts fear that "the increasing levels of dissatisfaction, accompanied by a lack of strong commitment to democratic values in the American public appear to create some potential for support of undemocratic leaders. In this light, the public's loyalty to political parties and commitment to traditional processes that inhibit aspiring undemocratic leaders become all the more important" (Flanigan and Zingale 1979, 196). The impressive voter turnout for the presidential candidate Ross Perot in 1992 was significant in that regard. Thus, higher levels of participation may be necessary to avoid social turmoil. What is more, in contrast to the assumptions of earlier researchers, many have concluded that there are no great differences between voters and nonvoters in overall political outlook, and no threat to democracy is likely to result from greater participation even if nonvoters have lower levels of information or political education (Bennett and Resnick 1990, 771–802).

The problem, according to consensus theory, seems to lie with "dysfunctions" in our political institutions. That is, our political parties, election campaigns, and voting procedures need reform in order to encourage greater participation. The primary focus is on registration laws and the role of parties in election campaigns. There appears to be at least some relationship between voter turnout and the stringency of state laws regarding voter registration. Many individuals concerned with increasing participation have thus proposed a variety of reforms to make it easier to register to vote. The new federal law referred to earlier will ultimately constitute a test of whether such reforms will increase voter turnout.

Other consensus theorists emphasize inadequacies in the political party system. Patterson and Caldeira (1993, 675–687) conclude that especially in gubernatorial elections, party organization, strength, and recruitment of candidates are critical for broader participation on the state level. One reason why turnout is greater in European municipal elections is that there is a greater connection between national and municipal politics and the parties therefore work harder to mobilize voters (Morlan 1984).

In any case, though, these theorists do not conclude that the political system itself is seriously flawed. Rather, there is a need for reform of election laws and improvement of party organization to motivate nonparticipants to involve themselves in the political life of the country, at least to the extent where a large majority of citizens will be willing to vote. Ruy Texeira (1992) blames the decline of voter turnout on "a reduction in the perceived benefits of voting" due to "a generalized withdrawal or disconnection from the political world, manifested most dramatically by declining psychological involvement in politics and a declining belief in government responsiveness." He therefore proposes reforms in campaign finance, media coverage of elections, and political party activity to boost voting participation to at least 70 percent.

Conflict theorists carry the critique of American political institutions much further. For them, it is not the individual who has to change; it is the system. They argue that the political system is designed to exclude the young, the less educated, and the poor. It serves the interests of those who rule to rely on a voting population that is disproportionately upper-middle-class or upper-class.

Tom DeLuca asserts that political apathy is a direct result of the structure of the political system:

Living today, Madison, and especially Hamilton, would be proud of their

handiwork. . . . They would know that lurking beneath the appearance of dominant explanations of nonparticipation as founded in mass apathy was some
careful planning that made it seem so. . . . Both men would read the years since
the adoption of their ideas as a time in which the liberal right of property had
been defended from the republican danger of full political equality and too vig-
orous political participation. (1995, 42)

Frances Piven and Richard Cloward agree with many consensus
theorists that restrictive registration rules discourage working-class participation. They argue, however, that in the late nineteenth and early
twentieth centuries "regional elites . . . crafted the step-by-step development of institutional arrangements to narrow the electorate precisely to
demobilize the groups whose politics were threatening and disruptive"
(1988, 120).

Working-class people are alienated from the system because they
perceive—accurately, according to conflict theory—that the candidates
of the two major parties have nothing to offer them. As Howard Reiter
(1984, 137) puts it, "With both major parties . . . geared to the maintenance of the corporate capitalist order, low-income whites see less and
less reason to vote. Indeed, instead of deploring their lack of civic responsibility, we might applaud them for their sophistication. They may
understand better than voters do how small the difference is between
America's major parties."

Public opinion polls show that Americans in general, but especially
nonvoters, have decreasing confidence in their political institutions. Beginning in the mid-1960s, an increasing proportion of Americans agreed
with statements such as "I don't think public officials care much what
people like me think" and "Government is pretty much run by a few big
interests looking out for themselves" (Stanley and Niemi 1994, 169).
Conflict theorists, sharply disagreeing with consensus theorists, claim
that these perceptions are correct.

Some conflict theorists, like Michael Parenti (1988, 194), argue that
although voting has some useful purposes for working-class people,
"politics has always been principally a 'rich man's game.' Ironically, the
one institutional arrangement ostensibly designed to register the will of
the many serves to legitimize the rule of the privileged few and often
excludes those most in need."

Others are less cynical and fatalistic. Many would agree with Walter
D. Burnham that working-class people may have no real alternative but
to abstain from participation, given the ideological monopoly held by the
two "status-quo" parties. But this does not necessarily mean that the

ruling class is strengthened. Rather, "if the two alternatives possible in this system both prove hopelessly inadequate to provide the political and economic means of a collective well-being for most Americans, then a full scale regime crisis . . . will erupt into plain view at some point" (1982, 313). This might provide an opening for a new political party, or at least a new and more open kind of political conflict. Indeed, many recent public opinion polls indicate a strong preference for a third party of some kind.

Obviously, evaluation of these differing perspectives depends a great deal on an assessment of American political parties, which are primarily based in the states and localities.

Political Parties

A political party is an organization whose purpose is to gain political power by placing its members or supporters in public office. Parties in most western democracies are usually private organizations unregulated by government, but this is not so in the United States. Until the late nineteenth century, parties handed out at the polls their own "tickets" listing their candidates. Voters would mark the tickets to indicate their choices. This made it difficult to cast a secret ballot; the states thus began to use the so-called Australian ballot, which contained the names of all candidates. This led to the development of a considerable body of regulation to legally define a political party and the circumstances of its access to the state ballot.

Each state has different definitions and rules. Some states make it relatively easy for new parties or independents to get on the ballot, at least for local or state legislative offices. Most states, however, make it quite difficult. In Florida, third parties or independent candidates must collect over 180,000 signatures and pay a "validation fee" of ten cents per signature (Harris 1990). In California, a third party must sign up 75,000 voters to register in its name, or collect ten times as many signatures on a petition. Oklahoma requires a petition with thousands of signatures, but each page must contain the names of voters from only a single county, and the petitions cannot be circulated between June and November of even-numbered years. North Carolina demands an elaborate bureaucratic procedure to determine the validity of each signature, plus a validation fee. New Jersey relies entirely on performance at the polls—a party will not be recognized unless it gains 10 percent of the vote in a state legislative election. Maryland requires 10,000 signatures, and adds the following restrictions:

> In a gubernatorial election year, such a petition may not be filed after the first Monday in August preceding through the 15th day following the general election in a year when a special primary and election are proclaimed by the governor, such a petition may not be filed after the fifth Monday preceding through the 10th day following the special primary, nor after the fifth Monday preceding through the 15th day following the special election. (U.S. Federal Election Commission 1995)

Well-financed candidates like Ross Perot or parties with "cult" followings—like the New Alliance Party or Lyndon Larouche's organization (which has gone by many names)—are able to meet these criteria; average citizens cannot. Staying on the ballot is an even more formidable task, usually necessitating 5 to 20 percent of the vote in a previous election. Most states also forbid "fusion," a practice by which third parties may endorse the candidates of major parties. New York is a notable exception, and this is part of the reason why several political parties regularly appear on its ballots. The U.S. Supreme Court in 1997 refused to declare such antifusion laws unconstitutional.

The ballot laws in the fifty states as a whole thus tend to limit competition to the Democratic and Republican Parties. On this matter, of course, the two parties are in agreement, and they use their position of power in state government to guarantee it. For all practical purposes, no other party has been able to break up the nationwide monopoly of the Republicans and Democrats, which began in 1856.

Perhaps the most important structural factor preventing the success of third parties is the single-member-district (SMD) system. Practically all federal, state, and local elected officials win election by gaining a plurality of votes within a particular geographical district. Most other nations rely at least in part on proportional representation (PR): candidates for legislative office are elected on the basis of the proportion of the total vote won by their political party. In a PR system, even a small percentage of the total vote may win a minor party a few seats in the legislative branch. Our system requires any third party seeking to expand beyond a local base to be well organized in a vast number of localities and to get more votes than the other parties in most of them. Thus the incentives for formation of a third party in competition with the Democrats and Republicans on the state and local level are few.

Third parties which persist in spite of this disadvantage either manage to build influence by endorsing major party candidates (where "fusion" is permitted) or ultimately end up merging with one of the major parties after a brief success as independent organizations. Examples of the former are the Conservative, Liberal, and Right-to-Life Parties in New York; examples of the latter are the Farmer-Labor Party in Minnesota and the Progressive Party in Wisconsin. There are in addition smaller third parties, such as the Libertarians and a number of socialist parties, which exist primarily to educate voters rather than to win office.

Development of Parties in the United States

Until recently, the American party system has to a certain extent adapted to changes in the pattern of social and political conflict in the United States. Most analysts agree that we have had at least five party systems since 1789. The first pitted followers of Alexander Hamilton and John Adams (Federalists) against followers of Thomas Jefferson (Democratic-Republicans). The Federalist constituency was composed of commercial and industrial entrepreneurs, especially those located in New England; the Democratic-Republicans had their base among farmers and workers in the South and West. The Federalists' aristocratic orientation led to their demise in the 1820s. The second party system came into being as Democratic-Republicans broke into factions supporting and opposing the policies of President Andrew Jackson; the former became the Democratic Party, the latter the Whig Party. The Whigs generally leaned toward business interests and a federal program to stimulate economic development (the "American plan"), but they split up over the issue of slavery in the 1850s. The Democrats also split during the election of 1860, resulting in the victory of Abraham Lincoln, presidential candidate of the Republican Party, which had been organized six years earlier to fight the expansion of slavery into newly admitted states.

After the Civil War this third-party system became regional in nature. The South went increasingly Democratic, as the Democratic Party became the standard bearer of white supremacy after Reconstruction; the North became generally Republican, with Democratic enclaves among immigrants and urban voters. The parties were evenly matched until 1896, when the Democrats absorbed a radical agrarian movement known as the Populists and nominated William Jennings Bryan for president. His defeat almost eliminated the Democrats as viable contenders in much of the North and rendered them a minority party for almost forty years.

The Depression changed all this by discrediting the Republicans, who took the blame for it through their president, Herbert Hoover. His defeat by Franklin D. Roosevelt in 1932 and the success of Roosevelt's economic program, the New Deal, forged a new coalition for the Democratic Party made up of Southerners, the urban working class, Catholics, Jews, and northern blacks. The Democrats became the majority party. It is this fifth party system which prevailed until recently. The problem for this particular coalition is that it has outlived its time and has not been replaced. It began to fall apart in the 1970s as political divisions created by the Depression faded and certain Democratic voting blocs became more Republican and vice versa.

The greatest changes, however, came in the 1980s. With Ronald Reagan's presidency, the Republicans became an almost exclusively conservative party; the liberal and moderate factions that had existed prior to 1980 have almost vanished. The Democratic Party had always been fractionalized between northern liberals and southern conservatives; the latter gravitated toward the Republicans, while the party as a whole became more conservative as working-class voting turnout declined and many Democrats felt a need to compete for the more "upscale" voters attracted to Reagan's program. The election of Bill Clinton in 1992 was attributed by many to a successful attempt by the Democratic Party to shed its liberal image. Thus both parties have become considerably more conservative.

In any case, exclusive identification with one or the other party is not so frequent among voters as in the past. The parties are less coherent as organizations representing distinct political interests. More specifically, in 1952 three-quarters of voters had described themselves as "strong" or "weak" partisans, and the remainder identified themselves as independents. By 1990, less than two-thirds indicated a partisan allegiance (Stanley and Niemi 1994, 158). Identification with a particular party is even weaker among younger voters. There is more "ticket-splitting" on all levels; it is much harder to find strong state or regional party allegiances. This raises the issue of whether the current party system is becoming obsolete, or whether parties themselves are increasingly irrelevant to the American people. The answers vary; we will consider them after examining party organization and functions on the state and local levels.

Party Organization

The hallmark of U.S. political parties is their complete decentralization. Decisions on organization, finances, programs, and candidates are made independently by thousands of state and local party organizations. This is quite different from the so-called "responsible" party systems in other nations, where party functions are more highly centralized and local party organizations are usually answerable to a national organization.

The basic units of American political parties are the 180,000 precincts, each containing a few hundred voters. If a party organization exists on that level (often it does not), a small precinct party committee and a chair or captain hold the responsibility for party functions. In their absence, the local unit may be the ward (several precincts), the legislative district, or the town committee, which may be composed of precinct representatives of those elected in party primaries. These in turn send representatives to the county committee (in some areas selected by the primary instead), consisting of anywhere from a few dozen to several hundred members or more. The county is the most active and most politically significant unit of political party organization, except in New England, where the town occupies that position. The county or town committee chair is thus an important figure in partisan politics. The state committee, usually composed of several hundred members, has various financial and organizational responsibilities on the state level. It is chosen by the county committees in about half the states and by primary or a state party convention in the others. Most of the state committees select a state party chair, who is chosen by a primary in about a dozen states. State party chairs have considerable authority and occasionally a good deal of real power, depending on the individual chair, party strength, and the chair's relationship to the governor. The national party committee consists of two delegates from each state; but although it is at the top of the structure, it has little power over state and local party organizations.

The party's electoral success often relies on its ability to coordinate these somewhat autonomous parts of its structure during election campaigns. The task of party committees and chairs is to raise money and coordinate party workers. Even though use of the media has become more important on the state and local levels, the crucial job of actually mobilizing voters to go to the polls, especially in primary elections, involves a direct personal effort by the local party organization. If the local organization is poorly led or no local organization exists, a party candidate without substantial personal resources faces an uphill battle.

In the early 1980s, local party organizations existed in most of the 3,600 county, town, and district units, but only 26 percent had a budget and only 13 percent had year-round headquarters. Nonetheless, three-quarters were involved in recruiting candidates for state legislative offices. On the state level, 90 percent of the organizations had a full-time chair or executive director, although 75 percent had ten or fewer full-time staff members. Only two-thirds had significant voter mobilization drives (Adamany 1984, 83–85).

American political parties are therefore essentially coalitions of autonomous local volunteer organizations, which often have little in common with each other except the party name and a desire to win elections. To a great extent this results from our decentralized, fragmented political system, which in combination with the single- member-district system precludes electoral success by a disciplined, centralized, programmatic party. The Democrats and Republicans have maintained their monopoly by adapting to this situation at the expense of any coherent program or organizational unity.

Party Strength and Competition

Ideally, a party system should be able to provide genuinely competitive contests among candidates for all offices across the nation. This would give the voters maximum leverage for maintaining accountability in government. Nowhere in the world is this ideal achieved, let alone in the United States. On the state and local levels, organizational strength and ability to compete vary greatly from place to place.

Most state parties are fractionalized, divided internally along urban-rural, liberal-conservative, or machine-reform lines. Factions may form around particular issues or individual leaders. Cohesiveness is the exception. California's parties are a prime example. Party structures and control over nominations were severely weakened as a result of reforms sponsored by the Progressive movement early in this century. This resulted in the formation of unofficial party organizations linked to individual candidates, which until recently had substantial influence. The ultimate effect has been to weaken the parties and strengthen interest groups and the mass media as organizers of public opinion in California elections (Gerston and Christensen 1991, 11–14).

Each state has a different pattern of organizational strength based on its particular political history and the quality of its political leadership. Lately, pluralist researchers have been optimistic about the overall pattern throughout the country; they see a resurgence after a period of decline in the 1960s and 1970s. According to Cornelius Cotter (1991, 1056), state party organizations are "stronger . . . than at any time in the twentieth century [and] have the capacity to be intermediating bodies, subordinating means to ends as they attempt to ally to control government and policy." Studies by James Gibson et al. (1985, 139–156; 1989, 66–89) claim that local party organizations have become more active in recent years, especially in the Northeast. Thad Beyle (1997, 41) asserts that not only have parties become more important in state governing institutions, but "in the 1990s some feel that the money these state parties can raise and the campaign services they provide to their candidates and local affiliates have made them a strong force in state politics." It should be added, however, that local elections in most areas are conducted on a nonpartisan basis, thus weakening party organizations on that level. Similarly, communities run by a nonpartisan manager deprive the political parties of a base in the executive branch of local government.

Considerable effort has gone into attempts to measure interparty competition in the states, with mixed results, depending on the criteria used for measurement. On a more general level, it is clear that over the last two decades the Republican Party has become much more competitive in the South, and "divided government"—the governorship controlled by one party and the legislature by the other, or even divided control of the legislature—has become considerably more prevalent. This follows from decreasing levels of straight party voting. Nonetheless, there are a few states in which one party has become dominant, and the primary election becomes an important contest, often more so than the general election. It can be concluded that at best party competition at the state legislative level or below is significant but inconsistent.

Parties in State and Local Politics

Issues of competition and voter affiliation lead to differences among the perspectives in evaluating the impact of political parties in state and local politics. It may be true that state and local party organizations are more active, well-organized, and competitive. But do they actually offer the voters a choice? And if they do, how much choice should they offer? Unlike political parties in many other countries, the Democrats and Republicans share an allegiance to the basic values of the existing political and economic system. Although the Republican Party became more conservative in the 1980s, the Democrats have also moved in that direction. There are few abiding or consistent differences on major issues, especially on the state and local levels, indicating that competition does not run deep. An ambitious office-seeker who is circumspect about publicizing his or her more outrageous ideas can find a home in either party, or even in both parties, using the primary election as a vehicle. The experience of David Duke, the Klansman and Nazi who in the 1980s was elected state representative, and almost succeeded in gaining the Republican nomination for U.S. senator and for governor in Louisiana, is instructive in that regard.

Consensus theorists see this as a strength of the system. Their criterion for evaluating the functions of political parties is whether the party system is able to moderate and mediate political conflict, that is, build consensus. If the parties fail to do this, there is a risk of intensified conflict and a structural crisis. In general, consensus theorists feel that decentralization, ideological consensus, and flexible structure are beneficial to the political system in promoting bargaining and compromise over political issues.

On the other side of the coin, however, the lack of structure may facilitate the takeover of state and local political parties by interest groups. The so-called Christian right, with its distinct ideology, its high degree of political unity, and its considerable money, has made significant inroads in its drive to control the Republican Party. In 1994, a survey by *Campaigns and Elections* magazine indicated that the influence of the Christian right was "dominant" in eighteen state Republican organizations and "substantial" in thirteen others (Persinos 1994, 22). Such a trend would obviously not lead in the direction of moderation or mediation of conflicts.

The major concern of consensus theorists is with strengthening party organization and promoting competition among candidates, but not necessarily ideological competition. Few want to see the establishment of European-style parties in the United States. If state and local parties can recruit candidates, mobilize voters, and offer alternatives within the mainstream of American values, they are doing their job. According to many consensus theorists, the political parties are slowly moving in that direction:

> To the foreign eye, the United States may seem to be engaged in nonparty politics, because the parties look so weak. But the state parties play an important role. Their nonbureaucratic organization belies their effectiveness. They engage in a remarkable array of electoral activities and have an independent and

potentially decisive impact on political outcomes. Furthermore, a good chance exists that they can become considerably stronger. In this sense, American state parties persist. (Patterson 1993, 209)

According to conflict theorists, the whole point of the American two-party system is to exclude alternatives to the status quo. "Whatever their differences," says Michael Parenti (1988, 177), "the two major parties cooperate in various stratagems to maintain their monopoly over electoral politics and discourage the growth of progressive third parties." Some analysts point out that notwithstanding their organizational strength, they do not hold the allegiance of voters; at best they may be cliques of activists who monopolize political life within their communities to the exclusion of average citizens.

Several analysts, not all of them conflict theorists, criticize the Democratic Party for going upscale and abandoning its historic working-class base. Thomas B. Edsall (1984, 64–66) claims that since the 1970s the Democrats have become more responsive to suburban middle-class constituencies interested in political reform and social issues instead of economic change. Rather than mobilize new or less affluent voters to beat the opposition, they have decided to play on the opposition's turf. The result is that the Democrats have failed to challenge the conservative Republicans ideologically and have therefore left many citizens unrepresented in political competition. In short, the two parties have become more alike on the issues and have therefore nothing to offer working-class, poor, and younger voters, who respond by failing to vote. The fact that Bill Clinton won the election of 1992 by presenting himself as a centrist "New Democrat" is therefore not necessarily an indication of a positive accomplishment.

From the point of view of elite theory in particular, this is a result of the increasing influence of money in politics. According to Thomas Ferguson and Joel Rogers (1986), the Democratic Party made a "right turn" because of the influence of contributors affiliated with the economic elite. Marxists agree, but they add that the upper class has also become more unified and more aggressive in terms of trying to reverse the gains made by the poor, women, and minorities in the 1960s; part of its strategy has been to recapture the Democratic Party.

Overall, then, pluralists are not entirely satisfied with the functioning of political parties, but they tend to see an improvement in their ability to mobilize voters and compete in state and local elections. Conflict theorists criticize the Democrats and Republicans for being too much alike and failing to offer voters the alternatives that might motivate greater participation. The question is whether voters will become increasingly impatient with the "sameness" of the two parties if they are unable to come up with solutions to the many socioeconomic problems afflicting states and localities.

Elections and Campaigns

The question of who is to occupy positions of power in state and local governments is, of course, decided by elections, which provide the basic means of public involvement in political life. But citizens' participation is low, and questions can be raised about the parties' effectiveness in contesting elections. Are elections, then, truly instruments of political accountability? Are the rules fair, so that all can participate? Are we able to make informed, intelligent choices on the basis of what we read and hear during campaigns?

Primary Elections

From around 1830 until the early 1900s the dominant method of choosing partisan candidates for state offices was the convention—a periodic gathering of local delegates who determined the party's standard-bearers. On the local level that decision was usually made by the local party organization. This generally reinforced the power of party organizations and allowed the leadership or party activists to maintain control of the nomination process. All this began to change with the advent of the Progressive movement, a group of middle-class political reformers. Under Governor Robert M. LaFollette in 1903, Wisconsin passed the first law requiring primary elections for all state and local offices. Within fifteen years these elections had spread to most other states, and they are used in all the states today.

In general, a primary election allows some or all voters to choose a party's nominee. There are several variations among the states. Most states have laws mandating direct primaries for all partisan elections; the rest do so by party rules. These laws and rules vary with regard to who may vote in a primary. As of 1990, fifteen states restrict voting in party primaries to people who have registered in that party in advance—this is known as a "closed" primary. Eight states allow unaffiliated voters to declare for a particular party on primary day. The remaining states have

Table 4.3: Primary Election Rules, 1990

Party Choice Required in Advance		Party Choice Not Required in Advance		
Unaffiliated do not participate	*Unaffiliated may declare at polls*	*All voters choose party at polls*	*Voters receive all party ballots, choose while voting*	*Other*
Arizona	Colorado	Alabama	Hawaii	Alaska
California	Connecticut	Arkansas	Idaho	Louisiana
Delaware	Kansas	Georgia	Michigan	Washington
Florida	Maine	Illinois	Minnesota	
Kentucky	Massachusetts	Indiana	Missouri	
Maryland	New Hampshire	Iowa	Montana	
Nebraska	New Jersey	Mississippi	Oregon	
Nevada	Rhode Island	N. Dakota	S. Carolina	
New Mexico		Ohio	Tennessee	
New York		Texas	Utah	
N. Carolina		Wyoming	Vermont	
Oklahoma			Virginia	
Pennsylvania			Wisconsin	
S. Dakota				
West Virginia				

Source: Council of State Governments, *Book of the States, 1990-1991*, p. 221

some version of an "open" primary. Either all voters are entitled to choose a party at the polls, or voters are able to vote for candidates in both parties. Louisiana has the most "open" primary; all candidates are listed together, and the top two vote-getters, regardless of party affiliation, compete with each other in the general election unless one of them gets 50 percent or more of the vote. Five other southern states also provide for some kind of run-off election.

A number of states still permit party conventions in certain cases. Alabama and Virginia leave the decision between primary and convention to party leaders; others, such as Colorado, Connecticut, New York, North Dakota, and Utah, permit some form of preprimary candidate endorsement by party leaders or conventions. Illinois, Indiana, Kansas, and Michigan allow conventions for certain state offices (Council of State Governments 1994-1995, 217–218). In states and localities with nonpartisan elections, "preliminary" elections are held, with the two top vote-getters challenging each other without party labels in the general election.

Obviously, the ability of parties to control nominations and the extent of party competition depends on the procedures used in the primary. Preprimary endorsements or conventions lend support to tight party organization. Primary runoffs in the South encourage competition within the generally dominant Democratic Party (which was the point in the days when the Democrats defended white supremacy). Open primaries weaken party discipline, and blanket primaries, in which voters can choose from more than one party, have the potential to eliminate it entirely. Primary competition depends considerably on whether an incumbent is running for election, whether the local party organization has endorsed a candidate, and whether a political party is dominant in the state or district. To the extent that these conditions exist, primary competition declines. In the last case primaries can have the effect of dampening two-party competition in the general election as potential candidates strive for the nomination of the "winning" party.

Overall, primaries may have democratized the nomination process, however, most likely at the expense of party organization and interparty competition. The problem is not so much the primary itself, but the fact that primary voters need not have a particular commitment to any party beyond advance registration, and often not even that. The state and local political parties, and increasingly the national parties as well, are in a position of having their most vital function—selection of candidates— largely in the hands of voters who have no organizational commitment or responsibilities. This has contributed greatly to problems of party incoherence and ineffectiveness.

Campaigns and Political Finance

The importance of money in political campaigns is hard to overstate, and campaign money has become a major source of controversy in recent years. The inconsistent role of party organizations in state and local election campaigns has largely left the responsibility of electioneering to the candidates themselves. For an incumbent who has made no serious political errors, this may not present a major problem. For challengers, or candidates in competitive races, there is a necessity for an aggressive campaign, which requires money. Challenging an incumbent in particular means building "name recognition"—the new candidate must find some way to make his or her name as familiar as that of the incumbent, whose political resources are usually superior to begin with. An even match between new candidates calls for even heavier financing.

The need for money is also a direct outgrowth of the increase in the number of uncommitted voters. They may be concerned with state and local issues, but the labels "Democrat" or "Republican" no longer imply a clear position on the issues to them or command automatic loyalty. Local nonpartisan elections eliminate party labels altogether. Thus the candidates themselves have to find a means of getting their messages across to voters. Person-to-person contact in various settings, such as rallies, group meetings, and even door-to-door canvassing, is certainly effective, but it is impractical and time-consuming in large constituencies. It also requires much more organizational work on the local level, which the parties are not always prepared to do. Yet until forty or fifty years ago this was just about the only method of campaigning.

The growth of the mass media, especially television, has changed all this. Candidates now have a means of immediate communication with voters, but only at considerable cost, in terms of both money and the quality of the message. Until recently, this was most apparent in national and gubernatorial campaigns, but it has now become more important in lesser state and local contests. The result is an increase in expenditures and a de-emphasis of issues in favor of the candidate's "image" and personality, which are more easily communicated in a thirty-second spot. This in turn has led to the hiring of political consultants—specialists who advise candidates on their strategies, especially their use of the media. The entire process is self-reinforcing: as the party organization weakens, candidates rely more heavily on media and money, and this in turn renders the party even more obsolete.

Media campaigns cost money; thus the trend in amounts spent has been steadily upward on all levels. In 1956, a race for governor cost on the average about $100,000, equivalent to $400,000 in current dollars. Most state legislative or mayoral races then cost a few thousand dollars or less. By 1986, the average gubernatorial primary and general election campaign cost over $3 million for each candidate. The combined cost for all candidates in Florida that year was $24 million; in California, $22.5 million. Four years later, the race for the California governorship cost a total of $43 million, in 1994, this race cost $60 million. Even in a less populous state such as Montana, candidates for governor spent $2.7 million, more than was spent by all statewide and state candidates four years earlier (Alexander 1992). In 1994, the governors' races held in thirty-six states cost a total of $418 million (Beyle 1996, 10). On the legislative level, spending for individual seats in 1988 ranged from an average of a few thousand dollars in smaller states to $370,000 in California (Gurwitt 1992, 49). In one California district in 1988, $2.4 million was spent just during the primary. During the 1980s, most states saw increases in legislative election costs of 100 to 200 percent (Singer 1988).

The bulk of this money comes from individual candidates themselves, their supporters, interest groups, and, increasingly, political action committees (PACs). When Congress passed laws in 1974 restricting and regulating individual campaign contributions in federal elections, it also allowed the establishment of PACs, which were authorized to collect donations from individuals and organizations and disburse them to candidates. There are now over 4,000 PACs, representing corporations, labor unions, trade organizations, ideological groups, and even individual candidates. Although they are especially active in presidential and congressional campaigns, their impact on state and local elections has increased dramatically. The overwhelming proportion of this money goes to incumbents. Since the point of their contributions is to buy access to the officeholder, PACs prefer to back incumbents, who are more likely to be winners. Thus incumbents in state and local elections, who already have an advantage in terms of name recognition, are given an additional financial boost over challengers. The result, of course, is a tendency for voters to reelect incumbent candidates.

Campaigns and State Regulation

Media-based campaigns have also given rise to the "negative campaign." "Mudslinging" has been a part of American politics from the beginning, but the use of television ads to besmirch the opposition has become a standard practice. Part of the reason is the obvious limitation of getting a message across in thirty or sixty seconds; it is far easier for a candidate to slander an opponent in that time than to communicate a positive image about himself or herself, or to promote a political platform. Thus Governor Ann Richards of Texas was the target of ads accusing her of drug use; Governor Douglas Wilder of Virginia was subjected to ads depicting a woman crying as an announcer described a bill introduced by Wilder that allowed court interrogation of rape victims on their private lives; and New Jersey's gubernatorial race of 1989 featured ads by each candidate showing his opponent with a growing Pinocchio-like nose, symbolizing alleged lying (Biemesderfer 1990, 24).

Most states have attempted some regulation of campaign finance, and some have attempted to restrict certain kinds of advertising. About half the states limit individual or PAC contributions in some way. Most prohibit or limit direct contributions by corporations or labor unions as well. Public disclosure of contributions is also prevalent. About half the states have enacted some kind of public financing of campaigns; a few accompany this with a limit on expenditures by candidates who accept public financing. It should be added here that the U.S. Supreme Court in 1976 forbade limits on how much of their own money candidates could spend. Although these laws have curbed some of the worst abuses of the system, they are still too limited to reduce the overall importance of money in state and local election campaigns. A number of states have enacted laws against "knowingly" making false statements in election campaigns. These are problematical because they run up against First Amendment guarantees of freedom of speech and the press; in three states, such laws have been struck down as unconstitutional. As a result, state officials are reluctant to enforce them (Biemesderfer 1990, 25).

State and local campaigns, like national campaigns, have thus become more "candidate-centered." The candidates act as political "entrepreneurs" who recruit themselves for office, finance their own campaigns out of personal funds or PAC contributions, and develop a marketing strategy heavily reliant on media advertising. The result has been an explosion in the cost of elections, and these costs are largely financed by special interest groups and wealthy individuals, including the candidates themselves. Candidates therefore have to spend far more time raising money, find much less advantage in basing campaigns on issues rather than personality, and end up insulting each other as a means of winning office. One result is increasing cynicism among voters about the entire electoral process; another is the lower quality of political dialogue in state and local government.

Consensus theorists do not view all this as a fatal flaw in the political system. Most would agree that money has become too important in elections, but this can be remedied by stronger party organization, limits on campaign spending, and public funding of candidates for office. In fact, public disapproval of the influence of PACs and other campaign contributors has forced the federal and state governments to adopt these measures over recent years, and the trend is likely to continue. Although money is critical, elections can still be won on the state or local level by

Table 4.4: Cost of Gubernatorial Elections, 1991-1994

State	Total Spent (Millions)	Cost per Vote	State	Total Spent (Millions)	Cost per Vote
Ala.	$19.5	$16.21	Mont.	$2.7	$6.52
Alas.	4.1	19.29	N.C.	13.3	5.15
Ariz.	8.2	7.23	N.D.	0.7	2.54
Ark.	3.6	5.03	Neb.	2.5	4.31
Cal.	60.6	7.00	Nev.	5.7	15.27
Col.	8.2	7.23	N.H.	0.8	2.68
Conn.	8.7	7.55	N.J.	22.4	9.24
Del.	2.7	9.78	N.M.	4.9	10.50
Fla.	21.1	5.02	N.Y.	32.3	7.21
Ga.	12.0	7.73	Ohio	6.9	2.07
Haw.	9.3	25.29	Okla.	5.5	5.51
Idaho	3.4	8.12	Ore.	6.4	5.26
Ill.	22.0	7.09	Pa.	36.1	10.06
Ind.	6.7	3.04	R.I.	4.1	11.46
Iowa	6.9	6.88	S.C.	12.3	13.20
Kan.	6.7	8.16	S.D.	2.8	8.83
Ky.	19.6	23.50	Tenn.	28.0	18.82
La.	9.8	5.66	Tex.	26.4	6.01
Mass.	6.1	2.83	Utah	3.9	5.18
Md.	13.4	9.53	Va.	13.5	7.58
Me.	5.3	10.43	Vt.	0.3	1.63
Mich.	11.0	3.58	Wash	7.0	3.08
Minn.	4.8	2.73	Wis.	6.1	3.87
Miss.	5.2	7.45	W.V.	3.9	6.00
Mo.	13.8	5.90	Wyo.	1.2	6.14

Sources: Council of State Governments, *Book of the States 1994-1995;* Beyle, 1996.

a combination of personal campaigning, amassing numerous small donations, and using volunteers.

Conflict theorists acknowledge that the richest candidate may not
always be the most successful, but they argue that the price of the admis-
sion ticket to the political arena has become too expensive for average
people. Candidates for office have no choice but to be obligated to the
source of their campaign funds, and this means that wealthy special interests have gained control of elections. Moreover, the emphasis on im-

age and personality in media-based campaigns makes an appeal to the electorate based on issues nearly impossible. Thus, state and local offices, which used to be accessible to people of average means, are now the preserve of those who have access to considerable amounts of money. The public policies produced by such officials will inevitably serve the interests of the wealthy.

Conclusion

If state and local governments are to be democratic in actuality as well as in theory, they must have effective institutions to facilitate and indeed encourage the maximum participation of citizens and the full expression of political views. There is a serious question as to whether such institutions exist.

Although the achievement of universal suffrage required a long struggle, the United States has a distinctly poor record of voter turnout, especially on the state and local levels. Turnout is related to age, income, education, and occupation. The issue is whether this is caused by some combination of voter apathy and minor flaws in our electoral system, as pluralists believe, or by the exclusionary effects of political party organization and the conduct of campaigns, as nonpluralists believe.

The state and local political parties are not consistently competitive either ideologically or electorally. They are not fully organized to encourage participation or to recruit and promote candidates for office. Voters are moving away from identification with the two major parties. Most consensus theorists, however, have not given up on the parties as institutions able to perform their function of articulating public opinion, developing consensus out of conflict, and maintaining political stability. They see improvements in state and local organizations and a larger role in campaigning that may ultimately draw more voters into participation. Conflict theorists, on the other hand, believe that voters have been "turned off" by the refusal of Republicans and Democrats to offer attractive candidates and viable policy alternatives. Unless they change, the existing political parties may become increasingly irrelevant and end by destroying themselves.

State and local elections used to be low-cost affairs based at least to some extent on ideological differences between parties and candidates. Today they tend to resemble national contests in their increasing expense and their emphasis on the candidate's image. Pluralists believe that this reflects a lack of public interest in political issues and a legitimate concern of many voters with the candidates' personalities and their professional qualifications. If campaign finance has gone out of control, it would not require a major transformation of our institutions to reassert limits on contributions and spending. Nonpluralists see contemporary election practices as symptoms of a deeper illness. The political system on all levels has become connected to a money machine that will not permit candidates to leave the ideological mainstream. Hence campaigns have become circuses, aided and abetted by the mass media, which use sensationalistic coverage to increase profits.

Many political and economic problems, particularly visible on the state and local levels, appear to be coming to a head as we approach the end of the century. The ability of the political system to articulate alternatives and develop leaders will be tested in this difficult environment and will demonstrate which of the perspectives provides the best explanation of how the process works.

Chapter 5:
Community Power and Citizen Action

Citizen action—direct participation by individuals in the process of promoting political change—is the most critical element of democracy. Without it, there is neither a day-to-day guarantee of political accountability on the part of state and local governments nor any means of consistent organized expression of public opinion. Those means do exist: direct democracy (initiative, referendum, recall, town meetings), the influence of interest groups, and the activism of community organizations. But increasing cynicism toward any political action has taken its toll on such involvement. Many people, especially the young, believe that citizen action is not worthwhile. Is that true? What does such activity accomplish? The impact of citizen action on state and local governments is argued among adherents of different points of view.

Community Power

The effectiveness of citizen action depends on the political relationship of state and local government to the community. If citizens organize to influence government, what kind of a response can they expect? Do its policies reflect a concern for public opinion? What is the structure of power within a state or locality? These questions have been raised by political scientists interested in community power. The specific application of consensus theory in this area of study is pluralist theory. In contrast to their positions on other matters, there are significant differences here between elite and Marxist theorists. Although any level of government can be used as a case study, local government is closest to its constituents and may therefore provide the best examples.

Pluralist Perspectives
Over time, pluralists have taken different approaches to the question

of who makes decisions and who influences decision makers. The classic statement was made by Robert Dahl in his study of New Haven, Connecticut, in the late 1950s. He described the political system as one of "dispersed inequalities": "a system dominated by many different sets of leaders, each having access to a different combination of political resources" (1961, 86). Each group of leaders specialized in influencing decisions only in its own area of interest. The only leaders consistently involved in more than one policy area were elected officials, particularly the mayor. Thus pluralist New Haven was neither a pure democracy nor dominated by an elite. Rather, a variety of elites competed for influence on elected officials, the ultimate decision makers, who were accountable to the electorate. Dahl has since changed his views, but his original study set the tone for further pluralist research in community power.

Pluralists emphasize the tremendous variety of interest groups within most urban settings. These groups do not have equal influence, but the potential exists for all groups to get a chance to exert influence on decision makers. Adrian and Press (1977, 84, 99), for example, assert that the power of business groups is limited because they spend much of their time opposing one another. The result is a situation in which "differences are settled by some form of compromise. For most communities it appears that officials make most decisions with the acquiescence of the large body of citizens. Desires of the more important interest groupings are anticipated. . . . The policy that results is a blend of administrative and political points of view."

Some pluralists feel that the process of interest group competition has gone too far. Douglas Yates (1979) describes the community power structure in many cities as "street-fighting pluralism"—an extreme fragmentation of urban politics in which groups in and out of government organize around the numerous different municipal services and fight it out with one another to impose their demands. A related thesis is that American cities are dominated by "functional fiefdoms"—separate turfs held by feuding municipal administrative bureaucracies in education, human services, transportation, and so on (J. Harrigan 1981, chap. 13).

Given the obvious impact of a declining economy and the fiscal crisis on local government, pluralists in the 1980s began to focus on how the political system functions within the context of the economic system. Economic changes are an outgrowth of forces that go beyond the jurisdiction of any community political system. As far as pluralists are concerned, the relevant question in an analysis of community politics is therefore how it works to adjust the locality to the "new reality." From this perspective, the language of market economics has become increasingly relevant. Paul Peterson offers an example of this kind of approach; he explains urban policy-making in the terminology of "public choice" theory:

> One explains urban public policy by looking at the place of the city in the larger socioeconomic and political context. . . . Cities select those policies which are in the interests of the city, taken as a whole. It is these city interests, not the internal struggles for power within cities, that limit city policies and condition what local governments do. (1981, 4)

That city interest, Peterson argues, is economic:

> Cities constantly seek to upgrade their economic standing. . . . I mean by this that cities seek to improve their market position, their attractiveness as a locale for economic activity. In the market economy that characterizes western society, an advantageous economic position means a competitive edge in the production and distribution of desired commodities relative to other localities. (22)

Local governments therefore make choices among policy alternatives to improve their "competitive edge" in the marketplace, and they respond to political pressures from different interest groups within the context of that process.

All these variations of pluralist theory share certain assumptions: (1) No single group can be said to dominate community politics—if there is such a group, it is the elected officials. (2) To a greater or lesser extent, opportunity exists for all groups to exert public influence on decision makers, although that opportunity is not always taken or effectively used. (3) Political conflicts usually occur within the context of consensus on fundamental values, such as the need for economic development within the framework of a market economy.

Elite Theory

Elite theory rejects these assumptions. In just about all communities, elite theorists claim, business interests predominate and have by far the greatest influence on political decision-making. By contrast, elected officials are generally either allied with or subordinated to them. Citizens and organized nonbusiness interests may exert pressure, but generally with little success at least in terms of big decisions such as taxes, education, welfare, and economic development.

The elite theory counterpart to Dahl's book is Floyd Hunter's study of "Regional City" (Atlanta) conducted in the early 1950s. Hunter's research method was "reputational": fourteen "judges" with extensive knowledge of Regional City were asked to identify the top leaders in several areas from a list of 175 possibilities drawn up by Hunter. Ultimately forty leaders were identified, researched, and interviewed. Hunter concluded that "the pattern of business dominance of civic affairs in Regional City is a fact" and that the structure "is that of a dominant policy-making group using the machinery of government . . . for the attainment of [its] goals" (1963, 76, 107). Studies such as Hunter's stimulated similar works on a national level, including C. Wright Mills's *The Power Elite* (1956). Pluralist responses have focused on the alleged inadequacies of Hunter's methodological approach.

Later studies used a broader set of methods. Edward Hayes's study of Oakland, California (1972) uses a framework similar to that of Peterson's later work: the private enterprise economy constrains decisions for all communities on the basis of the goal of profit. However, according to Hayes, the result in Oakland has been "systemic influence" on the part of Oakland businesses in shaping and staffing local government and "specialized influence" in developing public policies. This has meant segregated housing, removal of the poor from redeveloped areas, and corporate control of economic development.

Newfield and DuBrul (1977) make a distinction between the "permanent" and "temporary" governments of New York City. The latter, between 1953 and the mid-1970s, consisted of three weak mayors and an "almost irrelevant" city council. The former consists of an "invisible and unelected" confederation of elites who constitute an "interlocking network" of power. These authors assert that "there are about 1,500 or 2,000 people in New York City who have pieces of a power that is decisive, concealed, and therefore unaccountable" (77).

New York City provides another example of how elite control develops—the career of Robert Moses, who in the 1920s maneuvered himself into positions of control over several public authorities, in particular special district governments with responsibility for roads and parks. Within twenty-five years, by cleverly and aggressively expanding his power, he had risen to a position amounting to a one-man urban planner for the entire New York City metropolitan area, without ever having faced an election (except an election for governor in 1934, which he lost). It was not until the late 1960s that his reign was ended by an even more skilled practitioner of power politics, Governor Nelson Rockefeller (Caro 1974).

Such examples from the perspective of elite theory are merely a few among many. The particular configurations of community power may differ in each locale, but they add up to the same story: dominance by a small number of individuals who are either part of or connected to the business elite. Against such elites, community organizations and other middle- or working-class groups have little chance of promoting their political agendas.

Marxist Theory

The idea that the demands and constraints of a capitalist economy are usually inimical to working people distinguishes Marxism from pluralism; the idea that capitalists can lose political battles distinguishes it from elite theory.

Edward Greer's study (1979) of Gary, Indiana, demonstrates this perspective. Pluralism, Greer says, fails as an analysis "because it has no concept to incorporate the reality of monopoly economic power"; elite theory is even less satisfactory "because it assumes that everything that happens is more or less consistent with elite interests" (15–17). For Greer, the starting point of understanding political power in Gary is the overwhelming presence of U.S. Steel (now USX), whose interests "do prevail in a general overall sense." Reforms that would challenge its power "remain outside the political agenda." However, this power comes into conflict with, and most importantly is limited by, frequent opposition from the working and middle classes, to which the local government must in some measure respond. The corporation may sometimes have to pay higher taxes, or concede certain rights to workers, or be subject to government regulation as the result of "a shifting balance of power between various class actors [which] determines the actual outcomes" (19–20).

In a time of economic stagnation, local governments are pressured to create a "good business climate" by cutting taxes and social spending. The working and middle classes may choose to resist such demands—a more common occurrence before the 1980s. One side's gain becomes the other side's loss, and the local government is forced to choose sides. The tendency in a capitalist society is to side with business interests and implement probusiness policies, as pluralists like Peterson describe. Marxists believe, however, that ordinary people do not benefit from such policies; in fact, ordinary people pay a price with regressive taxes and service cutbacks. The argument that benefits to business "trickle down" to the community is firmly rejected by Marxists.

Capitalists do not always get what they want, however. Reviewing the process of urban redevelopment in five cities, Susan Fainstein and her colleagues conclude that

> while the processes and outcomes of redevelopment are broadly confined by the social relations of capitalism, the resolution of conflicts can differ in different places, with dissimilar results for comparable population groups. In other words we conclude that political pressure matters—that the difference between the condition of low income people in New Orleans and San Francisco stems in part from the higher levels of mobilization achieved in the latter. . . . We accept a class struggle model of the state, in which the state incorporates the gains that have been won by popular movements. (1986, 245–246)

They caution, however, that with economic decisions being made on ever higher levels of both industry and government, local political struggles have much less effect on policy. Nonetheless, from the Marxist perspective the importance of political organizing on the part of average citizens cannot be overestimated.

Citizen Action

Theoretical Perspectives

Different perspectives on community power necessarily lead to opposing views on whether and how citizens can affect the process of political decisionmaking. An argument for the futility of most citizen action can be found in elite theory. First of all, control by a powerful elite makes any significant change contrary to its interests unlikely. More important, organized groups that get involved politically and survive will probably lose their original sense of purpose. As Thomas Dye and Harmon Zeigler put it:

> Organizations perform a stabilizing, conservative function for the society. Formal organizations seldom cause social change. . . . Organizations gradually become more moderate. The goal of organization perpetuation takes priority over the original goal . . . In other words, as organizations grow older, they shift from trying to implement their original values to maintaining their structure as such even if they thereby sacrifice the organization's central mission. Organizations thus come to be dominated by people who have the greatest stake in the existing social system. (1981, 276–277)

The other side of this argument is that real political change cannot evolve from organization; rather, it must come from disruption. Richard Cloward and Frances Piven (1979, 36) make just that point in their book *Poor People's Movements*: "Whatever influence lower class groups occasionally exert in American politics does not result from organization, but from mass protest and the disruptive consequences of protest." The strategy is to put the power elite on the defensive with spontaneous aggressive tactics and then "take the money and run." Indeed, it is not an exaggeration to say that the politics of terrorism rests on elite theory, although few elite theorists favor terrorism. Elite theory therefore offers little to those who place any faith in the significance of political organizing. Pluralism and Marxism, on the other hand, have a good deal to offer, but from sharply differing perspectives.

According to pluralist theory, citizen action must be evaluated in terms of its impact on the need for orderly change in a stable political system. Direct democracy, for example, presents the possibility of drastic political change outside the established institutions of government. The intensity of conflict that may result from excessive or careless use of direct democracy may damage the consensual workings of the political system as a whole, even if it does provide a safety valve to protect against abuses of power.

Public participation in political action is considered highly desirable by pluralists as long as all concerned are willing to abide by the rules of the game—negotiation, bargaining, and compromise. Citizen action must operate to foster incremental change and maintain the system's overall balance in responding to public demands. In particular, political organizations should base their program on mainstream ideological values and avoid excessive confrontation.

Those who espouse the need for radical changes in the system, including Marxists, see citizen action as vital to their goals. Such action, however, must be of a form that effectively challenges the dominant values of society and the power structure that maintains it. Political organizations thus should ideally be based on a comprehensive program or ideology that has the potential for building connections among disparate groups making up the working class. The overall strategy is to establish coalitions among groups representing different neighborhoods and localities, as well as different racial, ethnic, and gender groupings. Particular organizing issues and tactics must be chosen in line with these basic principles. The ultimate goal is continuous pressure on state and local governments to accommodate demands for meaningful change.

Direct Democracy

Many states and localities have provided mechanisms by which citizens can "short-circuit" the system, passing or repealing laws without legislative approval or removing officials before the expiration of their terms of office. Some communities are governed through the direct participation of all their citizens. These methods of direct democracy are an important means of citizen political action. Consensus theory focuses on their relationship to the maintenance of political stability, whereas conflict theory focuses on their ability to produce change.

Initiative, Referendum, and Recall. The practice of placing questions on the ballot for the voters' approval is a legacy of the Progressive movement early in the twentieth century. It was designed to circumvent state legislatures' opposition to proposals for reform. The initiative allows voters to petition to place on the state ballot a proposed new law or constitutional amendment, which will take effect if approved by the electorate. Twenty-three states, of which all but six are west of the Mississippi, have provisions for initiatives; eighteen of these allow constitutional amendments to be added by this method. Initiatives may be indirect, requiring some kind of legislative action before a measure is placed on the ballot; or direct, with no such requirement. The petitions need to have a certain number of voters' signatures, usually equivalent to a certain percentage of the votes cast in a previous election.

The referendum by voter petition, used in twenty-three states, allows voters to petition for the repeal of an existing law. In these and many other states, the state constitution or the legislature itself may require a referendum on certain proposals, such as bond issues.

The recall for state officials, used in sixteen states, permits voters to remove an elected state officer before the expiration of his or her term. It is used in most of the states on the local level. Only eight states have all three methods of direct democracy.

James Madison explained in *The Federalist* number 49 why he was not partial to such mechanisms:

> It may be considered as an objection inherent in the principle that as every appeal to the people would carry the implication of some defect in the government, frequent appeals would in a great measure deprive the government of that veneration which time bestows on everything and without which perhaps the wisest and freest governments would not possess the requisite stability. . . .

Table 5.1: States With Initiative, Referendum, or Recall, 1994

STATE	INITIATIVE		REFERENDUM	RECALL
	Constitutional Amendment	Statute	(Citizen petition)	(Statewide)
Alaska		+	+	+*
Arizona	+	+	+	+
Arkansas	+	+	+	
California	+	+	+	+
Colorado	+	+		+
Florida	+			
Georgia				+
Idaho		+	+	+*
Illinois	+	+		
Kansas				+*
Kentucky			+	
Louisiana				+*
Maine			+	
Maryland		+	+	
Massachusetts	+	+	+	
Michigan	+	+	+	+*
Mississippi	+			
Missouri	+	+	+	
Montana	+	+	+	
Nebraska	+	+	+	
Nevada	+	+	+	+
New Mexico			+	
North Dakota	+	+	+	+
Ohio	+	+	+	
Oklahoma	+	+	+	
Oregon	+	+	+	+
Rhode Island				+
South Dakota	+	+	+	
Utah		+		
Vermont			+	
Washington		+		+*
West Virginia			+	
Wisconsin				+
Wyoming		+	+	

*Except judges

Source: Council of State Governments, *Book of the States 1996–1997*

The danger of disturbing the public tranquility by interesting too strongly the public passions is a still more serious objection. . . . But the greatest objection of all is that the decisions that would probably result from such appeals would not answer the purpose of maintaining the constitutional equilibrium of the government.

Contemporary consensus theorists have a somewhat similar concern. They worry that direct democracy can arouse conflict where it might not have existed. Until recently, the initiative and referendum were rather tame, if not conservative, political processes. But this tradition of moderation was violated by two drastic initiatives to cut property taxes: Proposition 13, passed in California in 1978, and Proposition 2 1/2, passed in Massachusetts in 1980, which radically altered these states' fiscal structures. To pluralists, and to the mass media, this was part of a grassroots "tax revolt," an authentic expression of popular sentiment against "big government" and excessive taxes. Pluralists therefore concluded that direct democracy could pose a threat to political stability by allowing voters to usurp a policy area usually dominated by experts or elected officials. In Alan Rosenthal's view, ballot initiatives constitute "sloppy democracy." He argues that they lead to less democratic decisions than those reached by the legislative process and that they create incoherent and irresponsible policies which hamstring government and undermine representative democracy (1995, 19–20).

Other analysts have concluded, however, that these two initiatives were not especially revolutionary. Propositions 13 and 2 1/2 were, in general, more consistent with conservative policy directions favored by both business and government since the early 1970s—lower taxes and less government spending. It could be argued that public opinion responded to a carefully orchestrated organizing drive on the part of certain sectors of business which were in no way populist and which manipulated public anger into a path serving their interests. Elite theorists in particular are skeptical about the initiative process for just this reason.

On the other hand, the process of direct democracy can be used to further more liberal or radical ends, although with a mixed track record. In Massachusetts from 1976 to 1992 voters were presented with the following issues: a total ban on handguns, establishment of a state-owned electrical utility, a graduated income tax, voter registration by mail, closing all nuclear plants, and requiring recyclable packaging (all defeated); and a state ERA, repeal of legislative salary increases, a bottle bill, a program to clean up hazardous wastes, and a liberalization of ballot access requirements (all passed).

Pluralists argue, however, that many of these issues are totally inappropriate for resolution by popular vote and may end up as expensive conflicts between rival interest groups. In 1988 there were no less than five ballot questions in California relating to automobile insurance rates. Proposition 103, sponsored by a Ralph Nader consumer group, called for a 20 percent cut in rates. In response, insurance companies offered three other proposals, along with yet another backed by trial lawyers. After tens of millions of dollars were spent, Proposition 103 passed, precipitating lengthy court battles over its implementation. From the pluralist point of view, direct democracy too often leads to this kind of fiasco (Moore 1988, 2296–2301).

Town Meetings. The six New England states still have hundreds of communities which conduct regular town meetings where citizens gather to decide on policy issues. This type of system also came under attack from James Madison in *The Federalist* number 10:

> A pure democracy, by which I mean a society consisting of a small number of citizens who assemble and administer the government in person, can admit of no cure from the mischiefs of faction. . . . Such democracies have ever been spectacles of turbulence and contention, have ever been found incompatible with personal security and the rights of property, and have in general been as short in their lives as they have been violent in their deaths.

Once again, the reality is quite different. In a situation where political conflict is settled in an open forum, individuals with good social and verbal skills can easily overwhelm those without such advantages. Moreover, attendance at such meetings has generally declined over the years and has varied within communities according to the issues on the agenda; thus town meetings may not be truly representative of the population. To a considerable extent the increasing centralization of government functions in the hands of state government has removed much of the purpose of town meetings. Elite theorists, in particular, are therefore skeptical about the town meeting as a democratic institution.

Others argue that town meetings have at least the potential to become arenas for political debate and discussion as well as decision making. In communities with a "representative" town meeting, in which only citizens elected from their precincts may actually vote, the problems of inconsistent attendance and representation are to some extent resolved.

With the expansion of community-access cable television, meetings are often televised, thus giving local residents an opportunity to learn about town politics. Marxists, and others interested in grassroots organizing for political change, might see the town meeting as a method of increasing political awareness and as a model for popular democracy.

Overall, then, direct democracy does not seem to confirm either the consensus theorists' worst fears or the hopes of those who want to promote mass organization. It has never seriously destabilized state and local government, but it does have the potential to articulate and sometimes implement the popular will.

Interest Groups

Interest groups are organizations of citizens that are formed to promote a particular political interest held in common. These groups may exist to advance economic interests, promote particular ideologies, provide public information, or pursue a single issue. There are thousands of such groups in the United States including business, labor, educational, farm, environmental, civil rights, religious, public interest, and women's groups, among numerous others. As instruments of citizen action to affect the political process, interest groups must be evaluated in terms of their capacity for representing the people and expressing the people's demands.

Groups use a wide variety of methods to accomplish their goals. To a considerable extent, this depends on whom they are trying to influence in state and local government. If a group wishes to have a law passed, pressure will be brought to bear on the governor and the state legislature or the mayor and the city or town council; if a group seeks a favorable administrative ruling, it will approach the bureaucracy; if a judicial decision is needed, a group may initiate a court case. Most interest groups employ lobbyists, whose job is to influence government officials on the group's behalf. A wealthy and well-established group may hire a law firm or seek out individuals with connections to government, such as a former legislator. Less influential groups usually rely on their own staff members or even volunteers. The goal of lobbyists is to influence decision-makers by gaining access to them, providing information favorable to the group's goals, and attempting to convince them that it is in their political interest to support the group.

In addition to the use of lobbyists, interest groups try to appeal to broader constituencies through grassroots campaigns publicizing the group's goals among potential sympathizers who are not members of the group. Mobilizing this kind of support can be useful in influencing legislators. For that same purpose, many groups have organized political action committees to collect campaign contributions from members and other voters. These contributions are then channeled to candidates who support the goals of the interest group.

Given the obvious importance of money in these activities, questions can be raised as to whether political influence in states and localities is distributed fairly among the various groups. Consensus and conflict theorists offer different answers.

Consensus Theory and Interest Group Politics. According to consensus theory, the main function of interest groups in the state and local political system is to represent the diverse interests of the American people and to compete for influence on all levels of government. Interest groups do this by applying political pressure to the appropriate group of decision makers, using whatever political resources are available. Overall, pluralists expect interest groups to stay within the rules of the game and be willing to make trade-offs with other groups. An effective interest group is one which can play by the rules and mobilizes whatever resources it has to achieve its goals. Money is certainly one of the most important of these resources, but by no means the only one. Others might include voter support, public opinion, organizational effectiveness, media attention, and the ability to build coalitions with other groups. Thus it is not necessarily the best-financed groups that win political battles.

There are two existing flaws in the system which consensus theorists recognize as having a potentially destabilizing effect in this regard—an upper- or middle-class bias in interest group representation, and a proliferation of uncompromisingly ideological or single-issue groups. First of all, citizens with more wealth and status seem to be "joiners" to a greater extent than are the poor. Whatever the reason, this tends to reduce the influence of those who have the most to gain from participation and increase the influence of those who have the most to lose. Thus, even consensus theorists acknowledge that the interest group system does not represent everyone equally. Second, the system cannot work unless all participants are ready to compromise at least part of their political agenda, but some are not willing. The 1980s gave rise to the "new right," which consists of ideological groups with a strong, often religiously based orientation on social issues allowing little tolerance for opposition. Single-issue organizations based on moral principles, such as the antiabortion movement, are often unwilling to bargain with those they perceive as their immoral enemies. This development disturbs many consensus theorists because the system needs room to maneuver, which such groups do not permit. If interest groups become too narrowly focused, consensus is impossible to maintain. If these groups take over or even establish themselves as political parties—as in the case of the Right to Life Party in New York—the situation is made even worse.

Nevertheless, consensus theorists still see an overall balance of power among interest groups, if not in each state at all times then in all the states considered together over the long run. In a summary of their ongoing study of interest groups in the fifty states, Ronald Hrebenar and Clive Thomas foresee "a continuation in the increase of group power at the expense of parties" and add that "money . . . will continue to play a significant role in group access and influence." However, they do not necessarily see this as a problem:

> If this means that the states are doomed to a future of domination by special interests, some consolation may be found in the fact that today more citizens in each state are represented by interests. Group activity is more visible than it was fifty or even twenty-five years ago, and the likelihood of conflict within and between powerful lobbies will work to restrain their influence. In addition, the success of groups that were formerly outsiders, such as environmentalists, is evidence that if new groups want to become part of the entrenched group system that they may do so if they become professionalized and employ the time-honored lobbying techniques, as well as the more populist methods. (Gray, Jacob, and Albritton 1990, 155)

Their preliminary listing of the most influential interests in each of the states features numerous business groups but also includes unions, farm groups, public employees, professional associations, and public interest groups (Gray, Jacob, and Albritton 1990, 560–567). The conclusion that no one group predominates is supported by a study by Hunter, Wilson, and Brunk (1991), who categorized over 39,000 lobbying efforts in fifty states between 1985 and 1987 according to types of interest groups. Out of fifteen types listed, none accounted for more than 15 percent, and governmental bodies and nonprofit groups each made 10 percent of the efforts.

Overall, then, citizen participation in organized interest groups is considered a healthy development if there is sufficient diversity, membership overlap, and political balance among groups and if they operate

within the consensual rules of the game. Although business groups of one type or another do appear to be the most active and influential in most states, this does not imply dominance of the political process by upper-class interests; it merely indicates that other groups must work harder to match their successes.

Conflict Theory Perspectives on Interest Groups. From the point of view of conflict theorists, interest group politics in states and localities has a built-in bias in favor of the ruling class.

On the state and local level a truly balanced system would require a relatively even match between business and labor and between special interests and public interest groups such as environmentalists and consumers. Conflict theorists claim that aside from occasional victories for the latter, special interests, especially business, have the upper hand. Labor unions have been forced onto the defensive by deteriorating economic conditions and declining membership, and they are increasingly unable to battle with the better-financed and more unified business groups. This is especially true of the once powerful public employee unions, which have been battered by fiscal crises in many states and localities.

Consensus theorists claim that business groups are not dominant in state and local politics because there are different sectors of business, which are not necessarily cohesive on most issues. Conflict theorists, on the other hand, point out that they are indeed united on the common goal of making business priorities as a whole number one on the agenda of state and local government, and that these groups work together to frame issues in terms of the business community's needs. Plotkin and Scheuerman (1994) cite "balanced-budget conservatism" as a position which corporate interests have sold to the middle class as a means of defeating progressive initiatives involving more government spending. Moreover, there has been a tendency in recent years for business groups to combine under larger "umbrella" organizations. This kind of ideological and programmatic monopoly, backed up by large sums of money distributed through business political action committees, is not easily broken by the likes of consumers, environmentalists, or workers. Marxists argue that a long-term coalition of such groups would be more effective, but it is much harder to build than a coalition of business interests.

In short, nonbusiness groups are far less able to play the political influence game in state capitals and city halls because they are usually up against a cohesive and well-financed opposition. Although business interests may compete in a pluralist pattern among themselves on less crucial matters, they band together to maintain their collective control over the entire state and local political system.

Community Organizations

Community organizations are the grass roots of state and local politics. A community organization is a nonpartisan citizens' group based in a specific locality or neighborhood that acts on issues directly affecting its residents. The geographic base is what primarily distinguishes it from an interest group, which has its base in a particular social, economic, or occupational segment of the population. However, there are some groups, such as the Public Interest Research Groups (PIRGs), inspired by Ralph Nader, which have characteristics of both.

The membership of a community organization usually consists of lower- and middle-income people and its primary but not exclusive political focus is usually local government. Community organizations attempt to improve the quality of life in their neighborhoods, particularly in regard to services involving government, such as housing, education, public safety, or health. They are by and large short-lived, but as some disappear, others form. Most exist independently, but many are part of some national or state coalition that allows them to retain considerable autonomy.

Some have adopted a "pressure" strategy of pushing governmental authorities to do their jobs more effectively. Quite a few of these organizations got their start in the 1960s with the massive outpouring of federal funds for urban problems, and many collapsed during the following decade, when the funds dried up. Currently, most community organizations pursue a "services" strategy—voluntarily providing them to the neighborhood or doing so in cooperation with a governmental agency. Most of them are self-financing, using a variety of fund-raising techniques to survive, although grants from government or private foundations may also be used. The most common form is the "community development corporation" (CDC), which spread rapidly during the 1980s as a response to a more conservative political environment. As Robert Fisher (1994, 14) describes them, "The new CDCs became less like community organizations and more like small businesses and investment projects. Most avoided political controversy, were dominated by professionals with a technical orientation, had narrow membership bases, and rejected social action activity."

There are thousands of community organizations across the nation, with tremendous differences among them in terms of political effectiveness. The question to be addressed here is which organizational approaches are correlated with political success, and there is substantial disagreement on this matter.

Political Programs: Opposing Approaches. An interest group generally does not have much internal debate over its programmatic goals. Organizations that influence government on behalf of, say, insurance companies, manufacturers, advocates of campaign finance reform, antiabortion activists, or private colleges have their goals pretty well defined by the nature of their constituencies. But community organizations have to decide program priorities explicitly. Should the organization assist the poor in connecting with government programs, or should it actively fight to improve the quality of those programs? Is it enough to start a "crime watch" program, or is there a need to reorganize local law enforcement agencies to provide "community policing"? Can a neighborhood pollution problem be solved without raising broader questions about environmental protection throughout the state, or even the nation? A community organization has to determine whether it will narrowly focus on immediate, specific issues or concern itself with a range of issues that involve the long-run welfare of the entire community. More generally, the ultimate question is whether it should work within existing political and economic "realities" or fight to change them.

Consensus theorists opt for the former approach. They believe that people will not get involved with any political organization unless they see a direct personal benefit. The best-known elaboration of this thesis has been made by the economist Mancur Olson, Jr. (1965, 61): "Group action can be obtained only through an incentive that operates . . . selectively toward the individuals in the group." In other words, a community organization must have a relatively limited and specific goal which is uncomplicated by explicit ideology and must sustain itself by rewarding its members—and only its members—with tangible material benefits which they could not obtain otherwise. A successful political group must always stand ready to answer the question, "What's in it for me?" According to Olson, most people act on the basis of "economic rationality" and will calculate the merits of joining a group on a cost-benefit basis. The group must therefore be nonideological, pragmatic, and designed to appeal to a specific constituency.

This approach in its numerous variations is the basis of most American community organizations today. Most aim for modest goals that relate to the immediate needs of those who are actively involved in the organization, and most do not try to challenge the existing distribution of wealth and power. They have decided that "efforts must be in tune with capitalist economic development and have a working relationship with the powers that be in the public and private sector" (Fisher 1994, 15).

Conflict theorists feel that mere reform on a local level is necessary but insufficient. If there are serious deficiencies in housing, health care, education, and public safety, they are related to the social and economic inequalities created by the capitalist system. From this viewpoint the purpose of a community organization must be to build toward a transformation of the society as a whole—to "think globally, but act locally." Summarizing his experiences in a Minnesota poor people's community organization in the 1970s, Senator Paul Wellstone (Democrat, Minnesota) wrote:

> The conclusion I have reached is that successful organizing is built not on "economic rationality," but rather on dignity and a sense of purpose. Poor people dedicated themselves to the Organization for a Better Rice County out of a sense of purpose. Once they realized that their voice could make a difference (the crucial importance of organizing victories) they viewed themselves in a different light as strong and independent people not afraid to speak up for their rights. . . . Through their efforts they could improve the community (country) and bring about more fairness and justice and a better life for low- and moderate-income people. These are the factors that sustained participation. (1978, 200)

The fundamental difference between this approach and consensus theory is the assumption that people can be motivated to organize politically on the basis of programs derived from an explicit value system, whether or not a short-term material incentive is forthcoming.

There is considerable debate among such organizers, however, as to which values should serve as a basis for organizing people in a community. Specifically, there are differences of opinion between those who adopt a "populist" strategy and those who choose approaches closer to Marxist theory.

The populist movement of the 1890s organized small farmers around programs challenging concentration of political and economic power in the hands of giant corporations and financial institutions. It based itself in what it considered basic American values of democracy and equality but rejected socialism; its primary goal was a change in the balance of power to strengthen farmers and workers. A contemporary populist approach was developed by Saul Alinsky, a Chicago-based community organizer during the 1940s and 1950s, who articulated a philosophy and organizing strategy that influenced many others in the following decades. His approach was to organize working-class people around issues they chose, using aggressive and frequently disruptive tactics to put the establishment on the defensive. The aim of all this was to gain power for the have-nots by employing whatever means seemed appropriate, but avoiding any explicitly ideological program:

> No [organizational] ideology should be more specific than that of America's founding fathers: "the general welfare." . . . The basic requirement for the understanding of the politics of change is to recognize the world as it is. We must work with it on its terms if we want to change it to the kind of world we would like it to be. . . . To the organizer, compromise is a key and beautiful word. It is always present in the pragmatics of operation. . . . If you start with nothing, demand 100%, then compromise for 30%, you're 30% ahead. (1971, 59)

In their advocacy of a nonideological approach, power and organizational expansion as a basic goal, and challenge followed by bargaining and compromise, Alinsky's ideas are an interesting—and perhaps contradictory—combination of consensus and conflict theory. In the 1970s, a number of community organizations advancing a similar ideology came to the fore. One example is the Association of Community Organizations for Reform Now (ACORN). Beginning in 1970 in Arkansas, ACORN spread into communities across the country over the next two decades. Its purpose was to organize the majority of the American people into a national network of community organizations capable of winning political power. ACORN's strategy was to focus on those issues which could unite disparate groups and which could also provide political victories. However, this meant adopting programs based on existing community values and traditions, which would be unlikely to challenge capitalism or the structure of the American political system directly. Such groups "employ the ideology of the new populism—decentralization, participatory democracy, self-reliance, mistrust of government and corporate institutions, empowering low and moderate income people— and at their best see themselves as grassroots groups to connect up with the national political process" (Fisher 1984, 134). In the 1990s, many of these "neopopulist" or "neo-Alinsky" organizations have become even less radical, adopting more moderate programs and strategies.

Others argue for a more radical stance. Unless a community organization is based on a broader ideological perspective that provides a thorough understanding of the systemic sources of community problems, it will ultimately be bought off by those in power or lose its force. In Kling and Posner's words (1989, 42), "Reliance on inherited [i.e., traditional community] values . . . prevents constituencies organized as publics from arriving at informed understandings of what policies and programs will directly attack the sources of their grievance." In fact, those inherited traditional values could end up being conservative or even reactionary, as in the case of antibusing community organizations such as Restore Our Alienated Rights (ROAR) in Boston in the 1970s. Thus, from this perspective, the program of an effective community organization should be based on an analysis of the relationships among classes, races, and sexes in a capitalist society. It should address local issues from a regional, national, or even global perspective, and on an ideological agenda.

Strategy and Tactics. There are various strategies available to community organizations, and generally these divide into what might be called "collegial-conventional" and "adversarial-confrontational." The former type, in accordance with consensus theory, emphasizes nonadversarial relations with government officials, acceptance of the political rules of the game, and conventional pressure tactics. The latter type is more consistent with the assumptions of conflict theory in viewing dominant interests and their allies in government as adversaries, and it accepts direct action, protest, and perhaps disruption as means of promoting the organization's agenda.

Specific tactical decisions involve a careful weighing of costs and benefits. At some point, any community organization has to be involved in negotiations with public officials to achieve its ends. A confrontational strategy may alienate officeholders; but, on the other hand, conventional tactics may allow officeholders to ignore the organization's demands. Media attention is vital for a community organization, and confrontation is far more likely to attract it—but what kind of attention is it likely to be?

A good example of the use of conventional strategies is the network of college campus-based public interest research groups (PIRGs), spawned by Ralph Nader's "public citizen" organizing efforts in the 1970s. The approach of PIRGs and similar organizations is to organize autonomous groups around specific issues (usually consumer-oriented) and use conventional techniques of political influence (lobbying, media campaigns, voter mobilization) to get laws passed. This pragmatic approach is considered politically realistic by its advocates in that it aims for what is possible within the rules and procedures accepted by all participants within the system, yet it tries to expand public control of both government and corporations. Going even further in this direction, Michael Eichler of the Consensus Organizing Institute argues that "many times, the causes [of difference] are not inherent conflicts between the parties that cannot be resolved, but miscommunication, misunderstandings, and lack of creative, constructive thinking." Thus, almost everyone can be seen as a potential ally, and therefore "the consensus organizer builds relationships with all the parties around respect, understanding, and genuine concern. The concern [in housing issues] is for the appraiser, the lender, the city official, the developer, the tenant—for everyone" (1995, 258–259).

Other community activists feel that something more is necessary, even within the framework of consensus theory. As mentioned above, Saul Alinsky had no aversion to open conflict and highly unorthodox means of achieving his goals, such as ending racial discrimination in hiring practices at a department store by organizing what might be called a "buy-in"—mobilizing 3,000 blacks to make small COD purchases and then refusing delivery (Perlman 1984, 49). Alinsky's Industrial Areas Foundation became known for advancing the interests of its working-class constituencies by using such methods, although contemporary "neo-Alinsky" organizations have largely abandoned them.

Any community organization whose program is based on conflict theory obviously has to consider the use of confrontational tactics. Robert Fisher (1994, 21) criticizes the entire conservative trend in both program and strategy. He argues that "community organizing must both build on and go beyond the contemporary context. . . . While the history of community organizing makes clear that national context is fundamental, it also instructs that conflict—ideological and direct action challenges—is essential to push the context, policies and programs toward meeting basic human needs and implementing more democratic processes."

Community organizers thus differ greatly on the goals and tactics of their groups. Consensus theorists favor a "pragmatic" program, achieved if possible through nonconfrontational methods. Organizers adhering to the ideas of Saul Alinsky agree, although they are more likely to address issues of power and are much more willing to use direct action of various kinds. Conflict theorists, on the other hand, favor a program that directly challenges the status quo, and the use of confrontational tactics if necessary. Whatever the particular approach, community organizations provide the most direct opportunity for involvement in state and local politics for those who choose to stay out of partisan politics. Each one in its own way contributes to the democratization of the political process, and their collective record of achievement is impressive.

Conclusion

According to both pluralists and Marxists, the structure of power in American communities can be responsive to citizen action; but they differ sharply on how community power is distributed and limited. Pluralists assume that certain basic political and economic goals, such as community economic growth, are widely shared. Within that context, all groups have an opportunity to get their share of the benefits through bargaining, negotiation, and compromise. Marxists, however, believe that the interests of different social classes are inherently opposed on almost all major political issues. Working-class groups must therefore adopt more aggressive, adversarial programs and tactics to protect their economic position.

The elite theorists' perspective on community power structure is consistent with their views on citizen action: economic and political elites are dominant and are not likely to be seriously challenged, much less defeated, by political organizing on the part of the mass public.

There are at least three political mechanisms available to citizens for the purpose of influencing state and local government: direct democracy through ballot questions and town meetings, interest groups, and community organizations. Elite theorists generally write them off as ineffective or in the case of many interest groups, hopelessly dominated by an elite. Pluralists, on the other hand, consider them of great significance in the political process.

Direct democracy has a proven track record of promoting political change. The issue is whether that accomplishment is positive. Pluralists tend to be leery of excessive direct participation and look at the so-called "tax revolt" as an example of ill-considered popular initiatives. Marxists see a potential for use by either side in achieving political change.

From the pluralist perspective, interest groups are the basic unit of political organization and as such can and usually do act as to represent the public in asserting political demands. The optimum condition is one in which the groups balance each other, reflect a broad range of public opinion, and are willing to bargain and compromise. This may, however, not always be the case in many states and localities. To conflict theorists, it is definitely not the case, because they believe that most interest groups represent the interests of upper-class people to the exclusion of average citizens.

Community organizations differ considerably in their approach to getting what they want from government. Most operate consistently with consensus theory, aiming for limited, negotiable goals and working within the system using conventional tactics. "Alinsky-type" organizations also limit their goals but are more willing to use confrontational methods. Yet others operate in line with the aim of promoting long-range programs based on a value system.

Achieving political change in state and local governments is in any case not a job for those with little patience. Placing an initiative on the ballot, lobbying the legislature, or getting neighbors together to pressure city officials requires long, hard work and careful organization. Many individuals feel that they have neither the time nor motivation. And yet, unless we accept the point of view of elite theory, we have no alternative but to accept responsibility for involvement on some level to ensure the accountability of those elected or appointed to positions in state and local governments. The instruments for that involvement are readily available.

Chapter 6: Gubernatorial Politics

Each of the perspectives offers a different concept of which factors are consistently important in shaping what the governors of the fifty states actually do, and what their roles and responsibilities are and should be. Consensus theorists see governors as professional managers capable of directing the executive branch, forging a consensus among competing pressure groups, and providing policy leadership for the legislature. Conflict theorists emphasize the impact of the relationship between the governor and the state's power structure.

Consensus Theory and State Governors

Consensus theorists in recent years increasingly draw an analogy between a governor—or even the mayor of a big city—and a corporate chief executive officer (CEO). They assert that managing a state bears a certain resemblance to running a large corporation; both involve maximizing efficient use of human and financial resources to produce goods and services demanded by the public. However, working as an elected official in the public sector adds certain complexities to the job. First of all, the governor faces certain constitutional and statutory limits to his or her authority. Second, public opinion is a crucial consideration in making decisions. Finally, governors have to deal with state and federal political institutions that are not under their control.

Formal Powers

In general, governors have had a harder job in recent years:

The 1990s are providing governors with new challenges. Falling revenues, rising needs, a retreating national government, and desperate local governments offer them and state legislatures the responsibility for making no-win decisions: raising taxes, while cutting services. . . . A new era of "go-it-alone" federalism has dawned . . . So far, governors, faced with considerable political roadblocks, falling economies, and changing system of government, and restrictions on

their powers, have been regarded by the public with a critical, if not jaundiced,
eye. (Beyle 1993, 107)

However, expansion of their authority over the last forty years has given
governors the tools to perform their jobs more effectively. There has
been movement toward a longer term of office. Governors serve for four
years in all states except Rhode Island, Vermont, and New Hampshire.
In about half the states, there is no limit on reelection. With few exceptions, strong veto and budgetary powers have become well established
for most governors. The average gubernatorial staff has tripled in number since 1960. Governors' salaries are now in the range of $75,000 to
$100,000, which is not comparable to similar positions in the private
sector, but respectable in contrast to salaries not so long ago. Administrative reorganizations in the 1960s and 1970s in many states strengthened the hand of the governor in choosing who will implement policy.
Larry Sabato, a political scientist specializing in the study of gubernatorial politics, could claim in the early 1980s that "the governor now works
in a political and structural environment less inhibiting than ever before,"
as a result of "the recent pace of constitutional revisions and reorganizations, [which] has been nothing short of astounding" (1983, 88).

The specific nature of the governor's formal authority, of course,
varies from state to state. Thad Beyle, expanding on previous efforts by
other researchers, constructed an index of gubernatorial power based on
tenure potential, appointment power, budget making, and organizational
and veto powers, among other factors. In 1990, half the states fell into
the "strong" or "very strong" category, which represented substantial
strengthening since 1960 (Gray, Jacob, and Albritton 1990, 228). Pluralists explain this expansion of gubernatorial power in terms of the need
for a state government that can deal with the political and economic
problems of a postindustrial society. This requires a strong executive
capable of difficult managerial decisions. This began to develop in the
1960s as a response to the proliferation of federal programs whose implementation required a greater degree of coordination in the executive
branch. More recently, gubernatorial power has expanded as the state
governments have stepped in to take over responsibilities delegated back
to them by the federal government. In addition, citizens have come to
expect that the state executive will provide political leadership; indeed,
they often anticipate more than the governor can deliver. This obviously
creates difficulties when the governor seeks re-election.

Public Opinion

Public opinion is a two-edged sword. It has increased the power of the governors; but according to consensus theorists, it also limits governors because it is the overriding, although by no means the exclusive, influence on the political choices they make.

Governors must, of course, be concerned with issues deemed important by the voting public. This varies from state to state and from time to time, and generalizations are therefore hard to make. One researcher, using gubernatorial state-of-the-state addresses as data, concludes that certain issues are perennial, that is, always important: education, highways, crime, and human services. Others are cyclical, rising to a peak and then steadily declining, such as environmental protection in the early 1970s and late 1980s. Finally, transitory issues, such as drug control in the late 1980s, appear suddenly and then vanish, but not before demanding gubernatorial attention (Gray, Jacob, and Albritton 1990, 230–232).

Public opinion is strongest on the issue of tax policy. Since the beginning of the so-called "tax revolt" in the late 1970s, it has become particularly risky politically for any governor to propose new taxes, or even to be associated with tax increases. That has been one of the most significant factors in defeating governors seeking reelection (Sabato 1983, 105–110). When Governor Jim Florio (Democrat, New Jersey) attempted to push through massive tax increases after being elected in 1989 on a no-increase platform, he faced massive protests and an attempted recall movement. He survived these only to be defeated in 1993 by a fiscally conservative Republican, Christine Whitman, who proceeded to cut state income taxes. However, she in turn encountered difficulties when she ran for reelection in 1997; she was blamed for the property tax increases implemented by local governments to replace the lost state revenue.

Institutional Conflict and Cooperation

Consensus theorists emphasize the fact that a governor's power relies on the ability to persuade other individuals and institutions to join in support. The essence of gubernatorial power from this point of view is coalition building in the administration, in the legislature, and within the governor's political party.

The governor's administrative appointment powers vary from state to state. Specifically, these depend on the number of separately elected officials in the executive branch; the number of departments, agencies, authorities, and boards reporting to the governor; and the governor's power to reorganize the bureaucracy. Also, the governor cannot expect automatic cooperation from an administration often largely made up of civil service employees organized into unions. The governor has no sanctions over them, although recently public employee's unions have been severely weakened by the financial crises facing states and localities.

Separately elected executives have a power base of their own which makes them independent of the governor as well as of potential political rivals. Indeed, they can be, and often are, from the opposition party. Occasionally, the governor may even feud with the lieutenant governor. In Massachusetts in 1978, the conservative Democrat Edward King was elected along with the liberal Democrat Thomas P. O'Neill III, an accident of separate primary elections which put the two on the same ballot (King had defeated O'Neill's preferred running mate, Michael Dukakis). There was little cooperation between them, and in 1982 they ran against each other for the gubernatorial nomination, which was won by Dukakis.

Another limit on gubernatorial power is the separation of powers, which is intended to guarantee institutional rivalry between the executive and legislative branches. Of course, governors have a considerable array of political resources at hand in moving the legislature in their direction. "Agenda setting"—the power of proposing a legislative program, especially in relation to the budget—is a formidable political advantage for governors. This puts the legislature in the position of spending most of its time dealing with the governor's programs. The power to veto bills passed by the legislature is an important weapon in the governor's hands, especially since, in most states, he or she has the power of "line item veto"—disapproving individual parts of bills. Governors may also have patronage—political jobs—to dispense as a reward for cooperation.

On the other hand, often the legislature may be dominated by the opposing party, or the governor's own party in the legislature may be highly factionalized. Legislators are beholden to their own local districts, which may not have the same interests as the governor's statewide constituency. Legislatures as a whole are increasingly well organized and professional, and members are less inclined than they once were to toe the party line, if indeed there is one. Governors therefore have to work very hard to persuade the legislative branch to pass their programs. This is especially true when states experience an economic decline, which forces governors to make unpopular decisions such as combining tax increases with service cutbacks.

The governor's political party may not be able to provide much in the way of support at election time, but it is certainly important to avoid intraparty opposition. In order to get the party's nomination in the first place, a governor must forge some kind of winning coalition within that party. Once a governor is in office, success or failure may depend in part on the ability to maintain that coalition. Party unity and ideology vary greatly from state to state. The relationship of the governor to the state party organization has consequences for the extent of his or her power. The governor may have to perform a difficult balancing act if the party has opposing ideological wings. Activists of the "religious right" have managed to capture the Republican state party organizations of many states in the 1990s, thus putting the organizations at odds with Republicans who are liberal on social issues. State Democratic parties can contain liberals, moderates, and conservatives.

Governors must also cope with the influence of the federal government. Although the massive expansion of federal programs that began in the 1960s ended with the Reagan administration, the impact of federal grants and mandates is extensive. Governors are still heavily involved in maintaining the flow of federal funds and administering the programs these funds help create. Categorical grants, such as those for welfare (until 1996), Medicaid, and environmental programs, involve federal regulations in the day-to-day state administrative process. Governors therefore have to act as lobbyists for state interests in federal agencies and Congress. They must pay considerable attention to the nature of federal-state relations in general. This requires effective liaison with the state's congressional delegation and the federal bureaucracy. Thus, although states can do more with federal money, their options are limited by federal regulations (especially those which do not include federal subsidies but require state spending) and by direct dealings between federal and local governments. This poses a political challenge for governors.

The Governor as Manager

Consensus theorists, considering all the conflicting demands on state governors, have concluded that the ultimate test of a governor's ability is the capacity for professional management. As stated earlier, they draw an analogy between the job of governor and the job of chief executive officer of a corporation and argue that to a considerable extent the same talents and approaches are needed.

In this regard, many are quite pleased with the development of gubernatorial power in the last few decades. Governors are better trained for their jobs because more of them have experience in other elective offices, notably the legislature, and their educational and professional credentials have improved considerably. According to Larry Sabato,

> It is reasonably clear to American political observers that a greater percentage of the nation's governors are capable, creative, forward-looking, and experienced. . . . Governors have gained major new powers that have increased their influence in national as well as state councils. . . . Governors have welcomed into their ranks a new breed of vigorous, incisive, and thoroughly trained leaders. (1983, 1–2)

From this point of view, governors can overcome the constitutional and statutory limitations of the office through effective management. According to Michael Del Guidice, corporate executive, and staff member to two New York governors and the Speaker of the state assembly,

> Today's governor must be a manager of resources, decisions, and systems. He is the elected official with overall management responsibility for the state equivalent to that which the corporate CEO has for the firm; thus the governor cannot avoid the variety of internal and external forces attempting to influence state government. . . . The governor must respond. His only choice is to become a gubernatorial CEO. (1986, 70)

As public sector CEOs, contemporary governors are challenged to draw on a variety of skills and talents their predecessors did not have to possess. In a collection of articles on how governors have coped with the problems created by the recession in the early 1990s, Thad Beyle notes that "they can do little to address this macro-level problem; they can only try to cope with its effect on state government." Thus to a great extent their personalities and political styles, rather than party or ideology, have become critical factors in successful management of state government during a period of prolonged austerity (1992, 6–7).

The measure of a governor, consensus theorists contend, is how well he or she applies management techniques and political resources to create a consensus that facilitates problem-solving. The ultimate goals are to resolve conflict and maintain political stability. The means to those ends is a higher degree of professionalism and the effective use of consensus-building techniques among those who occupy the top executive positions in the fifty states.

Elite Theory and State Governors

Conflict theorists argue that these perspectives on the role and responsibilities of a governor are not objective, scientific conclusions but rather are actually consistent with what the ruling class or power elite thinks a governor should be. A governor who acts and thinks like a professional manager is far more likely to take positions favoring business interests and opposing working-class or minority constituencies. According to elite theorists in particular, if governors have begun to see themselves as corporate CEOs, it is at least partly because their campaign money is coming from CEOs, and they themselves identify socially and economically with CEOs.

Money and Politics

The first task of any candidate for governor is finding the money needed to run. As discussed in Chapter 4, modern campaigns have become highly technological. It has become necessary to use the media, opinion polls, and professional consultants, and as a result, the cost of gubernatorial campaigns has escalated dramatically. The money, of course, comes from those who can afford to contribute, and the expectation of contributors is that they will be rewarded with political influence if their candidate wins. As pointed out in Chapter 4, there are few restrictions on campaign spending in the states.

The upshot of all this is that candidates must seek huge amounts of money from those with sufficient wealth to donate, and must inevitably return the favor in some form. According to elite theorists, the increasing amounts of money spent and the lack of effective controls have the effect of turning the governorship into a market commodity purchased by those who are wealthiest.

Social Background

Conflict theorists emphasize the fact that officeholders are highly unrepresentative of the population as a whole; they are recruited from a small segment of society. Only a handful of women have been elected governor on their own rather than as their husbands' successors: among the most recent are Madeline Kunin (Democrat, Vermont), Ann Richards (Democrat, Texas), Jean Shaheen (Democrat, New Hampshire), and Christine Whitman (Republican, New Jersey). There were no black governors until the election of Douglas Wilder (Democrat, Virginia) in 1989.

Of all governors elected between 1951 and 1981, half were lawyers, 20 percent were businessmen, and 8 percent were both (Sabato 1983, 26). That is an advantage as far as consensus theorists are concerned, but according to conflict theorists it only reflects the white, male, professional makeup of the national power elite. From the conflict perspective, this reduces the likelihood that working-class people, minorities, and women will find a sympathetic ear in the governor's mansion.

In some states political leadership has been the property of one family. Between the 1920s and the late 1960s the Byrd family dominated politics in Virginia. Huey Long's dictatorial regime in Louisiana sixty years ago began a tradition of Long family power there. The DuPont Corporation is the dominant presence in Delaware, and numerous members of the DuPont family have been highly placed in Delaware's politics. Although it has never elected a governor, the Kennedy family plays a considerable role in Massachusetts politics.

The best-known example of the combination of money, family, and gubernatorial politics was Nelson Rockefeller, governor of New York from 1959 to 1974. Acquiring and holding on to the office through liberal use of his own wealth in campaigns, he became one of New York's strongest governors. His approach to solving state problems was often high-handed, squarely in the family tradition. Although he launched massive state projects in higher education, housing, and highways, resulting in higher taxes and state debts, he was relatively conservative politically. One of the tangible results of his administration was the construction of a huge array of state offices in Albany:

> A forty-four story tower, visible from a distance of fifteen miles, clings gracefully to a steel core. Behind it stand four twenty-three story towers, identical children of the parent structure. Behind them, a low building runs unbroken for a quarter of a mile, a modern Temple of Karnak where drivers' licenses are processed. In front of the main tower, posed delicately on a shaft, is an enormous ovoid, inevitably called "The Egg." Within this space are two of the most boldly conceived theaters in the country. The Mall also contains the largest state library and museum in America. (Persico 1982, 203)

This complex is now fittingly known as the Nelson A. Rockefeller Empire State Plaza.

State Power Elites

Elite theorists in particular point out that in certain states there are economic or political elites which set the tone for politics. A governor will most likely have to adapt to that system or face intense conflict in resisting it.

James Lamare's analysis of politics in Texas starts with the presumption that oil and natural gas companies, agribusiness, and financial institutions make up the state's economic elite, which "influences elections in Texas through screening candidates, providing the chosen few with monetary resources, and curtails the opportunities of candidates who challenge economic privilege in the state" (1981, 72). The result, he says, is a series of governors who are responsive to the needs of the state's economic elite. In those states where one industry is the economic mainstay, as coal is in West Virginia, similar conditions may prevail. The vital importance of the "FIRE" economic sector—finance, insurance, and real estate--in many of the northeastern and New England states demands that their governors respond to the needs of that particular economic elite. In New Hampshire, the state power elite may well have consisted of one man: William Loeb, who died in 1981. He was the publisher of the Manchester *Union-Leader*, and he effectively used his paper to defame those who did not see eye-to-eye with him on his extreme right-wing brand of politics. Few state politicians could afford to offend Loeb. After his death, his wife inherited much of his influence.

According to some political researchers, certain states—Maryland, Louisiana, and Rhode Island, for example—have developed a tradition of political corruption. This usually stems from a political party machine which undemocratically dominates the political process for its own financial benefit. Often it may interact with economic elites, organized crime, or both. Thus the governor is either a product of the machine or has little if any success in fighting its power. Although the professionalization of the governor's office has made such arrangements scarcer, elite theorists assert that political insiders still prevail at most state houses, and many reap financial and material benefits from their connections.

From the perspective of conflict theory, then, the expense of gubernatorial campaigns, the upper-class background of many governors, and the domination of many states by economic elites or corrupt political machines or both, make the consensus theory at best naïve and at worst deliberately misleading for focusing on the importance of structural powers, public opinion, and executive management. Elite theorists see this domination as a permanent state of affairs.

Marxist Analysis of Gubernatorial Politics

Although Marxists, like elite theorists, reject the analysis of gubernatorial politics offered by consensus theorists, they argue that domination by moneyed elites is not the whole story, nor is it unchangeable.
Rather, the governorship, like all American political institutions, reflects
the changing patterns of class conflict.

The current emphasis on professionalism in government, Marxists
argue, represents a victory for the upper class. The assertion that political issues are merely problems solvable by effective management ignores
the fact that these issues are created by struggles over who will control
what society produces and how it will be distributed. These struggles
cannot be resolved objectively out of some textbook in public administration; they involve decisions about how people are going to live. Insofar as the upper class convinces everybody else that its point of view is
professional and objective, it will end up with most of the wealth and
power, and this is its real political goal. Thus from the Marxist point of
view, consensus theory is hypocrisy; "governor as CEO" really means
"governor as capitalist manager."

Elite theory, however, offers only an incomplete critique. Governors
are indeed limited by the constraints of capitalism as an economic system, but most are committed to that system personally and politically.
Gubernatorial candidates are not bought with campaign contributions;
rather, they sell themselves to donors with whom they already agree.
They represent a particular social class, and they attempt to impose its
agenda. Given the political power of the upper class, even governors
who are ostensibly liberal and from a working-class background ultimately make choices in favor of conservative, probusiness policies. One
such governor was Mario Cuomo (Democrat, New York). Plotkin and
Scheuerman (1994) point out that 25 percent of his campaign money
came from financial, legal, and real estate interests. But beyond that,

> Cuomo understood the significance of the ideology of balanced-budget conser-
> vatism and recognized the ability of business interests to define the political
> agenda and put progressives on the defensive. . . . Cuomo's liberalism was
> tempered by the strength of balanced-budget conservatism and the organized
> power of the corporate and financial communities. He had no place else to go.
> As Cuomo noted in an interview, he shared the values of labor and did not want
> to cut human services: "I want what they want," he said. But he cautioned, "I
> can't do what I want to do." In short, New York's governor knew his options
> were limited. (189–190)

Thus according to Marxist theory neither consensus nor elite theory fully explains the limits and possibilities of gubernatorial power. Governors generally work on behalf of capitalist interests, either willingly or because of the power of that constituency. On the other hand, however, governors can succeed and have succeeded in representing working-class and minority interests; some have even changed their upper-class allegiances. This happens when such interests are well organized and assert their own agenda. Three periods in the twentieth century were marked by the accession of governors in certain states who helped bring about important political and economic changes which were favorable to working-class people or minorities: the Progressive era from 1900 to 1920 in the Midwest and West, the New Deal period, and the late 1960s and 1970s in the South.

Progressive Politics

The Progressive movement was not Marxist or anticapitalist. In the East it was mostly composed of upper-middle-class liberals. In the Midwest and West, however, it was "radical" in representing the interests of farmers and workers against corporations, especially the railroads and the banks.

Progressives did not want to transform the whole economic system but were at least firmly committed to regulating it in the public interest— even, if necessary, to the extent of public ownership. They were profoundly disturbed by the increasing concentration of wealth and power in large corporations toward the end of the nineteenth century. They believed strongly in democratizing the political system by opening it up to increased public participation. This program was not favored by the corporate elite, and Progressives had to fight to get it implemented. They accomplished this by mobilizing farmers, workers, and reform-minded middle-class citizens against entrenched—usually Republican—political machines and the railroads and banks.

The prime example of Progressive politics on a state level was Robert M. La Follette, governor of Wisconsin from 1901 to 1907. He later became senator, and in 1924 he ran for president on the Progressive Party ticket. Fighting for dominance of the state Republican Party and finally winning, La Follette's administration passed a railroad tax and regulatory commission, an inheritance tax, an antilobby bill, and a civil service system.

Wisconsin was the proving ground of Midwest progressivism in its twentieth century phase. La Follette and his successors provided continuity of political leadership . . . For a quarter of a century, Wisconsin was the agrarian democratic commonwealth that the Grangers and the Populists visualized. And once rolling, progressivism was hard to stop. (Nye 1959, 201)

The "Wisconsin idea" spread to other state governments: Iowa under Governor Albert Cummins, Nebraska under George Sheldon, and Minnesota under John Johnson.

In the West, Hiram Johnson was elected governor of California in 1910, with a Progressive majority in the legislature. His accomplishments were considerable: popular initiative, referendum, and recall; home rule for localities; civil service; regulation of public utilities and railroads; child labor laws; and workmen's compensation. As one observer put it, "The social and political reforms enacted during the first burst of power of the Progressives have constrained California politics ever since" (Owens, Constantin, and Weschler 1970, 36).

The closest any state ever came to socialism was North Dakota in 1916, when it elected Lynn Frazier governor. Frazier was the candidate of the Non-Partisan League (NPL), led by A. C. Townley. It was a radical farmer's organization which used the primary elections to take control of the Republican Party. The NPL was a direct political response to domination of the state by the banks, railroads, and grain companies. The Frazier administration literally transformed the state government into a farmers' government. In 1919 it established a wide range of state-owned businesses and enterprises, largely related to agriculture, including a state-owned bank—the Bank of North Dakota—which is still in existence today. The NPL had considerable influence in neighboring states, especially Minnesota, although it failed to take power in any of them.

All of these movements declined in the 1920s. The repressive climate of World War I and its aftermath, internal factions, and counterattacks by conservatives all contributed to preventing the spread of progressivism. But the reforms generally remained. What is important is the fact that these were state administrations elected by people opposed to corporate power. They were not, as elite theorists might claim, meaningless elite-inspired reform governments. They were quite the opposite of the pluralist model of professionalism, yet they accomplished a great deal. The administrations of these governors are an example of what can be achieved by organized working-class political movements.

Radicalism in the New Deal Period

The aim of the New Deal, under President Franklin D. Roosevelt, was to save capitalism, not to transform it. The New Deal had its most significant effects on the federal level. Notwithstanding its relatively conservative goals, it created an atmosphere conducive to change. In a number of instances this found expression in state gubernatorial politics.

In many states the liberal wing of the Democratic Party was strengthened by Roosevelt's popularity and resulted in the election of New Deal governors and the implementation of economic reforms. The most dramatic examples of the effect of New Deal politics were in California and Minnesota.

In 1934, Upton Sinclair, socialist, author, and founder of the "End Poverty in California" (EPIC) movement, managed to capture the Democratic gubernatorial nomination but lost to a conservative Republican after a bitter campaign. Sinclair's race for governor was the closest any radical movement ever came to capturing a major state government. It had a profound effect on California politics in the years to come.

A new third party arose in Minnesota and captured the governorship in 1930. Floyd B. Olson of the Farmer-Labor Party was elected on "the most radical platform by a major party in the history of American politics." As Olson himself put it, "Now I am frank to say that I am not a liberal. . . . I am what I want to be; I am a radical . . . in the sense that I want a definite change in the system" (Fenton 1966, 165). His actual administration was more moderate, but much was accomplished before his premature death in 1936. His successors did not share his abilities, and the Farmer-Labor Party declined and merged with the Democrats after World War II.

Civil Rights Movement

In the southern states by 1900 most of the impact of Reconstruction after the Civil War had been erased. Black voters, along with thousands of poor whites, were totally disenfranchised and thus helpless to fight for their political and economic rights. The populists had made an attempt to build an interracial movement for change in the 1890s, but they were defeated. The governors who came to power in the South in the first half of this century were best known for their explicit racism, which they used as an effective campaign technique. The Democratic Party, espousing a platform of white supremacy, became the only party in most of the South. In Georgia, Eugene Talmadge was elected governor four times by putting together a coalition of rural whites to whom he appealed with racist invective. In Mississippi, James K. Vardaman, who referred to the black as a "veneered savage," and Theodore Bilbo, a demagogue who shared those sentiments, reached the state house the same way; Ben Tillman and Coleman Blease did the same in South Carolina. All of them used an approach combining a populist message of varying sincerity with race-baiting to attract poor and lower-middle-class whites.

What changed all this was the civil rights movement of the late 1950s and early 1960s, which challenged white supremacy throughout the South. Its greatest legislative victories came in Washington, D.C., with the passage of the Civil Rights Act of 1964, which banned segregation in public facilities, and the Voting Rights Act of 1965, which gave the ballot back to southern blacks. The resulting political changes were dramatic. A new generation of governors took office in the South, committed at the very least to political equality for blacks. Hundreds of black state and local officials as well as several black Congressmen were elected. Segregationist politicians, grudgingly or otherwise, had to change their tune or leave office.

At his first inauguration in 1963, Governor George Wallace of Alabama said, "I draw the line in the dust and toss the gauntlet before the feet of tyranny, and I say segregation now, segregation tomorrow, segregation forever." Twenty years later he was reelected, partly on the strength of black votes, and in his inauguration speech of 1983 he said, "In times like these we must turn to one another and not away from and against one another." As the *New York Times* reported on 18 January 1983, "This time a black man led thousands of Wallace believers in the Pledge of Allegiance to the flag. Another black man pronounced the benediction. And on the same podium that held George Wallace, a black man was sworn in as a justice of the Alabama Supreme Court. He was the first black elected to statewide office since Reconstruction."

One may question the sincerity of such conversions, and obviously the civil rights movement did not accomplish all of its goals, especially in the economic realm. But at least black citizens could expect treatment as political equals with whites from the governors they helped put in office.

The point of the foregoing history is that from a Marxist perspective the consensus theorists' focus on the evolution of professionalism and the elite theory emphasis on money, class, and power do not fully explain the political dynamics of state governorships. Class conflict ebbs and flows and takes different forms at different times depending on historical and economic conditions. Political mobilization by working-class people in the 1900s and 1930s, and by minority groups in the 1960s, produced governors more responsive to their needs. The conservative and upper-class forces were better organized in the intervening decades and produced governors more to their liking. This has been particularly true over the last twenty-five years, so that by the 1990s almost all of them, whether Democrat or Republican, have adopted the corporate capitalist agenda as their own.

Conclusion

Analysts of gubernatorial politics are sharply divided on what factors have shaped the development of the office of governor and the administrations of individual governors. Consensus theorists see steady progress in the prevalence of strong, professional chief executives who are increasingly able to cope with the institutional and political demands of the position. Conflict theorists see an increasing trend toward control by the upper class, but they offer different explanations for it. Elite theorists point to money as the basis of gubernatorial power, specifically that which the governor has as a result of personal wealth, connections with elites, or campaign contributions. Marxists see class struggle, broadly defined, as the context of gubernatorial politics, and they argue that the working class, which once placed progressive and even radical governors in office, has become fragmented and weakened, thus allowing business interests to take control. These contending theories have to be tested through application to the particular conditions in each of the fifty states.

Chapter 7: Bureaucratic Politics

There has been tremendous growth in state and local employment over the last forty years, as the demand for government services has expanded. The quality of those services depends largely on the work done by the more than 15 million employees of state and local executive departments and agencies. They have the ultimate responsibility for administering and implementing government programs in education, welfare, health, transportation, and public safety, among other areas. It is thus important to understand and evaluate the structural and political circumstances under which they operate.

The Structure of State and Local Bureaucracy

Institutional Characteristics

The concept of bureaucracy as a system of administrative organization was refined by the German sociologist Max Weber (1864– 1920). According to Weber, all modern societies are characterized by some form of bureaucratic organization, as opposed to "traditional" or "charismatic" organization in less developed societies. Bureaucratic organization is characterized by (1) jurisdictional areas ordered by rules and regulations; (2) an office hierarchy in which lower offices are supervised by higher ones; (3) management based on written documents; (4) a managerial class which possesses expert training and special technical learning for the job; and (5) full-time professional commitment to the office (Gerth and Mills 1958, 196–198). Bureaucratic organization thus rests on regulations, hierarchy, specialization, and professionalism. Although Weber presented this model as the most modern and "rational" method of social organization, later studies began to raise questions about its actual effects. Bureaucracy often seems to impede rather than facilitate efficient delivery of services, and its institutions and processes can appear to be inconsistent with democratic values. A number of issues

Table 7.1: State and Local Employment, 1992

	Number (1,000s)	Percent of Total	Change Since 1982 (Percent)
Total State	*4,594*	*100*	*+22.7*
Higher Education	1,909	41.6	+27.3
Hospitals	554	12.0	-1.7
Corrections	347	7.5	+90.0
Highways	261	5.7	+6.9
Health	166	3.6	+42.0
Natural Resources	164	3.6	+6.0
Financial Admin.	150	3.3	+27.8
Social Insurance	118	2.6	+5.5
Judicial/Legal	113	2.5	+52.0
Police	86	1.9	+13.8
Other	51	1.1	+20.0
Total Local	*11,103*	*100*	*+20.0*
Education	5,727	51.6	+21.0
Police	683	6.2	+15.0
Hospitals	608	5.5	+1.6
Utilities	430	3.9	+18.9
Fire	343	3.1	+15.5
Highways	299	2.7	+6.4
Parks/recreation	275	2.5	+30.7
Health	214	1.9	+64.3
Judicial/legal	209	1.9	+55.4
Corrections	194	1.8	+91.8
Transit	185	1.7	+15.9
Water supply	155	1.4	+23.3
Electric power	78	0.7	+18.2

Source: U.S. Department. of Commerce, *Statistical Abstract of the U.S., 1996.*

thus need to be examined: What are the effects of bureaucracy on how services are provided? What standards of performance are appropriate, and how are these to be achieved? What are the possibilities for public control and accountability? Consensus and conflict theorists have different answers to these questions.

Bureaucracy in State and Local Governments

If bureaucracy is a form of organization, the word "bureaucrat" is often used to describe someone who works within it. This term is not used as a compliment; rather, it has strong negative connotations, implying a lack of concern for individuals, a dedication to meaningless paperwork ("red tape"), and an obsessive concern with rules and regulations. Of course, such behavior is not inconsistent with what is required in a bureaucracy as Weber described it. At one extreme, a bureaucrat may be so efficient as to be devoid of all human feeling; at the other, he or she may use bureaucratic procedures to cover up laziness and inefficiency.

It is probably more accurate, however, to think of state and local officials and employees less monolithically in regard to their different functions and positions. First, a distinction must be made between "line" departments and agencies, which deal directly with the public (schools, police, welfare, etc.); and "overhead" departments and agencies, which perform purely administrative or supervisory functions (budget, audit, etc.). Employees within all these offices are arranged in a hierarchy. At the top are the various executive department and agency heads—commissioners, superintendents, directors, secretaries—who in most cases are politically appointed or popularly elected, and who thus hold office only temporarily. Officials in lesser supervisory and administrative positions—deputies, assistants, bureau chiefs—are, on the other hand, hired, promoted, and (infrequently) removed under the rules of civil service and generally hold their jobs permanently. Finally, there are those at the bottom of the ladder: teachers, welfare caseworkers, clerical help, police officers, librarians, inspectors, maintenance crews, and the like. Most of these employees also have civil service protection (or tenure, in the case of teachers) and many belong to unions, which represent them in their dealings with supervisors and employers in the process of collective bargaining.

Therefore, who is and who is not a "bureaucrat" and who is an "administrator" or a "professional" or a "worker" are distinctions which are not always easy to make. But perhaps it is not necessary to make them. The point is that what we call bureaucracy consists of different groups of people with varying functions and often conflicting interests. Their relationships with each other and with the public constitute what might be called state and local bureaucratic politics.

Bureaucracy and the Public

In private industry the chain of command and the organization of work are usually quite simple and direct: the employer is in charge and the employee, within certain limits, does what he or she is told or faces dismissal. In state and local government work the structure is quite different because the lines of accountability and responsibility are far more complex.

First of all, each level of the bureaucratic hierarchy has a different source of authority. For example, a chief state school officer (CSSO) may be chosen by the governor, whereas the state board of education, which the CSSO nominally heads, may be popularly elected. Workers in the state education department are likely to be civil servants, issuing regulations to popularly elected local school boards. These boards appoint superintendents who are responsible for hiring teachers and principals (within the limits of state regulations), who are in turn protected by tenure and their unions. Noninstructional personnel in the schools are hired through the civil service and may also be unionized. Therefore, although the board of directors of a private corporation can theoretically fire any corporate employee, the chief state school officer generally cannot hire or fire anyone. This means that different levels of the bureaucracy serve different constituencies rather than each other, and some are effectively insulated from serving any constituency at all.

State and local executive offices operate in an intergovernmental environment and within a structure of government based on the separation of powers. Departments and agencies responsible for programs such as welfare and community development are involved in administering a wide variety of federal grants-in-aid, consistent with regulations formulated by their counterparts in the federal bureaucracy. Thus the working relationship of a state welfare administrator might be closer to the Department of Health and Human Services in Washington, D.C., than to state officials. Some analysts call this "picket-fence federalism."

The lifeblood of state and local departments and agencies is appropriations from their respective legislative branches. Although in practice most bureaucracies are immune from complete elimination or, except in times of fiscal emergency, massive cutbacks, the attitude of a particular state legislative committee or a group of city council representatives may be a crucial factor in the future well-being of a particular bureaucracy. It becomes vitally important for administrators to cultivate good relations with specific individuals in the legislative branch. Furthermore, overhead agencies often have considerable power over line agencies in administering appropriated funds and controlling personnel actions. Some bureaucracies are thus more powerful than others within the overall structure. Finally, the judiciary may have a significant effect in controlling the actions of bureaucracies by issuing rulings in cases involving them.

The most distinguishing characteristic of public sector bureaucracies is the fact that most employees are hired on the basis of the "merit system," and their career paths are in many instances subject to civil service regulations. In the nineteenth century, public employees on all levels were hired and fired on the basis of their political allegiance. This "spoils system" distributed public jobs as patronage to adherents of the political party that controlled the respective governments. The resultant incompetence and corruption produced pressure for reform, which culminated on the federal level with the Pendleton Act of 1883. From that point on, civil service and the merit system replaced patronage as a means of filling public jobs, beginning with the federal government and spreading to states and localities over the next sixty years.

A public job covered by civil service is, first of all, defined specifically through "classification" and awarded to an individual on the basis of "merit," ostensibly measured by performance on an objective examination. This may be modified by preferences based on affirmative action regulations or policies favoring groups such as veterans. Promotion, tenure, and dismissal are governed by an elaborate set of regulations enforced by some type of civil service commission. At the present time almost all federal jobs below the top levels are civil service, along with most state and many local positions, especially in the uniformed services. By no means has patronage vanished, however, particularly in local government. Civil service thus severely restricts the hiring and firing prerogatives of public managers. There are, however, numerous ways of circumventing the regulations, such as hiring long-term "temporary" workers. It should be added that although elementary and secondary school teachers are not hired through the merit system or subject to civil service, the system of tenure, which grants more or less permanent employment after a probationary period, is widely used and has a similar effect.

Most public employees are also covered by formal agreements negotiated through the process of collective bargaining. In most states and localities, unions and other associations represent public workers in discussions with employers over wages, working conditions, personnel policies, and grievance procedures. The usual result is a contract, periodically renegotiated, which specifies the rights and responsibilities of both sides, and which often is far more important than civil service regulations in defining the nature of public employment.

Finally, public employees operate within the context of a peculiar combination of formal rules and regulations and varying degrees of administrative discretion. Moreover, since many employees are trained specialists, an attitude of professionalism often shapes how rules are implemented. Police departments, for example, are organized along military lines and are subject to myriad rules and regulations embodied in state and local laws. Yet police officers can and must use their professional judgment in making decisions on the street. Conflict often arises between regulations and judgment, and is usually resolved within the police hierarchy itself. Other line agency employees who are heavily involved with their clientele, notably welfare and education, frequently have to make difficult choices in implementing rules and regulations while trying to deal with individual cases which may not fit what is in the rule book.

This problem is intensified by a recent trend toward tighter restrictions on administrative discretion. According to William Gormley,

> State bureaucracies have paid a price for their growing importance, and that price is loss of discretion. In recent years, state bureaucracies have become more permeable, more vulnerable, and more manipulable. They are subject to a growing number of controls, as governors, state legislators, state judges, presidents, members of Congress, federal bureaucrats, interest groups, and citizens all attempt to shape administrative rule making, rate making, and adjudication at the state level. (1993, 171)

The overwhelming complexity and the numerous contradictions in the organization of state and local bureaucracies add a special dimension to the problems of maintaining accountability, establishing standards, and simply getting the job done. The web of connections among workers in an agency, between the agency and other agencies, and among branches and levels of government often seems to render futile any attempt to control state and local bureaucracy democratically. The fact that these bureaucracies produce services rather than tangible commodities makes the establishment of standards of work subjective at best and impossible at worst. The relative independence of public employees due to civil service, collective bargaining agreements, or tenure limits the ability of public managers, not to mention the public at large, to reward or punish their job performance as they see fit. Perhaps the most drastic move to reduce this independence has been taken by the state of Georgia, which abolished civil service protection for all employees hired after 1 July 1996. It is too early to judge the impact of this change, but it has received much attention from public managers throughout the country.

All this organizational complexity, however, does not necessarily make it impossible to improve the functioning of state and local bureaucracies. Each of the theoretical perspectives offers distinctive analyses of and solutions to their problems.

Theoretical Approaches to Bureaucratic Politics

Consensus Theory

Consensus theorists agree with Weber that bureaucratic organization is the hallmark of a modern, functional society, and they start with the assumption that state and local government employees share the same basic goals and values: efficiency, fair standards, rational rules, accountability, and compromise of differences. If any difficulties arise, it is in the implementation of these goals. The problems are structural and technical, and conflict over appropriate solutions is what constitutes bureaucratic politics.

Traditional public administration theory is based on the importance of organizational structures:

> Effectiveness, efficiency, and accountability in state government all hinge to a substantial degree on the nature of the organizational apparatus through which public officials and employees work. . . . The effectiveness and efficiency of competent personnel will be enhanced by properly designed governmental machinery. Ineffective organization can impinge upon their productivity. Accountability in particular depends heavily on structure. The coupling of authority and responsibility in an organization enables the public as well as the chief administrator to apportion credit and blame. (ACIR 1982, 113)

Although a number of scholars and researchers have developed approaches to reform with less emphasis on administrative structure, most of the efforts by states to improve the functioning of bureaucracy have focused on methods of organization.

Administrative Organization. Considerable effort over the last sixty years has gone into the reorganization of state bureaucracies. Until fairly recently, the direction was toward increased centralization, that is, consolidation of separate agencies into large groupings under more direct executive control.

In the past the combination of popular distrust of executive power, the influence of interest groups, and the concern of the Progressive movement with public involvement created a situation in many states where the bureaucracy was splintered into hundreds of boards and commissions. Although this structure was designed to prevent concentration of power and encourage citizen participation, according to professional administrators, it led to incompetence, domination by special interests, and inefficiency.

The cure, then, was to be centralization and coordination, as recommended in 1937 for the federal government by the Brownlow Committee, whose report served as an impetus to reorganization on the state and local level as well. Since then there have been several "waves" of bureaucratic reorganization in the states, the most recent being 1965 to 1978. During that time, as James Conant (1988, 898) points out, there were at least twenty-one comprehensive reorganizations of state executive branches: "In most of the states, the principal objectives were improved administrative effectiveness, efficiency, and economy; the principal methods employed to achieve these goals were constitutional, structural, and procedural changes aimed at shifting the balance of power over administrative management from the legislature to the chief executive." This was in line with the assumptions of consensus theory in political science.

Public Management and Productivity. Efforts at reorganization have been far fewer since then. The focus has been instead on the nature of management in the public sector. Since state and local government workers have a responsibility to provide services, they require intelligent management to do so effectively and efficiently. The question is, then, what are the appropriate methods?

The key word is productivity, which according to the Committee for Economic Development is defined as a "ratio of the quantity and/or quality of the results (outputs) to the resources (inputs) invested to achieve them." In the public sector the outputs—services—must be both effective (achieving objectives of service provision) and efficient (done at lowest cost). Improving productivity thus means "an increase in the ratio of outputs to inputs, that is, providing more effective or higher quality services at the same cost (or the same services at lower costs)" (1976, 14–15).

In private industry measurement of both inputs and outputs is not a great problem because profit is a good yardstick. But government outputs in the form of services are not so easily measurable. How does one measure the output of public education or the output of police protection? Notwithstanding that difficulty, increased productivity, measured in any practical way, is at least theoretically the major goal of public management. The fundamental question then is not whether higher productivity is desirable but how to achieve it. Here, too, there is a difference from private industry: civil service regulations and collective bargaining agreements preclude the effective use of promotion, demotion, or firing as a means of eliciting higher productivity. Thus there has been an incredible array of proposed solutions, almost all of which have been applied at one time or another by state and local governments.

An early approach was "scientific management," developed toward the end of the nineteenth century by Frederick Taylor; indeed, it is often referred to as "Taylorism." It emphasizes quantitative analysis of the time taken to perform each part of a particular occupational task through "time and motion studies." With this information, management is able to assume full control of the organization of work and has a standard of measurement to gauge workers' performance. The goal is increased productivity and therefore, in the private sector, higher profits. This, of course, requires a docile and preferably nonunionized labor force.

This technique was challenged by more "humanistic" methods. Group dynamics approaches, largely developed since the 1930s, stress the need to develop workers' internal motivation by organizing work in less rigidly authoritarian forms. Individuality, participation, and reduction of conflict become the preferred values. By treating workers as human beings, management can achieve the goal of increased productivity in less repressive and less antagonistic ways.

Garson and Williams (1982, 187) note that both approaches have been combined in attempts to make bureaucracy more efficient: "U.S. public administration has tended to stabilize around a reappreciation of the earlier hierarchical school, combined with a practical interest in various group dynamics people-management techniques. That is, the innovations of the group dynamics school are not so much replacing the hierarchical school approach as greasing its wheels." In state and local gov-

ernments there have been a number of specific applications over the last
thirty years or so.

Attempts have been made to increase productivity through changes
in the organization and nature of work. "Job enrichment" involves an
increase in individual accountability, authority, and freedom, more participation by workers in decision making, and the assignment of new and
more specialized tasks to public workers. "Quality circles" represent an
experiment in collective discussions between workers and management
on an informal basis to improve the quality of working life.   Specific
emphasis is laid on employees' suggestions for increased productivity.
"Participatory management" is an attempt to include workers in making
management decisions.   An elaborate attempt to combine parts of all of
these methods, known as "total quality management" (TQM), has become popular in the 1990s. In brief, TQM calls for breaking down hierarchical structures and improving communication to involve all members
of the workforce in a cooperative and ongoing effort to increase the
quality of the "product," which in the case of state and local government
would be the services provided to citizens.

Monetary incentives are a time-tested way of increasing productivity,
although given the financial constraints in the public sector since the
1970s they may not be affordable. "Performance-based" wage increases
are given to individuals in recognition of measurable improvement in
performance on the job. "Productivity bargaining" is an attempt to do
the same things on a mass level: getting public labor unions to agree to
tie wage increases for all workers to increases in productivity. Numerous
attempts were made, especially in the 1970s, to refine quantitative techniques of evaluating workers' performance. "Performance targeting"
uses as a standard of evaluation some explicit statement of the expected
performance of an individual or group. "Management by objectives" is a
technique applied to management that involves working together toward
certain stated goals (Greiner 1979, 2–5). The rapid development of
computer technology in the 1980s has led to its widespread use in state
and local government as a means of increasing productivity.

The idea of "reinventing government," popularized by Ted Gaebler
and David Osborne (1992) and enthusiastically championed on the federal level by Vice President Albert Gore, has become the buzzword of
administrative reform in the 1990s. Applying private sector models to the
public sector, it advocates the concept of "entrepreneurial government"
as an organizational framework. Instead of using a centralized, bureauc-

ratized, monopolistic structure to provide services, government should reorganize itself to satisfy "consumers" of these services by adopting more flexible, competitive, open-ended methods. These can include contracting services out to private vendors (or even outright privatization), introducing competitive bidding between public agencies and private companies, modifying or perhaps eliminating civil service, linking employees' salaries to performance in terms of "customer satisfaction," and increasing local administrative autonomy and responsibility.

Overall, attempts to guarantee bureaucratic accountability and efficiency within the limits of consensus theory have focused on organizational and managerial techniques. The task of state and local governments from this point of view is to improve on these methods or find new ones to guarantee efficiency and effectiveness in delivering public services.

Conflict Theory

From the perspective of conflict theory, the exclusive and obsessive concern with organization and management techniques is irrelevant. A bureaucracy has certain inherent antidemocratic tendencies no matter how it is organized. Any serious reform must deal with the goal conflicts that arise within public agencies.

If, as Weber asserted, bureaucratic organizations rest on regulations, hierarchy, specialization, and professionalism, they are obviously contradictory to any notion of democratic control. An accountable bureaucracy is a contradiction in terms. As Garson and Williams put it,

> Weber was sensitive to the ambiguous nature of bureaucratization. It was, he believed, a shackle on liberal individualism. Bureaucracy tended to give elitist power to experts, bureaucrats who through their control of information define the limits of what was possible for the politicians. Bureaucracy would use secrecy to maintain its power vis a vis politicians and democracy would be altered in meaning. And just as large-scale organization meant the workers' loss of control over production, so bureaucratization meant the public servants' loss of control over political administration. In each case, alienation and depersonalization were to be the prices of efficiency. (1982, 38)

A contemporary of Weber, Robert Michels (1962), formulated what has been called the "iron law of oligarchy": every kind of political organization tends to end up under the control of an elite because of the leaders' desire to retain power and the followers' inability to maintain the consistent involvement necessary to check that power. This, said

Michels, was true irrespective of the ideology of the political system or organization. Thus bureaucracy would naturally of itself become a tool by which the elite exerted control.

A good example of the nature of bureaucratic power is the structure known as the "iron triangle." This metaphor describes a situation in which policy making results from the interaction of a specific agency, the legislative committee which controls its appropriation, and organized interests with a stake in what the agency does. This goes on to the exclusion of any outside interference. Similarly, some agencies may become the captives of the clientele with which they deal. Regulatory agencies, especially those concerned with insurance or public utilities, have often been accused of serving the interests of the industries they are supposed to regulate.

Marxists in particular see bureaucracy as yet another arena of class conflict. Contrary to the assertions of consensus theorists, its component parts do not share the same goals and values, and managers and workers have opposed interests. In this context productivity means maximum output for the upper class at a minimum input cost, that is, lower wages and benefits for public employees. Marxists feel that this is actually the goal of top bureaucratic managers. This inevitably leads to conflict with public workers. What is more, public services benefit different social classes in different ways and to different extents. Many services are allocated more generously to corporate interests and to middle- and upper-class constituencies. Services to the working class are offered grudgingly and are generally the first target of budget cutbacks.

Unequal power in the bureaucracy is reflected in the racial and gender makeup of its different levels. Over the last twenty years there has been considerable talk about affirmative action in state and local employment—that is, an emphasis on hiring and recruiting more women and minorities in the interest of, among other things, democratizing the bureaucracy and making it more responsive. One study of the characteristics of state administrators shows that 2 percent were female and 2 percent nonwhite in 1964; by 1988, the proportions were 18 percent and 9 percent respectively, which is not a particularly impressive record of change over twenty-five years (Wright et al. 1991, 30–35). The record on the local level is worse. In 1974, 99 percent of a survey of 2,400 local managers and executives were male; in 1989, the proportion was still 95 percent, and only 1 percent were black (ICMA 1990, 44).

Table 7.2: State and Local Government Employment by Race and Sex, 1993

POSITION	TOTAL	% FEMALE	% BLACK	%HISPANIC
Officials/Admin.	273,000	31.5	9.9	3.6
Professional	1,206,000	51.3	13.9	4.9
Technician	465,000	41.9	14.8	6.7
Protective Svc.	846,000	14.2	17.1	6.9
Paraprofl.	360,000	72.2	30.8	6.4
Admin. Support	897,000	87.0	20.4	8.3
Skilled Craft	395,000	4.3	14.9	7.0
Svc./Maintenance	582,000	21.8	32.0	9.8

Source: U. S. Department of Commerce, *Statistical Abstract of the U. S., 1996.*

At the same time, the public service has become increasingly "professionalized". From the consensus theorists' point of view this is a laudable change, but to conflict theorists it simply means that the power of the white male administrative elite has been strengthened. This is considered especially detrimental in such policy areas as welfare, where women and minorities constitute a disproportionate amount of the clientele.

With all this in mind, the idea that reorganization by itself can make bureaucracy more effective and accountable becomes absurd. If decentralized administration results in control by special interests, centralization simply concentrates power in a different set of elites, probably those entrenched in the top levels of the executive branch. Nothing really changes. Moreover, techniques of management, humanistic or other, are simply variations of mechanisms of control to maintain the hierarchy. Conflict theorists argue that although certain reforms give the appearance of offering more independence and authority to employees, they are in actuality sophisticated methods of psychological manipulation. None of them will actually change the structure of power within the bureaucracy in any significant way; they merely deceive workers into thinking that management goals are in fact their own. In particular, "reinventing government" and privatization simply introduce all the inequities and injustices of corporate capitalism and the market economy into state and local government operations.

Conflict Theory and Bureaucratic Reform

Although they share assumptions about the nature of bureaucracy and a common critique of consensus theory, elite and Marxist theorists have some important differences on the possibility of change.

Community involvement in the administration and provision of government services is generally favored by consensus theorists, but conflict theorists put it at the center of their program for changing the bureaucracy. "Site-based management" of public education, if seriously implemented, offers the possibility of placing the governance of the schools in the hands of individual school councils consisting of parents, teachers, administrators, students, and community representatives. "Community policing" takes local police out of headquarters and squad cars and puts them back on the streets to work independently and directly with local residents and community organizations. Although crime control is the ultimate purpose, community police can become involved in a wide range of social service activities and develop personal relationships with citizens in the neighborhoods. Experiments such as these are designed to enhance public control of state and local government services.

From the perspective of elite theory, however, these can have only a limited and peripheral impact. It is in the nature of bureaucracy to create the conditions for domination by an elite. Changing the pattern of bureaucratic management or organization at best simply shifts power from one elite to another and usually works to guarantee the maintenance of a hierarchical structure overall. "Line" workers such as police and teachers can potentially be made more accountable; staff and administration in the central offices are unreachable. The problem of bureaucracy is therefore essentially unsolvable. Given the nature of bureaucratic organization as a whole, greater public accountability is highly unlikely. Thus state and local bureaucrats are likely to remain the rulers of what elite theorists call the "permanent government."

Unlike the elite theorists, Marxists see possibilities for change if the working class takes control of the bureaucracy. In the short run, Marxists advocate greater militancy by the public employees' unions as a means of asserting demands for improved delivery of governmental services. In the long run, they call for a radical change in the organization of work itself.

There has been a considerable expansion of unionism among state and local workers over the last forty years. The largest unions are the American Federation of State, County, and Municipal Workers

(AFSCME); the two teachers' unions, the National Education Association (NEA) and the American Federation of Teachers (AFT); and the various unions representing the uniformed services.

Until 1959 not one state had a law conferring on its workers the right to form unions and bargain collectively with the state over wages and working conditions. Aggressive political action by the unions, especially teachers on the local level, forced the states and localities to recognize them as representing public workers. Over half the states now have arrangements for bargaining with representatives of organized public workers; several more engage in some type of labor negotiations with employees. The exceptions are primarily in the South.

What distinguishes labor relations in the public sector from those in the private sector is the total ban on strikes in most of the states; only in a half dozen or so are public workers given even a limited right to strike. This ban is enforced ostensibly because of the peculiarly sensitive position of state workers. Many work in areas of public health and safety and thus a strike might imperil the physical well-being of citizens. From the point of view of union activists, which Marxists would share, this is simply a rationalization for keeping state and local workers in line. In the 1990s in particular, as fiscal conditions remain tight, the inability to strike limits the capacity of state and local workers to oppose cutbacks in vital services. Public employees' unions have responded by becoming less demanding and more conservative; Marxists, among others, would advocate a return to greater militance.

Marxists are strong believers in "worker self-management," that is, collective control of public services by workers in close partnership with the recipients of those services. Rather than have bosses issue orders which workers obey on pain of being fired, as in the private sector, or which are often disregarded, as in the civil service, the tasks of public agencies should be organized democratically. In other words, state and local employees should work as teams, perhaps with elected managers, who decide among themselves as a group how their jobs are to be performed and how particular duties are to be assigned. The assumption is that greater responsibility and control, along with the effects of peer pressure in a context of teamwork, will motivate employees to improve their work. Accountability to the public, rather than to appointed managers, would provide the necessary stimulus for efficiency and superior performance.

Case Study: The Criminal Justice System

The criminal justice system is a state and local bureaucratic institution. As such, and for its own importance as a function of state and local government, it provides a useful case study of bureaucratic politics. Although the federal government has significantly increased its presence in the nation's criminal justice system, the states and localities take on most of its administrative and financial responsibilities. State and local police make arrests, state and local courts dispose of the cases, and state prisons and local jails incarcerate those convicted.

If its goal is to reduce crime significantly, the criminal justice system has clearly not achieved it, as indicated in Table 7.3. The number of employees and the amount spent have increased dramatically between 1982 and 1992, yet the rate of violent crime increased, the rate of property crime did not change much, and fear of crime did not decrease. The crime rate, especially in certain major cities, has leveled off in recent years, but this may well be attributable to factors other than increased spending. Thus, there is a very valid question as to whether this massive investment of human and financial resources has been used wisely and efficiently. Nonetheless, this relatively straightforward question does not

Table 7.3: Criminal Justice System, 1982-1992

Area	1982	1992	Percent Change
Employees: police	668,001	769,977	+15.3
Employees: judicial/legal	219,109	322,843	+47.3
Expenditures: police	$16.7 Billion	$34.6 Billion	+107.9
Expenditures: judicial/legal	$6.4 Billion	$16.6 Billion	+159.7
Violent crime rate per 100,000 population	571.1	757.5	+32.6
Property crime rate per 100,000 population	5032.5	4902.7	-2.6
Opinion poll: more uneasy on the street compared with previous year.	41%	42%	

Source: U.S. Dept. of Justice, *Bureau of Justice Statistics Sourcebook, 1995*

lend itself to equally straightforward answers, especially because those answers depend on our theoretical point of view.

Consensus theory, it has been pointed out, assumes that societies are based on a consensus regarding essential beliefs and values, including acceptable social behavior. Crime, therefore, can be defined as behavior that deviates from what the community as a whole considers acceptable. The purpose of the criminal justice system is to maintain the stability of the social order by enforcing the law, which generally represents that community consensus. The system can thus be judged in terms of whether its structure is "functional" for that purpose, or in other words, whether the police, the courts, and the prisons are appropriately organized to do their jobs.

Consensus theorists see several problems along those lines. First of all, personnel within the system, especially the police, may not have a clear concept of what their function is supposed to be, or, if they do, may not be sufficiently trained or educated to perform it properly. Fragmented structure is another source of difficulty. The system is highly decentralized. The job of law enforcement rests on the shoulders of people in thousands of local police departments, and each state has its own unique system of organizing courts and corrections. Thus the solutions may lie in reorganization of the system and education of its personnel.

Conflict theory rests on fundamentally opposite notions. As stated earlier, it starts with the assumption that societies are divided by conflict between elites and masses, or among social classes, over whose goals and values will predominate. Therefore, crime is a political concept—its definition depends on which group or class is doing the defining. Since the criminal justice system is controlled by the ruling class, it becomes a means of imposing the values of that class on subordinate social groups. To put it more plainly, the elites decide what a "criminal" is, and they jail those who fit their description, within the limits imposed by constitutional rights and the possibility of mass protest. From the perspective of conflict theory, then, the overall problem with the system is that it is protecting the few at the expense of the many. Its structural and institutional problems are related to the fact that, despite its elitist purpose, it must go by rules that prevent it from operating entirely in the interests of the upper class. This necessarily creates contradictions and confusion in the administration of criminal justice.

Obviously, an evaluation of the criminal justice system as a bureaucracy depends on which theory we use as a starting point. A closer examination of the police and the courts illustrates the differences.

Police Forces

From the consensus theorists' point of view, major problems arise for the police because they have not sufficiently adapted, structurally or professionally, to changing societal demands and pressures. Conflict theorists, on the other hand, argue that the police face difficulties because of their position as enforcers of ruling class values and mandates on an increasingly resistant working-class and minority population.

Consensus theorists look at the history of police forces as evolving in relation to changes in society:

> American police have undergone significant change over the last 200 years. There have been a number of changes in the police role. Around the turn of the century, the police were concerned primarily with order maintenance and the provision of service to the community. This later changed to a focus on crime fighting. This focus was accompanied by the adoption of science and technology to create "professionalized" police forces. Today, American police attempt to balance crime fighting with order maintenance and service. . . . The changes in policing have paralleled changes in society with the police responding to economic, social, and cultural influences. (Gaines, Kappeler, and Vaughn 1997, 62)

Individual police officers may therefore feel pulled in several directions at once. It is this phenomenon which disrupts the orderly functioning of police departments by overloading them with contradictory or ill-defined tasks. Moreover, the "police subculture"—social isolation, insularity, and a feeling of separateness from the community—may make it even more difficult to adapt suitably to changing conditions (Reid 1982, 385). This creates a special problem when the police represent what is perceived by a particular community as an outside force, as in the case of white officers in an African-American or Hispanic neighborhood.

Consensus theorists seek solutions to these problems through changes in the training of police and the improvement of police-community relations. Although an individual reform, such as community policing, may improve the situation if properly implemented, it may also cause even more conflict and confusion about the proper role of the police. Thus, many consensus theorists argue that "to be successful, police departments have to be re-engineered all the way from the top to the bottom of the organization. All management and operational activities must be systematically examined and synchronized in their efforts to effectively accomplish goals and objectives" (Gaines, Kappeler, and Vaughn 1997, 354).

The picture looks quite different from the conflict theorists' perspective. Whatever the feelings of individual police officers about their jobs, there is no question that the role of the police as a whole in American society is essentially one of social control on behalf of the state and the dominant classes. This follows from the view of the criminal justice system as a protector of class values rather than community values. Historically, the police have been an instrument for suppressing labor struggles, especially early in this century, and repressing political dissent, most notably in the 1960s. More recently, it is their relationship to minority communities that has become a critical public issue.

The actual extent of what is called police brutality, particularly as directed against blacks, is a matter of hot debate. Clearly, its overt use was far more frequent in past decades, until the civil rights movement forced a change. Nonetheless, as the Rodney King incident demonstrated, the phenomenon has by no means disappeared. Conflict theorists argue that in fact it is still widespread as a conscious and deliberate method of social control. This makes ghetto residents contemptuous of the police and elicits more police brutality as a response, in a continuing circle of hostility. This continues as long as the police represent the dominant classes and act with relative impunity in dealing with blacks, Hispanics, and poor people in general. Conflict theorists see no solution short of changing the function of the police away from service to the ruling class. That is because at present "one of the reasons the offender at the end of the road is in prison is likely to be a member of the lowest social and economic groups in the country is that the police officers who guard the access to the road to prison make sure that more poor people make the trip than well-to-do people" (Reiman 1995, 99).

The so-called war on drugs is a case in point. So far, despite a time-consuming and expensive campaign, the war has clearly been lost. Consensus theorists argue that this is, once again, attributable to confusion about what the role of police should be, which stems from political differences over the issue of drug use: "The policy debate basically keeps the police in the middle and creates a basis for continued criticism as the police attempt to follow unclear, debatable social policies" (Gaines, Kappeler, and Vaughn, 1997, 394). Conflict theorists believe that the war on drugs is actually a war on minority communities. The importers and wholesalers, who are wealthy and politically connected, are rarely touched by law enforcement agencies, just for that reason. Instead, the street users, who are disproportionately African-American, Hispanic, and poor, face mass imprisonment and lengthy sentences. Drug use is simply a politically convenient excuse by the ruling class to get "social undesirables" off the street, which is the real purpose of the war on drugs—and that purpose is being achieved at tremendous expense to middle-class taxpayers. The role of the police, as always, is to act as enforcers of the law as defined by the ruling class; the difficulty of that task is what creates problems for police forces.

The Judicial System

The President's Commission on Law Enforcement and the Administration of Justice made the following observation in 1967:

> The Commission has been shocked by what it has seen in some lower courts. It has seen cramped and noisy courtrooms, undignified and perfunctory procedures, and badly trained personnel. It has seen dedicated people frustrated by huge caseloads, by lack of opportunity to examine cases carefully, and by the impossibility of devising constructive solutions to the problems of offenders. It has seen assembly-line justice. (Neubauer 1979, 428)

Almost twenty-five years later, it appeared that little had changed:

> Probably no other function of the legal system has come under as much public criticism as the courts' handling of criminal matters. Such criticisms are understandable given the dramatic increase in crime over the past three decades. . . . Particularly in the large metropolitan areas the local criminal justice system appears on the verge of a breakdown as a result of too many cases, various degrees of ineptitude among court officials, and general bureaucratic inefficiency. (Stumpf and Culver 1992, 107, 128)

From the point of view of consensus theorists, "the courts reflect American traditions and values. As such, the judiciary can represent the best and worst aspects of society. The broad goals of the courts are laudable—justice and equality before the law" (Stumpf and Culver 1992, 175). The continuing problems in achieving these goals are a result of the general fragmentation and disorganization of the system. Arbitrariness and discontinuities in the administration of justice have their roots in the localism and bureaucratic dysfunctions of the judicial system. First of all, the criminal justice system is characterized by a high degree of discretion at all levels, including the courts, and this inevitably creates inequities. What is more, the system is political in the sense that it has to respond to a variety of constituencies, especially when judges are directly elected; this creates inconsistency and role conflict. The result is that the system "is not as much a system as it is an assemblage of institutions and legal personnel who are involved in the common enterprise of dealing with those who violate the law." Such an assemblage cannot be expected to work in a coherent, interconnected manner (Stumpf and Culver, 109–110).

The reforms proposed by consensus theorists focus on court unification, more efficient administration, and other means of professionalizing the system. Yet where these have been implemented they have not worked, and in any case even minor reforms will face stiff political resistance from groups with a vested interest in the status quo. Given this situation, an incremental approach to change may be the best we can hope for. As one major study of court reform concludes, "If agents of change . . . adopt lower profiles, adjust their expectations, and move to take ameliorative actions, they might have more effect than is imagined. There are no easy answers, but if we are fortunate we might make some halting and partial advances" (Freely 1983, 224).

From a conflict perspective, the administrative and organizational problems have to be considered within a larger social context. It is no accident that criminal courts function as they do, because they deal with lower-class defendants. Processing has become the goal of the criminal justice system because genuine justice is not in the interests of the capitalist class. That police and the courts have been forced to recognize the rights of defendants at all is due in part to citizens' protests against arbitrary treatment. In short, the judicial system expresses the class values of its organizers. As Jeffrey Reiman puts it,

> The system works to make it more likely that those who end up in jail or prison will be from the bottom of society. For the same crime, the system is more likely to investigate and detect, arrest and charge, convict and sentence, sentence to prison and for a longer time, a lower-class individual than a middle- or upper-class individual . . . even when the crimes of the well off take more money from the public or cause more death and injury than the crimes of the poor. (1995, 126)

This is reflected in the socioeconomic characteristics of the prison population, and especially those on death row.

The inequities of the judicial system are therefore inherent in its purpose, which is not "equality before the law." Bureaucratic inefficiency affects primarily those without the financial and political resources to cut through the red tape and is therefore not of much concern to the ruling class. In this context court reform and reorganization become more or less irrelevant. Eliminating racism and class bias from judicial proceedings and protecting the rights of all equally will require changes that can only accompany a major transformation of the political and economic system as a whole.

The Criminal Justice System as a Bureaucracy

The criminal justice system in the states and localities has come in for severe and perhaps justifiable criticism. It has neither been able to cut back the crime rate nor deal consistently and equitably with those who come under its jurisdiction.

The central problem from a consensus theorist's perspective appears to be structural fragmentation and insufficient adaptation to changes in society, as well as confusion about roles. Thousands of police forces cannot deal separately with a national crime problem. Fifty different state court systems, many understaffed and unprofessional, cannot cope with caseloads. Prisons are overcrowded. Consensus theorists see a need for reforms of various kinds, even if the track record of such reforms has not been good. Professionalization of staff, unification and coordination of system components, and alternative, community-based methods of policing and adjudication may help, but the system has a long way to go before it is effective in protecting community values and maintaining social stability.

Conflict theorists see the central issue as upper-class control of the criminal justice system and the purposes it serves. The police, whether or not they are completely aware of it, serve the interests of the ruling classes and deal mostly with crimes which threaten those interests, especially crimes related to property rights. Thus minorities and poor people become the targets of arbitrary treatment and police brutality. The courts have been forced to deal more fairly with defendants, but they still handle their clientele on the basis of class origin and race. Prisons are for the losers in the struggle, and of late the ruling class has decided to put more losers away. The system as a whole must therefore be moved in the direction of serving the interests of working-class people: a redefinition of crime, new functions and greater accountability for the police, courts which really dispense equal justice, and a corrections system which serves a humane social purpose.

Conclusion

The politics of state and local bureaucracy deals with its internal conflicts and its relation to other branches of government and to the public. The nature of its structure and authority raises serious questions about its capacity to perform its tasks effectively and accountably.

Consensus theorists see the problem of bureaucracy as resting in inappropriate organization and insufficient productivity. They propose solutions in terms of revamped structures and new methods of personnel management. Conflict theorists believe that bureaucracies are generally designed to strengthen ruling-class control over citizens; most reforms are therefore little more than window dressing to make that control less visible and less painful. Any real change requires a fundamental shift in power relations within the system, but elite theorists hold little hope for democratization of an inherently antidemocratic system of organization. Marxists see a possibility for a change in the political direction of bureaucracy, away from serving the interests of the capitalist class, if public workers and local communities became better organized and more militant in asserting their right to control it. The question of how to control a bureaucracy is in fact most crucial for democratic theory. If we adopt the goal of making state and local governments fully accountable to the people, the most formidable obstacle is that part of government which is least amenable to change—those who are on its payroll.

Chapter 8: Legislative Politics

Representative government involves delegating the power and responsibility of political decision making to a small number of citizens chosen by the majority of voters. In the case of the states, some 7,400 legislators determine on behalf of 250 million people what public policies are to be implemented by state governments. But do we have a rational and effective system for choosing them? Do the rules and procedures by which they operate facilitate democratic policy making? Do they really have to take our opinions into account? Affirmative answers would certainly be reassuring, but whether they are accurate depends on our individual theoretical perspectives.

Perhaps the most significant change in the state legislatures over the past forty years is what can be called increasing professionalization. Until the middle of this century, most state governments had rather limited responsibilities. Thus most had part-time "citizen" or "amateur" legislatures, meeting for a few weeks or at most a few months yearly or even every other year. Those who served in them received minimal salary and little or no staff assistance, and most did not serve more than a few terms. Their educational and professional credentials were unimpressive since people who possessed impressive credentials had no financial or career-related incentive to seek legislative office. The result was a policy-making process that could not accommodate the growing demands placed on state governments.

In most states, this is no longer the case. The expanding policy agenda of state government since the 1950s has demanded more time of those elected to state offices. This has led to the development of "professional" legislatures, which meet most or all of the year, pay adequate salaries, provide sufficient staff support and office space, and reward those who commit themselves to service over a longer period of time. Legislative service has generally become more challenging and remunerative, and therefore more attractive to individuals with superior educational and professional backgrounds. According to the National Conference of State Legislatures, as of 1995 ten out of the fifty states had fully professional legislatures: California, Florida, Illinois, Massachusetts, Michigan, New Jersey, New York, Ohio, Pennsylvania and Wisconsin. Seventeen states, mostly in the South and West but also including Maine, Vermont, and New Hampshire, still had citizen legislatures. The rest were "hybrids" (Mahtesian 1997). This change from part-time citizen legislatures to full-time, professional legislatures has become a focus of contention among analysts of legislative politics.

From the perspective of consensus theory, the purpose of state legislatures is to maintain the social consensus which underlies the stability of our political system. Greater professionalism, which will usually reduce the level and intensity of political and partisan conflict, is therefore desirable. This purpose also necessitates developing policies based on compromises among competing groups, facilitated by negotiation and bargaining. Consensus theorists assert that this is generally being accomplished. The method of selecting legislators may be imperfect in many respects, but it has produced a higher level of legislative professionalism in most states. Legislatures may have flaws in their internal structure and may have complex or even undemocratic rules, but they generally, if unevenly, produce the gradual policy adjustments required by a changing society. Some groups certainly have more influence on the legislature than others, but not consistently or permanently; the voter has the last word.

Conflict theorists believe that the legislative process is rigged in favor of the ruling elites or upper classes. They believe that our choice among candidates is limited by the power of money and incumbency, that the range of policy alternatives is limited by rules and procedures which discourage innovation, and that public influence is limited by the vested interests of lobbyists and their legislative clientele. The increasing professionalization of the legislatures, so valued by consensus theorists, actually works in favor of the interests of the upper classes. The power of the upper classes is further enhanced by rules and procedures that ensure minority rule in the legislatures. The mass constituency may be heard at times, but the response is shaped and limited by the ideological predispositions of the state legislators themselves.

An examination of how legislators are chosen, the nature of legislative organization and procedure, and the structure of influence and power in the legislature gives us the information we need to evaluate these contending points of view.

Recruitment and Selection

Legislative Campaigns The first step toward entering the state legislature is gaining the nomination of one of the two major parties, unless a candidate wants to run (and almost inevitably lose) as an independent. Would-be legislators either recruit themselves or are recruited by community groups, political parties, or sometimes both. The extent to which the local party organization is involved at this stage depends on its strength, which varies among and within states.

If there is more than one candidate for a party's nomination, a primary election is held. The rules governing primaries vary, as discussed in Chapter 4. The different rules affect the chances of the candidates as well as the influence of the party organizations. A primary that is open to independents or members of the opposing party is harder for parties to control, and hence is easier for self-recruited candidates to win. A closed primary tends to strengthen the party's hand, since independents are excluded.

Levels of competition within a primary depend first of all on the desirability of a particular party's nomination. If the party's chances of winning the general election are poor, few if any candidates will enter its primary. States with stronger party organizations have less primary competition, and there are fewer close races.

The important point, however, is that incumbents have an overwhelming advantage. As Alan Rosenthal states (1981, 23), "There is not much reason for an incumbent—one who wants to win and works at the job—to lose in a bid for reelection." This is largely because "the accouterments of a modern legislature—professional staff, longer sessions, better pay, adequate office facilities, and computer resources—enhance the ability of state legislators to get media attention, communicate a public policy record, and claim credit for legislative accomplishments." This is in addition to "an incumbent's edge at raising money from interest groups, lobbyists, and party sources" (Simon 1986, 32). In the 1990s, however, perhaps as a reaction to the imposition of term limits, there has been an apparent increase in legislators who choose not to run for reelection (Hansen 1997, 50).

Legislative elections are also becoming more expensive, for reasons discussed in Chapter 4. In most states, the money for these campaigns comes from individual contributors, political action committees (PACs), interest groups, and the better-organized political parties, as well as the

candidates themselves. Contributors, especially PACs, tend to favor incumbents. As pointed out in previous chapters, controls and limits on
campaign contributions and expenditures in the states are not especially
widespread or effective.

Candidates for the state legislature thus have to raise funds on their
own from a number of sources, and therefore must be reasonably well-
known in the community to connect with those sources. State legislative
office is not reserved for the well-to-do everywhere, but a substantial
amount of money is necessary, especially in larger urbanized states. As
discussed in Chapter 3, frustration among many voters with the seeming
impossibility of dislodging well-financed but unresponsive or ineffective
incumbents has spawned a highly successful "term limitation" movement
in those states with the initiative process.

Who then ends up in the state legislatures? Overall, state legislators
are from the upper middle class. One survey taken in the 1980s found
that 37 percent were lawyers, business owners, or real estate executives.
Farmers, educators, and business managers or employees constituted ap-
proximately 10 percent each. Another 10 percent were retired, home-
makers, or students; and 11 percent defined themselves as full-time professional legislators (Paterson 1986, 22–23). These proportions, however, are not consistent across the fifty states. Farmers, for example, are
more prevalent in midwestern state legislatures.

More significant is the distinction between full-time and part-time
legislatures. Rural and less populous states still tend to have part-time
legislatures, which therefore are more likely to have a higher proportion
of "citizen-legislators," middle-class people with conventional jobs who
spend part of the year in the legislature. For example, the Colorado legislature, which pays $17,500 annually,

> is now composed almost entirely of people who can devote most of their time
> to it without having to worry about holding down a full-time job somewhere
> else. . . . There are some who are independently wealthy. There are retired
> military officers collecting comfortable pensions, and aging ranchers. . . . There
> are a few lawyers and oil company executives whose firms understand the
> power of the legislature and don't mind subsidizing an employee who is absent
> for months at a time. There are men whose wives are highly paid professionals
> . . . . Most of all, however, there are women—highly educated, affluent subur-
> ban women. (Ehrenhalt 1992, 199)

Legislatures in urban, industrialized states, on the other hand, are
generally full-time; their legislators tend to be more professional, in

terms of both social position and orientation to the job of representation.

In all these cases, however, legislatures tend to be demographically unrepresentative. African-Americans, Hispanics, and especially women are underrepresented. A 1993 study found that although women constitute over 50 percent of the voting-age population, no state legislature was more than 40 percent female. The national average was 20.4 percent; the proportion of women was especially low in southern states. Out of seventeen states with a significant percentage of African-Americans in their population, only in California and Florida were they represented in proportion to that percentage. Out of nine states with large Hispanic populations, only two—New Mexico and Colorado—matched those percentages in their state legislatures (Stanley and Niemi 1994, 402–404).

Recruitment and selection can be summed up as a process in which individuals are largely responsible for their own election, with varying amounts of support from a party organization. Entering the arena of legislative politics is much like starting a business: The "entrepreneur" comes up with the idea, arranges for financing, finds the market, and promotes the product. Sharp competition and effective challenges against incumbents are exceptional as campaign finances and incumbency have become important factors. This produces, on the whole, a rather homogeneous group of legislators.

Theoretical Analysis

Consensus theorists, as stated earlier, are primarily concerned with the legislature as an instrument to promote consensus and stability in the political system and in society as a whole. The most significant recent event in legislative politics has been increasing professionalization of state legislatures and their membership. Thus consensus theory focuses on the impact of that change on the effectiveness of state legislatures as consensus-building institutions.

For most consensus theorists, a higher proportion of legislators who consider politics their career represents an improvement. The business of governing requires professionals with a permanent commitment—preferably with the appropriate credentials, such as a law degree—rather than dilettantes or status-seekers. Some see problems in that a professional attitude may destroy the sense of community and political enthusiasm that often characterizes citizen or part-time legislatures. Generally, however, consensus theorists tend to see lower turnover and higher social background, if balanced with responsiveness and greater diversity, as positive factors in developing a state legislative branch that is capable of accepting full-time responsibility for policy making. As Alan Rosenthal puts it, "Legislatures have made considerable progress with respect to their competence in policy making and the power they exert. They want to continue to be professional as a legislature while avoiding complete careerism as legislators" (quoted in Jones 1990, 25).

Consensus theorists, therefore, generally oppose term limits. As mentioned in Chapter 3, twenty-one states have passed initiatives limiting the number of terms state legislators may serve. It is still too early to be certain about their impact, which will not be fully felt until after 2000, when many legislators will be forced to leave office. Nonetheless, consensus theorists agree with the assessment of most legislative leaders, who offer

> a sobering view of what term limits may mean to legislatures: no institutional memory in elected officials; discord among legislators who try to maneuver for legislative positions; disrupted balance of power in which the executive branch becomes, by default, stronger; state agencies where career officials need merely outwait lawmakers with whom they disagree; special interest lobbies more capable of wielding influence over inexperienced lawmakers; a loss of rural and minority influence. (Hansen 1997, 50)

Conflict theorists view the selection process as vesting representation of the majority in the hands of a particular social class or elite. The increasing expense of campaigns has effectively excluded the average citizen who might want to run for the state legislature. The only viable candidate is one who is well connected with the local party organization, if any, or with a community elite or interest group PACs able to finance a candidacy. This means the nomination and election of white male lawyers, managers, and business owners. Conflict theorists argue that these legislators cannot be expected to represent the interests of working-class people, women, and minorities. Moreover, professionalism cultivates an elitist point of view toward politics; that is, if public policy questions are to be resolved through the application of specialized expertise, only the "experts" will have a voice in developing solutions, and public opinion becomes secondary. Thus a professional legislature dominated by one class of people is inimical to democracy in state government, and will result in the passage of legislation favorable only to the interests of that particular class.

Structure and Process

Legislative organization and lawmaking procedures have a tremendous impact on policy making. These include the selection of leaders, organization of committees, determination of financial and staff amenities available to members, prescription of formal rules of lawmaking, and promotion of informal codes of behavior. The nature of their impact, however, is subject to debate. Overall, many observers have noted a trend toward "congressionalization" of state legislatures. This refers to an increasing similarity between the structure, procedures, and norms of the U.S. Congress and many, if not all, state legislatures. To different extents and for very different reasons, all three perspectives are critical of that direction.

Leadership

In all states the principal officer of the lower house is the speaker, elected by the whole house. In the state senates the principal officer is called the president. In the majority of states the lieutenant governor automatically becomes president, usually having only formal powers, with the real power vested in the hands of the majority party leader. In many states that leader is also the elected senate president, sometimes called the president pro tempore.

Normally, legislative leaders are chosen by a process that begins when legislators of each party meet as a caucus to agree on their respective candidates for speaker and senate president, as well as to choose their own party leadership. Each party then usually votes as a block for its own candidates. The nominees of the majority party thus generally win. In a few cases a bipartisan coalition has elected a leader, especially where the majority party is divided and the margin of control is slim. One such instance was the accession of the Democrat Willie Brown in 1980 to the speaker's position in the California assembly, with the help of Republican votes.

Until the mid-1970s there was a fairly rapid turnover in state legislative leadership, but this changed as some leaders began to treat their positions as a career. In a few states there is an explicit tradition of rotating leadership after a few sessions; and, of course, in states with strong party competition, leadership will change with the partisan composition of the legislature. Most leaders, however, leave voluntarily to run for higher office or to find a better-paying job.

The ability of legislative leaders to control the lawmaking process depends largely on their ability to use persuasion as well as rewards and punishment to create a consensus. One of the most important resources for this power is control of the legislative committees, specifically in determining their membership and chairs, a power which leaders in the U.S. Congress do not have. House speakers have the exclusive power to appoint committee chairs and members in all but a handful of states. Senate presidents have this power in about half the states. Such appointments are sometimes made with the participation of other majority party leaders as well as the governor. In some cases the minority party may be consulted on the allocation of its committee seats. In certain states the speaker and senate president also appoint the other party leaders.

Additional powers of legislative leaders usually include the ability to influence or regulate the scheduling of bills and control over the allocation of benefits and perquisites for individual legislators, such as support for bills, patronage, staff assistance, and so on. All these resources can be used for the purpose of directing the legislative process by negotiating agreements to build the consensus necessary for the passage or defeat of bills according to the wishes of the leadership.

There was a time when legislative leaders would use their powers aggressively to enforce party discipline and pressure wayward legislators to toe the line. The former U.S. House Speaker Thomas P. ("Tip") O'Neill described his tenure during the 1950s as speaker of the Massachusetts house of representatives:

> Because we needed every vote, I did everything possible to maintain our majority. I once chased Joe Leahy, a Democratic member, for a vote after I learned he had made a commitment to an outside lobbyist to vote against us. I had locked the doors of the chamber, so the only places he could be were the reading room and the lavatory. When I couldn't find him in the reading room, I tried the other place. I didn't see anybody there, but it occurred to me that he might be hiding in one of the stalls with his feet up on the toilet. "I know you're in there, Joe," I shouted, "so you better come out because we need you." My hunch was correct, and a red-faced Joe shuffled out and gave us his vote. (1987, 65)

Indeed, under the leadership of William Bulger, the Massachusetts state senate operated in a similar, if more politically sophisticated, manner until his retirement in 1995. In most cases, however, this kind of leadership style began to die out in the 1980s:

Many [legislators] are career politicians and some are full-time legislators. They win election largely on the basis of their work in the constituency. On policy issues, they may be less responsive to leadership and more to interest groups. . . . There are probably fewer legislatures where the norm of strong party discipline exists than was true a generation ago. Under these conditions, effective leadership requires more bargaining skill, more sensitivity to members' needs, and more flexibility than in the past. Those legislative leaders who have been deposed, or have had their power curtailed, have often been ones who have failed to adapt to the demands of today's legislators. (Jewell 1989, 11)

Thus, in New York, the senate majority leader Ralph Marino and the assembly speaker Mel Miller succeeded "iron-fisted, powerful" leaders, and adopted a more casual, democratic, and responsive style of managing their respective chambers (Gallagher 1989, 18). Willie Brown's power as assembly speaker in California was strengthened by "his ability to change with the times" (Paddock 1989, 22). And the Texas house speaker Gib Lewis "got where he is by being friendly and unthreatening to the other 149 members of the Texas House" (McNeely 1989, 27). Yet all of them were effective legislative leaders. There are still exceptions, but for the most part the old legislative party boss has become obsolete and, from the consensus theorist's point of view, rightly so. A more professional legislature requires a more professional management style.

The Committee System

All state legislatures organize standing (i.e., permanent) committees to perform the task of evaluating bills introduced by members, as well as analyzing policy issues and overseeing the administration of executive agencies. In all but three states these committees generally operate separately in each house. In Connecticut, Massachusetts, and Maine they are set up as joint standing committees, which include members from both houses deliberating together. They are usually organized around specific legislative subjects and given appropriate titles: education, agriculture, judiciary, and so on. Numbers of standing committees in both houses of the legislature vary from under a dozen in several states to more than sixty in New York. State senators usually sit on four or five committees, members of the lower house on one or two. As pointed out earlier, the presiding officers usually have control of the committee appointment process.

Once a bill is referred to a committee, as is usually the case, the

committee has the option of recommending the bill as it stands to the full
chamber, modifying or changing it, reporting it negatively (in some
states), or simply letting it die. Theoretically, this means that committees
have considerable power, as they do in the U.S. Congress. But in fact the
screening process in the states is often not that strict. Alan Rosenthal
estimated in 1981 that two-thirds or more of all bills going into committee receive favorable reports, with considerable variation from state to
state (199).

In general, state legislative committees lack the prestige and power
of their counterparts in Congress, since in most legislatures they tend to
become instruments of the party leadership, and most do not retain a stable membership from session to session. Thus, although committees
play an increasingly important role in the legislative process, their impact
is not uniformly strong in all fifty states. According to a study by Wayne
L. Francis in 1985, only ten states had legislative chambers in which
committees alone were important centers of decision making (255–256).
In most states power is shared by committees and party leaders or scat-
tered among three or more centers.

Staff and Salaries

The most dramatic change toward greater professionalism is the increase in salaries and staffs. Higher salaries ostensibly provide the necessary incentive to do a full-time job of lawmaking; larger staffs provide
the means. Both were generally inadequate before the 1960s.

In 1963 one-third of the states paid legislators on a per diem basis
plus expenses. Daily pay ranged from Rhode Island's $5 for up to sixty
days to Louisiana's $50 for up to ninety days. Most of these states also
granted $15 to $20 per day for expenses. Biennial salaries ranged from
$200 in New Hampshire to $20,000 in New York, usually plus expenses.
The median was $1,500 a year (Lockard 1966, 112–113). Since then the
trend has been upward, although it has slowed in recent years, partly because of increasing public cynicism about the value of high salaries for
legislators. As of 1995, nine states paid on a per diem basis. Rhode Island still paid $5, but Kentucky, Nevada, and Wyoming paid $100. New
Hampshire still paid its part-time citizen legislators $200 per session, but
twelve states paid over $25,000; California was the highest at $72,000.
Almost all states pay $50 to $100 per day in expenses, and many pay
additional stipends to legislative leaders (Council of State Governments
1996, 80–81).

Staffs were practically nonexistent until the late 1960s. Research work was done by legislative councils consisting of legislators meeting between sessions to perform necessary background work. This has changed dramatically. Initially there was simply a growth in the number of staff members assigned to the legislature as a whole. By the mid-1980s, most state legislatures provided personal year-round staff for individual legislators as well as legislative committees. By 1995, almost all states did. Technological sophistication has increased:

> Computer-related staff positions have grown tremendously in the past decade. Automation of bill-drafting, statutory retrieval, roll-call voting, bill status and general word processing got off to a big start in the 1970s. But it was in the 1980s that computers have blossomed as a legislative tool. Almost daily, new applications have been introduced for political redistricting, fiscal analysis, information retrieval, constituent communications, data manipulation, and information sharing. (Weberg 1988, 25)

From the consensus theorist's point of view, higher salaries, more experienced and qualified staffs, and the use of high technology are necessary adjuncts to a professionalized legislature.

Lawmaking Procedures and Legislative Norms

There are variations among the states in how a bill becomes law, but a general pattern can be described. In most of the states, any member of the legislature may introduce an unlimited number of bills. In some states these bills may be requested or even written by individual constituents. Generally, legislators receive assistance from a legislative agency in drafting the bills properly.

In the regular legislative sessions of 1994–1995, well over 200,000 bills were introduced in the fifty state legislatures, up to 33,000 in New York and 15,000 in Massachusetts alone. Normally the number is 2,000 to 5,000 per state (Council of State Governments 1996, 105–106). Each bill is filed with the clerk of the house or secretary of the senate, depending on where it is introduced. It is subsequently announced on the floor by its title (the "first reading"), assigned a number, and referred to the appropriate committee by the presiding officer, whose discretion in that decision is usually limited by rule or tradition.

The committee, if it chooses, looks into the bill, discusses it, and possibly holds public hearings on it. If the bill is reported favorably, it proceeds to the floor of the chamber for consideration. Some states allow committees the option of reporting bills favorably or unfavorably. In some states a bill may proceed directly from the committee to the floor; more frequently the leadership, usually through the rules committee, will schedule it on the legislative "calendar." At this point the bill is given its "second reading," and is discussed, debated, and amended on the floor. A third and complete reading of the bill precedes a final vote, which in most states requires a roll call.

The same process is repeated in both chambers. If there are differences between what has been passed in each house, a conference committee, consisting of members of both houses, is selected by the leadership to resolve them. The report of the conference committee must then be approved by both houses. It is then sent to the governor, who may sign it into law. In all states but North Carolina the governor may veto the bill. A veto can be overridden by the legislature. In most states this requires three-fifths or two-thirds of all elected legislators in each house. There is generally a time limit after which an unsigned bill becomes law. In about a dozen states the governor can use a "pocket veto": if the legislature adjourns before the time limit expires and the governor does not sign it, the bill dies. In certain states, the legislature may reconvene to override postsession vetoes. In all but five states the governor may suggest changes or veto a particular item in appropriations bills, a process known as a line-item veto. This power was recently, in part, granted by the U.S. Congress to the president, but in 1998 the Supreme Court ruled it unconstitutional.

Obviously, this process functions as an obstacle course. Unless there is a strong consensus behind a bill, special attention from its advocates is required to get it passed. Determined opponents, even if they are in the minority, have numerous opportunities to block it. The most significant legislative power is thus negative: the ability to prevent something from happening. Only about one-fifth of legislative bills become law.

The complexity of the process requires a certain amount of individual conformity to specific behavioral standards if anything is to be accomplished. The existence of such norms is historically well established in the U.S. Congress, where they generally concern the individual's relation to the institution of Congress as a whole. In the last thirty years, however, legislators in both Congress and the state legislatures have become increasingly individualistic, as the ties of party loyalty and the rigid rules of seniority have lost importance. By the 1980s, it could be said that "those who do not conform to norms, insofar as norms exist, generally are left alone to do their own thing. It would seem, in fact, that today fewer members are concerned about norms; more are willing to challenge them" (Rosenthal 1981, 206). Thus, for better or worse, legislators act increasingly on the basis of their individual inclinations rather than on the basis of institutional traditions or party discipline.

Theoretical Analysis

Consensus theorists evaluate the structure and processes of the legislature in terms of how they reflect adaptation to the increasing demands made on government. The key word is, again, professionalism.

In the 1960s the literature on state legislatures came down heavily on the so-called amateurism of legislators. Duane Lockard (1966, 124–125) referred to legislators as "struggling, sometimes not very successfully, to cope with an alien and bewildering world" and predicted that, without changes, "the state legislature will wither away." Herzberg and Unruh (1970, 3–13) felt that the bureaucracy was usurping legislative powers because of the legislature's "ineffective" committee system and the "disproportionate" influence of lobbies in the absence of staff, as well as the lack of an "executive salary."

The answer was to be structural reform. Numerous reports were issued by professional and scholarly organizations, such as the report of the Citizens Conference on State Legislatures (1971), which saw a need "to propel state legislatures into the twentieth century" and "to transform the horse and buggy legislatures into modern, competent, supersonic, decision-making vehicles" (Herzberg and Unruh 1970, 103). By 1990, Rich Jones, a staff member of the National Council of State Legislatures, could report:

> The reformers succeeded; state legislatures are stronger. In 1988 there were over 33,000 staffers working in state legislatures, 40 percent of them full time professionals. In 1990, all but seven states met in annual sessions. Legislative compensation has been increased in most states (although barely keeping pace with inflation) and legislators in 42 states are eligible for retirement benefits. . . . The turnover in state legislatures has declined. . . . In 1988, almost one out of every five legislators viewed the legislature as a career. (22)

Alan Rosenthal (1991, 200) feels that "there can be little doubt that the contemporary legislature exercises influence over the executive branch not only in making policy and in determining budgets but also in running state government. . . . [There is] a condition of true co-equality between the two branches of government."

Consensus theorists are split, however, in their evaluation of these changes. Although none question the greater effectiveness of the legis-lative branch as a participant in making policy, some question whether the departure from the model of the citizen legislature has gone too far. First of all, conflict is not always inversely related to professionalism. According to Charles Mahtesian (1997, 16), the professional Minnesota legislature "has sunk into a humiliating morass of bitter partisanship and personal scandal," and the "amateurish" Tennessee legislature has "con-ducted an efficient, productive, and thoroughly civilized legislative ses-sion, something it has done every single year during the 1990s."

That may occur because too much resemblance to the U.S. Congress, with its increasingly sharp and contentious partisan conflict, can be dam-aging: "At a recent conference on the future of state legislatures . . . the participants—current and former legislators, political scientists, and me-dia representatives—generally agreed that legislatures should try to avoid becoming highly professional bodies like the U.S. Congress." Burdett Loomis states that "the central problem remains today what it was, in many ways, 20 years ago: how to balance the value of citizen legislature against the need for enhanced expertise and experience in dealing with the increasingly large, difficult, and complex problems facing the states" (Jones 1990, 25).

Others, like Alan Rosenthal (1986b, 5), are concerned with "institu-tional maintenance": "Political careers, re-election campaigns, constitu-ent service, interest group demands and the lengthy agenda of public problems . . . exercise centrifugal force. Members . . . neglect matters such as structure, procedure, staff, image and community. . . . Although the legislature is a durable institution, it needs constant care and attention from its members. I am troubled that its needs are not being met."

From the perspective of conflict theory, this entire discussion is ir-relevant. Modernization and professionalism have nothing to do with representation of people in making policy. Indeed, they actually mini-mize public influence.

Elite theorists concentrate their attention on how legislative struc-tures and processes concentrate power in the hands of a particular elite. The sheer complexity of the process and the increasing volume of busi-ness mean that legislative power depends on information and position, which are not shared equally among all legislators. Thus, even if the leadership can no longer exercise dictatorial power, its control over rules, scheduling, and the committee system means that most legislation cannot be passed without its support. Individuals representing particular vested interests can and do maneuver themselves into strategic positions on committees or in the leadership to promote or block legislation. Professional staff members have the capacity to become an "unelected legislature." The whole system is biased against majority rule by providing multiple opportunities for well-entrenched minorities to obstruct it, which is consistent with the original intentions of those who drafted the U.S. Constitution in the first place.

Marxists agree, but they would add the language of class analysis. From their perspective, state legislatures overrepresent the interests of businesspeople and upper-middle-class white males, because that is who the legislators are. Part of the ideology of that class is the idea that social problems can be resolved by the application of expertise by "objective" professionals such as themselves. This tends to lessen the value of mass public opinion in making policy decisions, especially when it contradicts the class interests of the legislators. Policy issues are dealt with as technical problems rather than as political conflicts. Power is therefore concentrated in the hands of technicians and specialists in the legislature. All of this works against the interests of working-class people.

Policy Making

The ultimate test for a representative institution of government is its accountability, as reflected in the way it makes decisions. The central question here is what influences those decisions, and each theoretical perspective offers a different answer. Consensus theorists, adopting a "multi-influence" perspective, see each individual legislator as subject to different influences on different issues. The result is that the legislature as a whole decides policy on the basis of constantly shifting coalitions. There is a tendency toward building consensus among competing and conflicting pressures on legislators from their political party, the governor, interest groups, and their constituency. Conflict theorists, on the other hand, emphasize the disproportionate influence of interest group lobbyists and the influence of ideology. We review the facts and the theories at the same time by discussing each source of influence in turn.

Political Parties

There is no uniform pattern of party cohesion or competition among the fifty states. The dominant party often becomes highly factionalized

along regional or ideological lines. Sharp statewide party competition
for legislative seats is relatively uncommon. Thus one cannot draw consistent conclusions about policy direction simply on the basis of partisan
control of the legislature.

Professionalism has diminished the role of parties. Changes in the
Connecticut legislature serve as an illustration:

> In the 1950s, when a legislator . . . described himself as a professional, he
> meant a member of a political party, an organization, someone who grasped the
> rules of that organization and worked patiently to secure the benefits member-
> ship brought. . . . The only way to qualify for these fruits of office was to be a
> team player, to practice the political self-discipline that party loyalty required. .
> . .To be a professional [today] means, of course, almost exactly the opposite. . .
> . One doesn't work months on end and give up all other gainful employment
> for the privilege of going to Hartford to sit around and take orders. (Ehrenhalt
> 1992, 147)

Nonetheless, many studies conclude that partisanship is the best single predictor of legislative voting. But even if that correlation exists, it
neither proves that partisanship actually influences voting behavior nor
means that there is a great deal of party competition. It is reasonable to
conclude that parties continue to have a distinct influence on legislative
voting behavior, although party allegiance and discipline have declined
considerably as a factor.

The Governor

The influence of the governor on legislative policy making varies
considerably from state to state. To some degree this depends on the
formal institutional powers mentioned in previous chapters. Although
legislators belonging to the governor's party may be more apt to cooperate with him or her, this by no means constitutes a guarantee, given what
has been said about party cohesion.

More often it comes down to a question of the governor's political
acumen in dealing with the legislators as individuals. Specific rewards
such as patronage or reelection support may be useful. The governor's
ability to mobilize public opinion as well as to cultivate working relationships with the legislative leadership and to pay attention to legislative
needs are important and will heighten executive influence. Thus the nature of gubernatorial impact on legislative voting and political direction
cannot be generalized; it depends on how effectively the governor uses
available formal and informal powers and how strongly the legislature

resists.

The Constituency

The basic assumption of consensus theory concerning the influence of constituents' opinion on a legislator's political choices is best expressed by Malcolm Jewell: "Most districts are fairly homogeneous; the major interests are clearly recognized. There is a dominant point of view and the legislator usually shares the viewpoint. If there are divisions of opinion, he is likely to recognize which one dominates among his supportive constituency. . . . Most legislators believe that they are typical of the mainstream of attitudes in the district, and most of them are probably correct" (1982, 103–105). The constituency is characterized here in typical consensus-theory fashion as embodying a general agreement on basic issues, with conflicts arising on matters relevant only to the particular district on noneconomic questions.

Within this context, Jewell concludes that legislators generally are able to act as more or less "free agents" because constituents' opinion "often cannot be followed because it is poorly informed, not clearly articulated, or sharply divided" (1982, 112). This does not mean that the legislator can ignore the constituency. Citing another analyst's approach, Jewell states:

> When conflict arises, the legislator begins by asking whether the issue is salient to his district, and if it is, the interests and demands of the district must be taken into account, if not always followed, as the decision is made. Although the legislator makes many decisions without any regard to the constituency, taking cues from other sources, he does this after he has considered and rejected the possibility that the issue is salient to the district. (1982, 130)

Constituency influence also extends into another area: legislative "service." Many legislators are asked to do individual favors for their constituents—helping to obtain government benefits, interceding with an unresponsive bureaucracy, or perhaps finding a job. Alan Rosenthal (1986a, 29–30) concludes that "where the professionalization of legislatures is advanced and electoral considerations powerful, service tends to be a major operation." He states further that the trend toward increased service to the constituency is likely to continue and is positive for both incumbents and constituents, since both benefit. The disadvantage is that although the legislative staff usually performs this function, it does take time away from attention to policy making and the needs of the legislature.

Not all researchers agree that legislators tend to reflect the views of their constituencies. Eric Uslaner and Ronald Weber (1979, 579) concluded that "American state legislators in general do not have the views on public policy that correspond closely with their constituencies. These men and women misperceive public opinion more than one might have guessed. . . . [They are] a 'poorly informed elite.'" Even Jewell himself notes that "legislators who say that they are typical or think like their constituents may be referring to those groups that are in the majority and that contributed to their election" (1982, 120). It also needs to be remembered that most legislators cannot know what is taking place in the lawmaking process at all times. It is impossible for any individual to cast intelligent votes on all the bills which come through. Outside the legislator's own constituency and committee interests, votes are generally cast on the basis of "cues" from other legislators—party leaders, committee chairs, or simply friends in the legislature—rather than the constituency. David Ray (1982, 1086) found this to be true especially in "professional" legislatures, leading him to conclude that "the policy actions of less professionalized legislatures . . . were more representative of the public's policy preferences than were the actions of more professionalized legislatures." Finally, one may deduce from the strength of the movement for term limits that many citizens are profoundly unhappy with their state legislatures and feel that regular elections do not ensure accountability.

If there are questions even among consensus theorists as to the extent of constituency influence, that debate should lead to a discussion of other political influences on the legislature—interest groups and ideology—which are more related to the concerns of conflict theorists.

Interest Groups

There are sharp differences between the two theoretical perspectives on the subject of interest groups' influence. From the consensus theorists' perspective the ability of any particular group to get what it wants from the legislature depends on its use of political resources to gain access to the legislators themselves. In other words, those interest groups best able to mobilize public opinion, communicate their point of view, and reach decision makers will get what they want. Moreover, lobbyists—individuals hired to represent the political interests of a particular group—are seen by consensus theorists as performing necessary functions:

Lobbyists play an indispensable role in the legislative process, providing a crucial link between legislators and various organized groups which often exist outside the lawmaker's district constituency. . . . Frequently legislators find their electoral constituencies are either irrelevant to the policy under consideration, uninformed, or not interested. Legislators . . . turn to information sources outside their electoral districts—the governor or other executives, the bureaucracy, legislative staff, or lobbyists. (Bell 1986, 12)

Among the functional activities of lobbyists from this point of view are such tasks as developing proposals, supplying information, transmitting attitudes of client groups, developing coalitions around policy proposals, and providing campaign assistance to friendly legislators. According to Jewell and Patterson (1977, 298), "lobbying is part of the conflict management process. It is an aspect of legislative bargaining, negotiating, and compromise. The legislator-lobbyist relationship is not a one-way street."

A common stereotype, supported by conflict theory, is that lobbyists for moneyed special interests dominate the legislative process. Consensus theorists reject this idea. According to Alan Rosenthal:

> On minor issues, the lobbyist's influence is likely to be central, and may in fact carry the day. On major issues, other factors play a much greater role, and a lobbyist's influence is likely to be marginal. . . .Those who have money also have an edge, other things being equal. This is more likely to occur on the narrow, special-interest issues. Other things are less likely to be equal on broader issues. . . . Money is certainly an important resource in interest-group politics, but it is by no means the only or the most important resource. . . . What we have is neither a closed system nor one in which every participant is equal. Just how participants weigh in depends on who they are. It also depends on the particular issue in contest, the politics of the time, the people in government, and more immediate circumstances. (1993, 214, 224)

To a conflict theorist, all this is naive. By acting as the primary sources of information, lobbyists effectively cut off opposing viewpoints. Presenting such information requires research and full-time representatives in the state house. Thus, as David Welch (1989, 19) reports, lobbying activity in state capitals is intensifying and "lobbyists are increasingly professional, just as legislators are. . . . Lobbyists acknowledge that more and more they must support their case with solid arguments." This has led to the growth of "contract lobbyists," law firms that offer lobbying as part of their services. Many of these firms have begun to operate across state lines; an example is Multistate Associates, located in Great Neck, New York, which maintains a network of nearly 1,000 state and local lobbyists, whom it matches with clients according to particular needs (Welch, 21). Obviously only wealthy groups can afford this, and thus only their voice will get a full hearing. Moreover, legislators are more likely to listen to lobbyists who come from the same legal or professional background as themselves. And, of course, the promise of campaign support and contributions is most important, a promise which can be fulfilled only by those lobbies with the appropriate financial resources. In fact, conflict theorists reject the "multi-influence" perspective, arguing that lobbyists, especially those representing corporate or other elite interests, are the primary source of influence on a legislature, particularly since the public usually lacks sufficient organization and resources to oppose them in any coherent way.

Ideology

Some political scientists emphasize the importance of the legislator's political value system, or ideology, in making policy choices. Corey Rosen (1974, 671) claims that "there is a strong if not insurmountable bias in legislatures toward a moderate approach to politics," which is related not to consensus in constituencies but to internal organizational characteristics of the legislature that promote this kind of thinking. Ambrosius and Welch (1988, 206) claim that in the five states they studied, "legislators are inclined to see business interests as more important than labor interests. And they are so inclined for reasons beyond the . . . resources that business can bring to bear on policy decisions." Robert Entman (1983, 178) concludes that "economic development, party competition, and elite ideological liberalism seem to reinforce each other, and the latter appears to have an independent impact on policy decisions."

Marxists in particular would assert that this research supports their position that most legislators, by virtue of their upper-middle-class social position, operate within an ideological framework consistent with their class interests. They may be conservative or liberal, but few will ever respond to arguments based on challenges to the existing distribution of wealth and power, because they have a stake in that distribution. From the Marxist point of view, this excludes the views and interests of minority, female, and working-class constituents and limits policy alternatives to "politically realistic" ideas consistent with capitalism and its unfair allocation of resources. This would lead to policy choices that are unfavorable to those interests, especially in the areas of economic development, education, and welfare.

Conclusion

To what extent, then, do state legislatures serve as accountable and effective institutions of representative government? Consensus theorists offer an optimistic answer. State legislatures may once have been narrow, parochial, part-time bodies dominated by political oligarchs and interest groups, but this is true no longer. Most legislatures are becoming capable of dealing with and adjusting to the pressures of the political environment. An increase in legislative professionalism; modernization of procedures facilitating negotiation, bargaining, and compromise; and responsiveness to a variety of cross-pressures are, in general, positive factors leading to the development of a viable and functional social and political institution. If there are imbalances as a result of these changes, they are most likely resolvable by institutional reforms.

Conflict theory sees the legislative branch as overrepresenting elite elements of the population. A legislature is structured so as to enhance the power of minority factions or of particular individuals. Legislators are more or less isolated from their constituents and respond most readily to the lobbyists for special interests. The result is a political institution that supports the continuing dominance of the state's power elite.

Marxists add that the state legislature reflects the relatively limited ideological spectrum of the upper middle class, which for the most part composes its membership. Increasing professionalization is an advantage primarily to those who seek policies consistent with the interests of that class. Increasing public dissatisfaction with state legislatures reflects the alienation of those institutions from their constituencies.

Consensus and conflict theorists are divided on the question of whether resolving political conflicts is a matter for political professionals and specialists or for average citizens. Given the continuing trend toward professionalization of the state legislatures, that controversy is likely to continue.

Chapter 9: Ideology and Public Policy

The concept of ideology as a tool for the study of politics in the United States has a controversial history. Few political scientists regularly use it; until recently, most denied that it had any relevance. Nonetheless, the discussions of state and local public policies that make up the remainder of this text, will be based entirely on comparison of ideological perspectives. This choice warrants a discussion of its own.

Why Ideology?

The word "ideology" itself has been subject to different definitions depending on the point of view of the definer. In the 1950s most consensus theorists identified ideology with any set of political ideas which was not in line with what they considered the American political value system. From their perspective, American politics was "nonideological," that is, pragmatic and based on negotiation and compromise. Communism, fascism, and socialism were systems based on ideologies. American politics, on the other hand, was supposedly based on a looser, more tolerant "creed" of widely shared values such as democracy, private enterprise, and individual liberty.

The political turmoil of the 1960s, which challenged American political and economic values, to some extent undermined this comfortable analysis, but most consensus theorists interpreted the events of that decade as atypical or pathological reactions to unusual episodes such as the civil rights struggle or the Vietnam War. The apparent political calm since that time has seemed to support that argument, and most political scientists continue to disregard ideology as a factor in evaluating state and local politics or public policy. The collapse of the Soviet Union has led some commentators to conclude that ideological conflict between capitalism and socialism is over, and the future of the world will be based on acceptance of political values dominant in the United States.

Among the political scientists rejecting this analysis is Kenneth M. Dolbeare (1982, 10), who defines ideology as "a set of beliefs about how the social order does and should work." This is one of several factors "external to the public decision-making system itself that appear to have shaped policy choices in the past." Although most Americans do share certain ideological assumptions, there are nonetheless significant differences among them. These differences, says Dolbeare, shape the conflicts around approaches to health care, welfare, and energy, among other policies. It is this approach which is to be applied here. The goal of this text is to help students develop their own points of view on the structure and policies of state and local governments. We have thus far examined governing institutions and processes from the theoretical perspectives of consensus and conflict theory. These theories are attempts to assess how state and local politics actually work. In determining where we stand on issues such as taxes, education, or welfare, we must look at them from the standpoint of social and political values, that is, ideology. This shift requires additional explanation.

For example, a theory of state and local government may explain how the legislature decides on a particular welfare policy, or what the relationship is between interest groups and the governor on the subject of taxation, or how the bureaucracy administers educational policies. But if our question is what kind of a welfare system we need, or why a decision maker chooses certain alternatives in tax policy and rejects others, or how state government should reform the education system, then we must explore alternative political value systems—ideologies—to evaluate these choices. A theory will answer how government works and provide a basis for an opinion as to how it relates to its constituents. An ideology is the foundation for understanding the policies it produces and for proposing changes in those policies.

Since a theory in and of itself cannot provide policy alternatives, adherents of each theory of politics are divided ideologically. There are conservatives, liberals, and socialists among both pluralists and elite theorists. Pluralists, for example, are increasingly divided on the question of whether pluralism can be preserved in a corporate capitalist system. Also, they do not agree on the proper role of government in the lives of people. A small minority of elite theorists favor the elite rule they see, but most call for reform, and some seek the outright destruction of the ruling class. Marxists are all socialists, but there are many kinds of socialists, and many non-Marxists have socialist ideas.

Whatever conclusions we may have drawn on the basis of theory must be supplemented by evaluation of state and local public policies. Therefore, the remaining chapters use ideology as the tool of analysis. Ultimately, as a result of reading this text, the student should have a well-developed set of ideas on how state and local governments work, why they work that way and whether they should, and what policies they should be implementing.

All this implies that we do not have to be experts to formulate alternative policies and that we do not have to defer to those who claim they are. A mastery of facts is certainly necessary and desirable, but it is worthless without an understanding of the ideological basis of public policies. What ought to come first is an idea about what kind of society we should have in relation to what now exists. We should then examine the facts to see what is possible.

Comparing Ideologies

As is the case with the concept of ideology itself, it is almost impossible to develop universally acceptable definitions of individual ideologies. The adherents of each one often differ among themselves as to its "true" meaning. Opponents of a particular ideology will ascribe negative connotations to it. Ideologies themselves change as time goes on and new issues come to the fore. Thus we make no attempt here to develop a comprehensive definition of the various ideologies. Our focus will be on the basic values that underlie the variations of each ideology, and how these are applied to the specific issue of the relationship between government and the people. This is adequate for evaluating state and local public policies.

This text considers three ideologies: conservative, liberal, and socialist. These are sufficient to cover the ground of political debate on the state and local levels. In considering the definitions of these ideologies, we should remember that these are general descriptions of overall approaches to political thinking, not a list of rules. One may be "moderately conservative" or "liberal with socialist leanings." One may to some extent also be liberal on one issue and conservative on another. At a certain point, however, combining different ideologies becomes simply inconsistent.

Conservative Ideology

It is perhaps necessary to start by stating what conservatism is *not*. It does not mean "keeping things the way they are" or "going back to old ways." On the contrary, conservative ideology applied to state and local politics might mean radical changes. Moreover, one can be conservative on political and economic issues—which are the emphasis here—without holding what are called conservative positions on social issues such as abortion, gay rights, drug use, or religion and politics.

The basic social value underlying conservative ideology is individual freedom of choice, meaning the right of the individual to make his or her own choices in life. Although conservatives are divided on whether this applies to the social issues mentioned above ("libertarian" conservatives believe it does), they are unanimous in applying this value system to the economy and, in particular, to the role of government.

Conservatives believe that if decisions need to be made on what a society should provide and how it should be produced and allocated, they must be made among individuals acting free from coercion. If a certain good or service is needed or wanted, it should be produced by those who volunteer to do so on the basis of the incentive provided. If no one volunteers, then perhaps it is not a necessary commodity.

The social mechanism favored by conservatives to get things accomplished is the economic "free market": the ongoing and unrestricted exchange of goods and services among producers and consumers in competition with each other. If individuals want a particular good or service, they should be prepared to pay its actual cost. It will be available to the extent that other individuals make a profit by producing it. The providers will compete with one another in the "market" to offer the best good or service at the lowest price to attract buyers, who will choose among them. The result ought to be an ongoing process of competition and bargaining which would provide goods and services at the "equilibrium price," the point at which an exchange becomes equally advantageous to both buyers and sellers. If the market is allowed to work this way without any outside interference or coercion, the production and distribution of what people need or want will be arranged as if by an "invisible hand." The market itself will regulate supply and demand. There will be no need for any outside force, especially government, to tell an individual what to produce, how to produce it, or what to buy. Society will not and should not limit or control an individual's choices by subsidizing them with other people's money. Such subsidies constitute an abridgement of the freedom of all concerned to use their own resources as they see fit and to have an understanding of the true cost of their choices, and as a result subsidies hinder the efficient operation of the free market.

The allocation of goods and services would thus be determined by impersonal, objective, and nonpolitical market forces. People will work to the extent that they want to be able to participate as consumers, and what they earn will depend on their individual ability to market their labor to producers, who will profit depending on their ability to satisfy the market for their products.

The fact that the real world does not now operate this way is obvious to conservatives. They believe that it could and should, and in capitalist societies it does, at least to some extent. The major obstacle to that goal is government, which arbitrarily and clumsily makes rules and regulations that obstruct the otherwise smooth workings of the market. It seems to follow, then, that "the best government is that which governs least."

The economist Milton Friedman (Friedman and Friedman 1980, 19–25) offers the clearest expression of conservative ideology in relations to the role of government. He sees four duties which the government must fulfill, of which the first three are derived from the philosophy of Adam Smith, the eighteenth-century founding father of capitalist economics. The first is the protection of society from threats of coercion, which involves the task of national defense. The second is the protection of individuals within society from coercion by other individuals, which requires the establishment of a judicial system. The third is the provision of "public goods." This is an economic term for a good or service for which a user charge cannot be calculated in the market or which cannot be practically collected. For example, the market cannot decide how much someone who pollutes the air and water owes those who are burdened with the pollution. Therefore, government needs to find methods of controlling pollution, preferably through a system of financial incentives. City streets are necessary for commerce, but it would not be practical to levy a user charge by establishing toll booths at every corner. Thus government must provide this "public good" and pay for it out of tax money. Limited-access highways, of course, are a different matter.

Fourth and finally, the government must protect the interests of those—and only those—who are utterly unable to make free choices, a category which Friedman limits to "madmen or children." This does not include the physically handicapped, the aged, unemployed people, college students, or any of the other categories of people now benefiting from government programs. These are individuals intellectually and legally capable of choosing for themselves how they will use whatever resources they have; they are to be given the freedom to do so.

Conservatives do differ among themselves on what specifically might be included in these four tasks of government, but they all agree that the tasks clearly exclude the bulk of responsibilities now assumed by governments on all levels. The program for conservatives is to divest government of these tasks and to assign the remaining ones to the private sector if at all possible, or otherwise to the lowest level of government which can possibly handle them. The federal government, then, would be left with little more than the responsibility of national defense; most other duties can and ought to be handled by state or local governments. The result would be a society in which individuals would largely be responsible for themselves, governmental coercion would be at a minimum, and the free market would make most of the decisions for the society as a whole.

It must be emphasized that few conservatives would advocate an immediate transformation of society in line with these goals or expect to achieve them in the near future. Conservatives favor policies such as those of the Reagan administration, which were in general consistent with these aims and values and which were designed to lead ultimately to their fulfillment.

Liberal Ideology

Liberals, like conservatives, place a high priority on individual freedom and see the market system as worth preserving. But they reject the conservative program as inconsistent with their own highest value: equity. The goal of liberalism is to maintain the capitalist system in its broad outlines, while at the same time mitigating its tendency to produce highly unfair and inhumane outcomes:

> The market system provides little or no payment to individuals who cannot or do not produce what other people want. . . . People can occupy strategic economic positions because of fortuitous circumstances as well as because of hard work and foresight. The resulting distribution of income and wealth is not always considered just. (Committee for Economic Development 1979, 34)

The uneven distribution of wealth in particular is, according to the economist Arthur Okun (1977, 30), "the big liability on the balance sheet

Table 9.1: Comparison of Ideologies

	Conservative	Liberal	Socialist
What values are most important in society?	Economic freedom of choice.	Fair and equitable distribution of economic rewards and political power.	Collective responsibility for social well-being; political, social and economic equality.
What is the source of our political and economic problems?	Too much governmental authority and interference with the economic system.	Unfair distribution of wealth and power.	Inherently undemocratic and exploitive nature of capitalist system.
How should the economy be organized?	Free-market capitalism.	Capitalism modified to reduce inequities.	Production for use rather than profit through public ownership and democratic planning.
What should be the role of government?	Responsibility only for what the market cannot control or provide.	Social programs and economic regulation as needed to balance equality and efficiency.	Facilitate democratic social control of economic life and guarantee equality.
How should responsibility be allocated among levels of government?	States and localities assume primary responsibility for limited functions of government.	Federal government to assist and work with states and localities.	Federal government ensures fairness and uniformity; states and localities implement policies.

of capitalism [that] cannot be defended ethically as the outcome of fair races in which the prizes go to those who make the greatest contribution. . . . There is no excuse for inhumane penalties for losers." Indeed, increasing inequalities of wealth and income are becoming an important political issue.

Thus government ought to have a responsibility to see to it that the capitalist system is equitably balanced between efficiency and productivity on the one hand and fairness and humaneness on the other. This can be difficult to achieve because the more the government intervenes, the more the market is restricted. Yet if it does not get involved, people will suffer. The job of liberal decision makers is to find the appropriate trade-offs. Such a goal is also expensive; it entails a good deal of taxing and government spending.

Government has four methods available to it to accomplish this goal: (1) progressive taxes, (2) categorical social programs and transfer payments, (3) equal opportunity programs, and (4) regulation of the economy. Progressive taxes increase rates as the taxpayer's wealth increases (see Chapter 10). The liberal rationale is that wealthier individuals ought to bear a greater responsibility for the costs of maintaining a system that benefits them. A categorical program is one that grants benefits only to those individuals who fall into a particular category of need. Public elementary and secondary education, for example, is a universal social program, since all children qualify for free schooling. Welfare, however, is categorical, since an applicant must meet certain criteria of income, family status, work history, and so on in order to qualify. Liberals for the most part do not favor cash grants or programs that allow universal eligibility (such as "family allowances" in Canada and Europe, which pay benefits to all families with children). For this reason, liberals are divided on questions of national health insurance and low-cost public higher education. Generally, liberals feel that help should be extended only to those in need (not just "madmen or children," however). Thus government must establish suitable categories. The purpose of progressive taxes and categorical programs is to redistribute wealth without seriously infringing on basic individual freedoms or disrupting the capitalist system. This, again, calls for careful trade-offs.

Liberals recognize that women and minorities for a variety of reasons have not fared as well as white males in the economic system. The free market cannot solve this problem, they argue, so government must have a responsibility to guarantee equal opportunity. This does not mean economic equality. Liberals reject the idea that everyone should have similar incomes or shares of wealth. Rather, all citizens should have similar chances to make it on their own. At the very least, this means rigorous antidiscrimination laws. The purpose of school integration, for example, is in part equal access to education and thus equal opportunity. Most liberals favor some kind of affirmative action in employment, that is, special consideration for women and minorities in the hiring process to compensate for past exclusion and discrimination.

Finally, liberals believe that society cannot rely on the market alone to ensure economic growth and prosperity or to fill all social needs. They do not share the conservatives' faith in the "invisible hand." Sometimes, they argue, the profit motive and the public interest do not coincide. Therefore government must intervene in the economy. Using its fiscal powers, it must establish budgets that help stimulate economic growth. It must also set up regulations to ensure fairness in employment—minimum wages and maximum hours—for example, as well as to protect the rights of labor unions. The environment must be protected, natural resources conserved, consumers given guarantees that what they buy is safe and effective, and unprofitable but socially necessary services provided. Only government can accomplish these goals.

So-called "neoliberals" go even further. Following the models of Japan, Taiwan, Germany, and South Korea, they advocate a form of national economic planning that would use the expertise and financial resources of government to stimulate the economy by subsidizing "growth" or export-oriented industries, such as high technology, and phasing out obsolete ones, such as steel. In addition, they call for government funding of the physical and intellectual "infrastructure" necessary for economic growth. This would include, for example, modernization of highways and mass transit, development of energy resources, and aid to education.

Liberals see capitalism as imperfect but far superior to the alternatives. By government action, they believe, the imperfections can be remedied without destroying the system as a whole. In this regard it is the federal government which must assume much of the burden. It alone has the resources and authority to deal with problems on a national level. State and local governments are viewed as junior partners with considerable responsibilities of their own. In conclusion, as Arthur Okun puts it:

Democratic capitalism is a workable compromise if people see it as a compromise and want to make it work. It means facing the issues of equality as matters of more or less rather than all or none. It means recognizing that "profits" and "rich" are neither dirty nor sacred words. It means developing specific measures that offer a greater equality at a low cost of inefficiency or shrinkage of the national economic pie. With such measures, we can establish a right to a decent standard of living, end the transgression of dollars on rights, and reduce the handicaps in the races for jobs and funds. And we can do all that within the framework of efficiency and private enterprise. (1977, 33)

Liberalism has been under tremendous attack since 1980, but its basic policy accomplishments are still in effect. The vast array of services provided by federal, state, and local governments; the extensive amount of economic regulation; and the existing efforts to guarantee the rights of women and minorities—all these stem from the predominance of liberal ideology. However, liberalism is on the defensive, and its future at this point is open to question.

Socialist Ideology

The lack of broad support for socialist ideas in the United States, as well as the demise of the Soviet Union, raises questions about why the socialist point of view should be included here. This was dealt with to some extent in our discussion of Marxism in Chapter 1, but it bears some elaboration here.

First of all, socialist politics has a long history in the United States, reaching its peak in the early part of this century. The Socialist Party at that time elected hundreds of state and local officials and two congressmen, and it polled almost a million votes for its candidate, Eugene Debs, in the presidential election of 1912. Even though there has been no active socialist movement in many decades, socialist ideas had significant influence in the activism of the 1960s, and they still have a constituency among social scientists, organizers, and political activists. This has not changed, despite events in the former Soviet Union, because American socialists have always taken pains to distinguish their democratic brand of socialism from the authoritarian and bureaucratic types which existed in the Soviet Union and China and which still exist in Cuba and North Korea. Thus as far as most American socialists are concerned, the end of communism does not necessarily invalidate their point of view. It can be argued, therefore, that socialist ideology still has relevance for analysis and evaluation of public policy in the United States, if only to make the point that conservative and liberal ideologies do not exhaust the possibilities for change.

Socialism of all kinds is, of course, based on the ideas of Karl Marx;

individuals who proclaim themselves Marxists are therefore necessarily socialists as well, but the reverse does not have to apply, depending on how one defines the ideology. Both, however, accept the same basic assumption: that capitalism is inherently unfair to working people. This assumption is based on the Marxist concept of how capitalists make a profit. To put it as simply as possible, Marx argued that profit came out of "surplus value," which he defined as the value added by labor in processing raw materials into marketable commodities. Although that added value really belongs to the workers who produced it, the capitalist appropriate it and pays the worker as little as possible for it. Thus capitalism is, in a sense, the use of power to steal what belongs to the worker—his or her productive powers. From this point of view, conservatives are merely protecting the interests of the capitalist class, and liberals are trying to fix a system that cannot and does not deserve to be repaired.

Michael Harrington (1989, 197), an activist and writer who until his death in 1989 was chair of the Democratic Socialists of America, argued that "the growing centralization and interdependence of capitalist society under the control of an elite" will ultimately destroy any vestige of political and economic freedom in the world. The solution is democratic socialization of the economic system: "The democratization of decision making in the everyday economy, of micro as well as macro choices. It looks primarily but not exclusively to the decentralized, face-to-face participation of the direct producers and their communities in determining the matters that shape their social lives." Democratic socialism, said Harrington, involves "the democratization of the workplace and the creation of new forms of community, both within the nation and throughout the world . . . the democratization of information and education, the vesting of real power in decentralized institutions that give the citizen a pragmatic reason for participation" (277). In short, this means a system in which society as a whole owns and controls the means of production, and all citizens are involved as directly as possible in making the political and economic decisions that affect them.

The basic values asserted by socialists are equality and social responsibility. They believe that the difference among economic classes has little or no connection with the inherent abilities of individuals within each class. If some are rich, many poor, and others in between, it is the result of the arbitrary and unjust distribution of wealth and power in a capitalist system, which benefits a few at the expense of everyone else. There is no justification for the extent of inequality under capitalism, especially when considered on an international scale. Society must be organized so as to guarantee economic equality, at least to the extent of a far narrower range of differences in wealth than exists today. This will require some measure of public ownership and control of the major industrial and financial sectors of the economy.

The other side of this is political equality, and this is what would differentiate democratic socialism from what existed in the Soviet Union. Each individual should have more or less the same right and responsibility to take part in making decisions which affect him or her. This implies neither that everyone must participate in making all decisions nor that each person gets whatever he or she wants. It means that all people are entitled to have a say in resolving economic and political conflicts in which they are involved, and that no one has the right to make arbitrary decisions for others by using wealth, social position, or political power.

Social responsibility as a value means, first of all, that society as a whole should see to it that every one of its members is guaranteed certain goods and services as a matter of right to ensure a proper standard of living for all citizens. Thus education, health, child care, and related services should be "entitlements" financed by very progressive taxes and available at nominal prices or even free of individual charge. Employment at decent wages should be guaranteed for those who are able to work and a livable income provided for those who are not. Decent housing should be a right supported by appropriate government programs. The publicly owned economy should be planned with this overall goal in mind, consistent with the need to protect the environment.

Most socialists would add that this responsibility goes both ways. If decent jobs are available for all, then individuals have a responsibility to work if they can. If higher education is free, then perhaps there is a responsibility to use it in a socially beneficial way. Democratic socialism is not just a "welfare state." Similarly, if democracy is to function and "authoritarian collectivisms" (Harrington's phrase) such as the Soviet Union are to be avoided, there is a certain responsibility to participate actively as a citizen. Democratic socialists believe that the political cynicism which exists today is the result of a capitalist system that discourages participation on the part of ordinary citizens. Encouraging such participation would obviously call for changes in the way we educate people to become politically active.

Accomplishing this would obviously mean a radical restructuring of the economy and government. Democratization of all aspects of the economic system would probably require changes in the current political system, with its emphasis on built-in stalemate and limitation of majority rule. There would have to be a new relationship between the national government and regional and community governments and among the branches of each government to facilitate thoroughly democratic decision making. As with conservatism, all this is a long-range program which democratic socialists certainly do not see as an immediate possibility. Strategies differ, but most favor using the existing political process in some manner to build support for candidates who favor these ideas. Unlike Marx, American socialists generally do not favor revolution as a means of achieving their objectives, although they recognize that the political struggle to achieve them would be, to say the least, very intense.

Conclusion

Political debate on the state and local levels today is limited to a spectrum ranging from conservatives on one end to liberals with some socialist sympathies on the other. On a national level the conservative point of view was dominant until 1933. The New Deal brought liberal ideas to the fore, and these ideas more or less prevailed in Washington, D.C., until the 1970s. Ronald Reagan changed all this, and conservatism has dominated the agenda since the 1980s. The accession of Bill Clinton did not reverse that course in any significant way, and the Republican victory in the elections of 1994 appears to have strengthened the hold of conservatism on national politics in the near future.

The changes on the state and local levels are too numerous to describe, but in general the national pattern has been reflected there as well. It is perhaps more accurate to describe the ideological differences as regional in nature. Each area of the country has its own balance of ideological forces. Liberal candidates, mostly Democrats, have fared best in urban areas in the Northeast and upper Midwest, and on the Pacific coast. Conservative strongholds prevail in the deep South, the Southwest, and the Rocky Mountain states. Texas, Indiana, Wyoming, Idaho, and New Hampshire have a well-deserved reputation for conservatism; other states, such as Massachusetts, for liberalism (the conservative former governor William Weld notwithstanding). States like California and Wisconsin have all three ideologies in their political history and culture. Within states like New York, liberal-conservative differences generally correlate with urban-suburban-rural differences. In the South, the correlation may well be racial, with whites more conservative than blacks.

The remaining chapters in this text will deal with public policy issues facing state and local governments by outlining the problems and offering alternative solutions from each of the ideological perspectives.

Chapter 10: Public Finance

When the national economy boomed in the eighties, growth in state spending soared. As the national economy went bust in the nineties, growth in state spending slowed. State governments were caught in a fiscal squeeze. (Raimondo 1993, 31)

Entering the year [1992] better than one out of four cities faced budget gaps in which revenues lagged at least 5% behind expenditures. Many of the most pronounced problems were not in the large cities but in small cities and towns. Local governments all over the country responded to the crunch by freezing hiring or, in some places, by reducing the number of municipal workers. (Berman 1992, 51)

With overflowing "rainy day" funds and investment accounts swimming in black ink, state budgets across the country are bulging with record surpluses. The reasons: a healthier economy, sizzling stock market and careful government spending, economists concur. (*Boston Globe* 7 June 1996, p. 1)

The early 1990s were indeed financially difficult for most states and localities. Yet by 1995, the states were in the strongest financial shape in a decade. "Boom and bust" cycles characterize state and local finances. The purpose of this chapter is to explore the reasons for that phenomenon.

States and localities have been subject to recurring fiscal crises. The massive expansion of state and local government programs in the prosperous period after World War II, aided by generous federal grants, was slowed in the early 1970s and ground to a halt during the recession of 1974–1975. Following a few years of economic recovery during which inflation eroded the value of additional spending, the recession of 1982–1983, combined with cutbacks in federal aid, once again forced states and localities to take drastic actions to balance their budgets. The economic expansion of the middle and late 1980s gave a temporary, unevenly distributed boost, but the recession of 1991–1992 once again created disastrous fiscal conditions, though these were eased considerably by the recovery that followed. Of course, not all states and localities are affected the same way. Some manage to remain in healthy fiscal condition, but others never seem to escape financial difficulties, even in good times.

Why is it so hard for state and local governments to maintain a consistently sufficient revenue flow? In particular, why are state and local budgets so vulnerable to economic conditions? What are the solutions? Answers vary depending on one's point of view, which must rest on a basic knowledge of state and local finance. Fortunately, this is not so hopelessly technical as it sounds. We will examine where states and localities get their money, how they spend it, and how their current financial predicaments have arisen. In that context, we can evaluate solutions to those problems.

Sources of Revenue

States and localities get most of their money from three sources: taxes and fees, intergovernmental aid, and borrowing. The structural characteristics of each have distinct effects on the direction of fiscal policy.

State and Local Taxes and Fees

Since the 1930s, states have relied on taxes levied on two items: income and consumption. The former includes personal and corporate income taxes; the latter, retail sales, excise (selective sales), and numerous miscellaneous taxes and fees.

As of 1994 forty-five states collected general sales taxes ranging from 3 to 7 percent. Most states exempt food, prescription drugs, and utility bills; several have other exemptions as well, such as clothing. All states tax—at varying rates—gasoline and cigarettes, and most tax alcoholic beverages as well or, in some cases, retain a monopoly on their sale. Sales taxes have both economic and political advantages. They yield fairly consistent amounts of money from year to year as long as the economy does not fluctuate too sharply, and as "hidden" taxes they are less painful to taxpayers than income or property taxes. Taxes on alcohol and, especially recently, cigarettes, can be justified as "sin" taxes, that is, the extra price a consumer pays for a bad habit.

Individual income taxes were levied in forty-three states. A few of these states charge a flat rate, that is, the same percentage for all income levels. The others have graduated income taxes: the percentage rises as income increases. Certain states have sharper rate increases than others. In Alabama and Maryland the top bracket is reached with an income of $3,000, whereas in Iowa the tax rises to 10 percent in nine steps up to an income of $48,000. States such as Massachusetts charge differential rates depending on the source of income: 6 percent for wages, 12 percent for dividends. After exemptions, deductions, and loopholes, however, the actual ("effective") rate may be quite different, and difficult to calculate accurately (Council of State Governments 1996, 260 ff.).

Forty-five states had corporate income taxes as of 1994; very few were graduated in any real sense. Smaller businesses are most directly affected because, unlike some larger businesses, they are unable to pass the tax on to consumers. There has been considerable controversy about the methods of state taxation of multinational corporations, which are often able to organize their profit taking in such a way as to avoid paying state taxes. Some states have responded by adopting the "unitary" method of taxing such businesses, which divides the company's worldwide receipts according to a formula into proportions of business done in each place, and then taxes the proportion done in the state.

In addition to these taxes, most states impose user charges for a wide range of services such as hospitals, recreation, and education. Tuition at public colleges is an example of such a charge. These constitute an important source of revenue, increasingly so as states reach limits in imposing new taxes or raising old ones.

Lotteries and legalized gambling have become more popular in the last few years as a means of raising revenue. Although they have the political advantage of financially affecting only those who choose to gamble, they are highly controversial. What is more, in most states they do not produce a large proportion of income despite increased yields (Gold 1994).

Local governments are generally left with tax sources that are not used by the federal and state governments. Indeed, it is state law that determines what taxes may be imposed by counties and municipalities. About half the states authorize local sales taxes, and about a dozen allow county or municipal income taxes. User charges have become increasingly important on the local level also, especially in providing water and sewer services, or in those communities owning their own utilities. But the most important source of all locally raised revenue is the property tax.

In 1643, New Plymouth Colony (Massachusetts) began to assess all

**Table 10.1: Sources of State Government Revenue, 1994
(Billions of Dollars; Total: $841 Billion)**

Federal aid	204.5
Taxes	373.3
Individual income	117.1
Corporate income	25.6
General sales	123.0
Selective sales	62.8
Charges and miscellaneous	114.4
Higher education tuition	32.8
Insurance trust revenue	142.6

**Table 10.2: Sources of Local Government Revenue, 1994
(Billions of Dollars; Total: $720 Billion)**

State aid	242.0
Taxes	252.2
Property	188.8
Sales	37.8
Charges and Miscellaneous	145.0
Hospitals	29.2
Utility and liquor store revenue	63.2
Insurance trust revenue	18.3

Source: U.S. Department of Commerce, *Statistical Abstract of the United States, 1997.*

residents "according to their estates or faculties, that is according to goods, lands, improved faculties" for the purpose of taxation (Tipps and Webb 1980, 20). For the next 250 years taxes on real and personal property were the mainstay of both state and local finances. The tax on personal property fell into disuse in the nineteenth century. In the 1920s and 1930s states began to develop sales and income taxes, turning the property tax entirely over to local governments. Thus the tax on buildings and land has become the major source of money for local government services, particularly public education.

Administration of the property tax has become a major political issue. The process begins with an elected or appointed local assessor or board of assessors, who may or may not have professional training. These officials are responsible for compiling a list of each parcel of taxable property in the community together with its estimated value ("assessment"). Assessors use a variety of methods to come up with these figures, which are in theory objective and equivalent to market value; the particular proportion, known as the "assessment ratio," varies among states and communities. Some states have forced localities, often over stubborn resistance, to assess at full market value, that is, an assessment ratio of 100 percent. The result is a tremendous variety of assessment practices throughout the country. This, of course, creates inequities and inconsistencies, in that similar properties may be listed on the tax rolls at widely divergent values depending where they are located.

Once the assessment is set, the municipal government sets the tax rate, which is usually expressed as the amount due per $100 or $1,000 of assessed value. These rates vary widely as well and are generally highest in large cities and lowest in rural areas. In Massachusetts in 1980, before the tax rate limitations of Proposition 2 1/2 took effect, the tax rate on property assessed at full market value ranged from $5 to $10 per $1,000 in rural areas, to around $50 in smaller cities, and to $114 in Boston (Levitan and Mariner 1980, 199–204).

The property tax is thus highly visible and political. It is directly billed to the taxpayer, included in the mortgage payment, or part of a tenant's rent. Any change in assessment practices or tax rates is immediately apparent and is bound to trigger a reaction from taxpayers. The tax is in most cases unrelated to the income of the property owner. However, some states have developed "circuit-breaker" systems—programs of state tax rebates to selected groups of low-income individuals with excessive property tax bills. As a result of all this, the property tax has borne the brunt of the taxpayers' resentment of what appears to be inherent unfairness. It is, as one observer puts it, "the tax the public loves to hate" (Snell 1991b).

Who Bears the Tax Burden? There is no such thing as a "fair" tax, because what is fair to one group may be distinctly unfair to another. There are no objective standards for making judgments about the equity of a particular tax. However, a distinction can be made between "progressive" and "regressive" taxes. The former is a tax that takes an increasing share of income as a taxpayer becomes more wealthy; the latter does the opposite. Inheritance taxes and, for the most part, corporate taxes are progressive because they take a small share of income from the poor and a larger share from the rich. Graduated income taxes are more or less progressive depending on their structure. Several states with graduated taxes establish income brackets that favor the rich. Oregon, for example, has three brackets: The first $2,000 is taxed at 5 percent, the next $3,000 at 7 percent, and all income over $5,000 at 9 percent. As Barlett and Steele (1994, 295) point out, "This places a middle income family in the same top tax bracket as a millionaire."

All flat rate taxes, such as sales and excise taxes, are regressive. A twenty-cent gasoline tax is likely to take a smaller share of income from the owner of a Porsche than from the owner of an old Chevrolet; a 5 percent sales tax on clothing is a greater burden to those who shop at discount stores than to those who can purchase boutique clothing, even if the cash amount differs. Property taxes can be very regressive; a retired person with an expensive home pays a high tax despite a lack of cash income. Wealthy persons do not generally buy lottery tickets; hence state lotteries are also very regressive, though this depends in part on how the proceeds are distributed.

To judge whether state and local tax systems are progressive or regressive, we must know who is paying and how much is being paid. This is not always easy to determine. Sales and individual income taxes are obviously paid by consumers and wage earners, respectively. But who pays the corporate income tax? Who pays the tax on commercial and industrial property? Economists have reached no consensus on the extent to which business owners and landlords are able to shift taxes onto consumers and tenants. Moreover, official tax rates are not necessarily the same as effective tax rates.

Notwithstanding these questions, the available evidence seems to show that, considered nationwide, state and local taxes as a whole are highly, if somewhat unevenly, regressive. A widely cited study by Joseph Pechman (1985, 60) estimates that in 1980 state and local taxes levied an effective rate of 18.1 percent of income from families earning under $5,000, 7 to 8 percent from families earning between $5,000 and $500,000, and 9 percent or more from the wealthiest families. More specifically, the property tax took about 1 percent of the income of the poorest one-third of all families and no more than 4 percent of the income of the richest 1 percent of all families. Sales taxes were consistently regressive, taking 7 percent from the poorest tenth and only 2 percent from the richest tenth (80). These calculations assume maximum impact on wealthy taxpayers; actual regressivity could therefore be even greater. In 1991, a study by Citizens for Tax Justice, a liberal organization favoring progressive taxes, calculated that the richest 1 percent of all families, earning $875,000 on the average, paid 7.6 percent of their income in state and local taxes, while the poorest 20 percent, earning $12,700, paid 13.8 percent. In forty-six states, the middle fifth of all families paid higher rates of state and local taxes than the top 1 percent.

Of course, the pattern varies from state to state. New Hampshire, up to now, has no income or sales tax and relies heavily on regressive excise and property taxes. Wyoming has no individual or corporate income tax and relies on a 4 percent sales tax on everything but prescription drugs. North Dakota, on the other hand, has steeply graduated personal and corporate income taxes, along with a "circuit-breaker" on property taxes for senior citizens (Council of State Governments 1996, 263 ff.). The study by Citizens for Tax Justice lists what it called the "terrible ten": states whose rates on the poor vastly exceeded rates on the rich. The most regressive was Nevada, which took 10 percent of the income of the poor and only 1.8 percent from the rich, and which, of course, depends heavily on gambling revenues. All of these states had either no income tax or a flat-rate income tax. As a whole it seems clear that the system of state and local taxation imposes a disproportionate burden on lower-income groups.

Public Opinion and the "Tax Revolt." Public reactions to state and local taxes are little affected by such technicalities, however. In 1981, when a survey asked respondents to name the "least fair" tax, 36 percent named the federal income tax, 33 percent the property tax, 14 percent the state sales tax, and 9 percent the state income tax. A majority favored higher user charges over any new tax or tax increase on the local level (ACIR 1981). Thus public opinion is not necessarily directly related to progressivity or regressivity or even to which taxes are increasing the fastest. Rather, whatever tax seems most visible or appears to be burdensome or unfair in a particular time and place draws the most fire, deserved or not. The very complexity of the tax system tends to confuse the public's perceptions. Thus the property tax was the initial focus of what came to be called the "tax revolt."

In the late 1970s, accumulated anger at the excesses and inequities of the tax system took the form of ballot initiatives to limit taxing and spending by states and localities. Between 1978 and 1982 voters in twelve states imposed limits on increases in expenditure, voters in four other states limited revenues, and voters in five states imposed limits on local property tax rates. Although widely perceived as a grassroots movement, these initiatives were generally organized by conservative groups seeking to limit the size of government—these groups took advantage of the public's resentment over taxes. In any case, the movement was politically successful.

The most dramatic limits were those imposed by popular initiative in California in 1978 (Proposition 13) and Massachusetts in 1980 (Proposition 2 1/2). The former limited property tax rates to 1 percent of market value, the latter to 2 1/2 percent. Both were passed overwhelmingly. The immediate results were cutbacks in local government spending, reduced services, and layoffs of public employees. After the recession of 1982–1983, however, the states increased local aid, thus mitigating the worst effects. The recession that began in 1991 forced the states to cut back aid, thus once again intensifying local fiscal crises.

Overall, however, the tax revolt had a less drastic direct impact. Its real significance was to make state and local officials much more cautious about proposing increases in income, sales, and property taxes. They relied instead on higher user fees and excise taxes, which were less visible but also less lucrative. Thus the proportion of personal income taken by state and local taxes has remained relatively stable since the late 1970s. This has made it harder for states and localities to relieve the fiscal pressures created by economic downturns.

Ideology and Taxes. Those states that need and want more tax revenues have the problem of squeezing more out of a regressive tax structure at a time when lower- and middle-income citizens are hard-pressed. One alternative is a more progressive tax system, but one that goes to the heart of the political and ideological conflicts over tax policy. Among the political problems is that public opinion is by no means automatically in favor of taxing the rich. Moreover, if one state should increase taxes on businesses or wealthy individuals, neighboring states can and do attempt to lure them away with promises of lower taxes. Notwithstanding this, a number of states have recently moved toward higher income taxes on the affluent as a result of "concern about fairness and the alleged inequities, a concern that developed in the 1980s, as the distribution of income became more unequal" (Gold 1991, 14–15).

The crucial issue, however, is the ideological conflict over what really constitutes a fair tax system. From a conservative point of view progressive taxes are first and foremost a violation of the principle underlying free market capitalism: that individuals are entitled to the rewards of greater effort. Any system which takes away more as an individual earns more is destroying incentive and dampening economic growth. Thus the fairest revenue system, according to conservatives, is one that relies on flat rate taxes on consumption, thus encouraging saving and investment, and user fees, which leave it to the individual to decide whether a particular good or service is worth the price.

Socialists take a diametrically opposite stand. If equality is to be the basic value of a political system, then the tax structure should be used, among other things, to facilitate the redistribution of wealth. Nothing socially useful is gained by allowing unlimited profits on investments, particularly given the socialist point of view that exploitation is the source of profit. In addition, the wealthy owe something to a society that provides the physical and educational infrastructure that enables them to make money. A sharply graduated tax on income, inheritance, and wealth is thus both necessary and justifiable.

Liberals take a compromise position. A certain level of progressivity is desirable to guarantee sufficient state and local revenues and to ease the burden on lower- and middle-income people. Yet the need for appropriate financial incentives for business investment cannot be ignored. Thus a political balance must be struck, based on the particular situation in which states and localities find themselves. State and local tax structure needs to balance "equity" with "efficiency."

A consensus on tax policy is not easy to ascertain. The result has been a strategy of incrementalism in most states—that is, slow, moderate changes in the tax structure, to avoid offending too many interests. If fiscal crises continue, and if public cynicism and indignation about politics and government intensify, this kind of approach may well prove inadequate.

Intergovernmental Aid

The second major source of state and local government funds is federal aid to states and federal and state aid to localities. Even though the demand for such assistance has increased, the federal government has cut back sharply, and most states find it financially difficult to subsidize localities, especially during periods of economic decline and recession.

Chapter 2 offered a history of the development of intergovernmental fiscal relations and briefly surveyed some of the changes made in federal aid programs early in the Reagan administration, in particular consolidation of many categorical grants into block grants, and reduced appropria-

tions for both. Federal grants-in-aid to states and localities had doubled from 1970 to 1975 and almost doubled again by 1980 to $91 billion, amounting to 26 percent of state and local government outlays. By 1989, however, the total was $123 billion, representing only 18 percent of such outlays; the early 1990s saw an increase, reaching $210 billion and 23 percent by 1994 (U.S. Department of Commerce 1997, 302). The states responded with different combinations of cutbacks and tax increases; the uneven economic expansion of the mid-1980s provided a larger tax base for many states, thus making even more drastic cuts or increases unnecessary. Local governments were in worse shape. The tax revolt had forced them to reduce or at least not increase property taxes. In 1979, federal aid had made up close to 12 percent of local budgets; ten years later it was down to under 4 percent. The termination in 1986 of federal revenue-sharing with local governments (rebates of tax money with no strings attached) was particularly damaging (Snell 1991b).

The other major form of intergovernmental aid is state assistance to localities. In 1994, $225 billion in state money was sent to local governments; almost two-thirds of it went for aid to elementary and secondary public schools (Council of State Governments 1996, 406). Although this is double the amount ten years previously, it has not fully kept pace with increasing local expenditures and has not compensated for the loss of federal aid. Combined federal and state aid to localities was 39 percent of local revenue in 1979, falling to 28 percent in 1989. Moreover, while state aid to education more or less kept pace with inflation and increased expenditures, other areas, such as capital improvements and public safety, were cut back (Snell 1991b). Thus, just as demand for state aid was increasing, the flow of funds was restricted.

For almost twenty years, until the late 1970s, the constantly increasing amount of intergovernmental aid stimulated state and local spending on a wide variety of programs in health, housing, welfare, education, and infrastructure. As aid declined, states and localities, especially the latter, were left high and dry, forced to make choices between increasing taxes and fees or cutting programs, or to do both.

Other kinds of federal spending also have an effect on state and local economies, and hence on their budgets as well. Most of this effect is more or less evenly distributed among states and localities, but certain programs benefit some more than others. Social Security benefits, for example, have a stimulative effect on the economies of states with large elderly populations, such as Florida. More significantly, military spending is targeted to locations that have defense installations or production facilities. Thus Massachusetts, Connecticut, California, and Virginia benefited disproportionately during the 1980s, when the Reagan administration substantially increased the military budget. Of course, there was a considerable negative effect when spending for defense leveled off in the following decade.

The devolution of financial responsibility from federal to state governments has in many cases been passed on down to local governments, which are generally less able to cope with additional fiscal demands. What is more, in the long run the conversion of categorical grants into block grants, as was done with the welfare program in 1996, will put states and localities in the position of attempting to maintain social programs without any guarantee of consistent, predictable federal help.

Borrowing

The third source of funds for states and localities is borrowing. States and localities borrow in the same manner as the federal government and private business: by issuing bonds. These may be long- or short-term bonds and are backed by either all the financial resources available to the government ("general obligation" or "full faith and credit" bonds) or specific sources of revenue, such as a user charge for the facility financed by the bonds ("nonguaranteed," "limited liability," or "revenue" bonds). Over 90 percent of all state and local debt is long term and about 40 percent of that is nonguaranteed. States and localities usually borrow to finance capital spending, that is, the construction of public facilities such as schools, roads, sewers, housing, hospitals, and public colleges. Accordingly, as the volume of services has increased, so has state and local debt, increasing from $133 billion in 1969 to $335 billion in 1980 to nearly $1 trillion in 1992 (U.S. Department of Commerce 1997, 304). Most localities face state restrictions on amount and type of debt. Many states require public approval of state and local bond issues through a referendum. One-third of this debt is held by commercial banks, another third by individual investors, and most of the remainder by insurance companies (Aronson and Hilley 1986, Chapter 9).

States and localities have to compete for sales with other issuers in the bond market. In the 1960s state and local bonds were considered a good investment, since revenues were holding up and the bonds were (as they still are) exempt from federal taxes. State and local governments thus found borrowing a convenient and relatively painless way to finance their growth. In the 1970s, however, as a declining national economy pinched the revenues needed to redeem the bonds, as inflation increased interest rates, and as rival borrowers crowded the bond market, states and localities found fewer buyers. As the fiscal condition of many governments became visibly shaky, their bonds became less desirable. This situation was brought to a head by the recession of 1974–1975 and the fiscal collapse of New York City.

New York City was distinguished by a tradition of extensive public services, including a tuition-free municipal university. By the early 1970s, its declining economic base was unable to support these services, and in an attempt to avoid cutbacks, the city government indulged in budgetary sleight of hand and excessive short-term borrowing. As the financial problems became more obvious, the banks that held New York City bonds dumped their holdings and refused to purchase any more. With default imminent and with the federal government unwilling to help, the state government stepped in and established an Emergency Financial Control Board, which took charge of the city's finances. To restore New York City's credit, it mandated wage freezes, service cutbacks, increases in user fees (including an end to the 140-year tradition of tuition-free higher education), and layoffs of municipal employees. By the mid-1980s this goal had been accomplished, but only at severe cost to those who depended on the services offered by the municipal government.

An object lesson of what could happen if a city resisted pressure from the banks occurred in Cleveland in 1978, when its mayor, Dennis Kucinich, essentially declared war on the banks and defaulted on municipal bonds. In the end, however, the banks won when Kucinich overplayed his hand and lost the next election to his Republican opponent, who was more willing to cooperate with the financial establishment.

Massachusetts in 1975 found that it could not sell its bonds to finance public housing unless it satisfied the demands of Boston banks for a "credible" state budget, thus forcing Governor Michael Dukakis to raise taxes and cut services, thus violating his campaign promises of the previous year. Ultimately this helped cost him his re-election in 1978.

A somewhat different scenario ensued when, in December 1994, Orange County, California, a prosperous and highly conservative suburb of Los Angeles, declared bankruptcy and defaulted on its bonds. The banks did not directly crack down on the county government, but this event had the effect of making banks even more cautious, thus driving up interest rates on municipal bonds across the board (Petersen 1996, 28–30).

In the late 1970s, then, banks became the arbiters of which states could and could not borrow. Since that time, states and localities have kept a careful watch on their standing in the credit markets and have disciplined themselves accordingly. In that context, considerable power is held by two investment firms, Standard and Poor Corporation and Moody's Investors Services, which rate state and local bonds according to their soundness. A low rating means that bonds will be more difficult to sell and will therefore require higher interest payments to attract buyers. Thus a decrease in a bond rating may well cost a state or city millions of dollars in additional interest expenses.

Borrowing has enabled states and localities to invest in needed capital improvements, but at the same time has made them hostage to the fiscal policy preferences of the financial institutions that make the funds available.

The National Economy and Fiscal Conditions

To a considerable extent, the ability of states and localities to raise money is affected by forces beyond their control, most notably the national economy. In a time of reasonably full employment and low inflation, such as the 1960s, income taxes and sales taxes will produce sufficient revenue, costs will increase only slowly and predictably, borrowing will be easy and inexpensive, and demand for government services such as welfare will be relatively low. A chronic combination of high inflation and unemployment, as occurred in the 1970s, will reduce tax revenues, increase costs, and make banks more choosy about their lending. The generally stagnant economy of the early 1990s exacerbated these problems while at the same time increasing the need for greater social spending. The present methods by which states and localities gain their income actually reduces the amount just as the need becomes greatest.

Overall, vanishing tax revenues, shrinking intergovernmental aid, and the difficulty of borrowing have combined to make it impossible for many states and cities to find enough money to maintain, much less improve, public services. The intensity of the problem makes it unlikely that incremental solutions will be of help. The continued stagnation of the economy over the long run, and recessions in the short run, bodes ill for the future, even if temporary upturns lighten the burden. This constitutes one side of a fiscal crisis. The increasing demand for services is the other side. This brings up the issue of what particular kinds of services state and local governments provide. Is a solution to fiscal crises to be found on the expenditure side of the budget?

Expenditures

In the mid-1990s, state and local governments spent well over $1.5 trillion annually. Education and public health and safety are the consistent priorities of local governments across the nation. State priorities differ. Aid to local school districts is the top priority for most states, but welfare, especially Medicaid, consumes an increasing share. Highways are important objects of expenditure in western states; public higher education receives a lower priority in the Northeast than it does in the South and the West. As a whole, the trend since 1960 has been steadily upward in all areas; if the trend has slowed since the mid-1970s, that is due to severe cutbacks in the growth of spending, in line with revenue scarcity, rather than to lower costs or decreased needs.

Pressure for more spending has come from several sources. For instance, the public has come to expect more of government, even as it demands lower taxes. Strong demand for low-cost higher education pushed states into making it widely available. Receiving welfare became less of a stigma in the 1960s, and states were often forced by federal regulations to accept more recipients. Public employees' unions organized extensively during the 1960s and 1970s and pushed the wages of their workers up considerably, especially for teachers. The availability of federal aid and the ease of borrowing during the 1960s made it easier for states and localities to respond to pressure for more services; but when the aid vanished, the commitments continued. More recently, two expenses in particular—environmental management and health care— have become increasingly burdensome. The cost of maintaining a clean water supply and adequate waste disposal systems has risen considerably. And in no other area of consumer expenditure have prices increased as rapidly as health care. In both cases, federal programs (environmental protection and Medicaid) have forced greater spending by state and local governments. These topics will be discussed in greater detail in the chapters to follow.

In the late 1980s, there was a considerable increase in the volume of intergovernmental "mandates." These are requirements imposed by the higher levels of government on the lower levels to implement a particular

Table 10.3: State Government Expenditures, 1994
(Billions of Dollars; Total: $775 Billion)

Aid to localities	224.7
Public welfare (including Medicaid)	148.2
Insurance trust (pensions)	82.6
Higher education	77.1
Highways	43.8
Hospitals	28.0
Interest	23.7
Administration	22.2
Corrections	21.2
Health	18.9
Natural resources	11.1

Table 10.4: Local Government Expenditures, 1994
(Billions of Dollars; Total: $719 Billion)

Elementary and secondary education	$244.6
Utilities and liquor stores	81.4
Hospitals	37.0
Administration	33.5
Police protection	33.3
Public welfare	31.6
Interest	31.2
Highways	28.2
Sewerage	20.3
Housing	17.9
Health	16.4
Fire protection	16.1
Parks and recreation	13.9
Higher education	13.7
Solid waste management	12.7
Insurance trust (pensions)	12.7
Corrections	11.0

Source: U.S. Department of Commerce, *Statistical Abstract of the United States, 1997*

kind of program and in many cases to pay for it as well. This was espe-cially true in environmental policy. The federal Safe Drinking Water Act, for example, requires states to adopt strict standards for water qual-ity and to guarantee enforcement on the local level. The amendments of 1986 to that act require particular kinds of filtration systems to be installed by small localities. In 1990, according to one observer, Congress added twenty mandates which had the potential of costing the states $15 billion (Fabricius 1991, 28–33). Similarly, states have found it politically convenient to impose mandates on localities without the necessary funding. Although a number of states have passed laws prohibiting these unfunded mandates, they have not always been consistent in enforcing them (Hosansky 1995, 26–27). Once again, this is particularly true of programs dealing with land, air, and water quality, especially in relation to the disposal of solid or hazardous wastes. These mandates have been cited by critics as examples of unreasonable "devolution" of responsibility from federal to state to local governments. Given the fact that local governments have the least capacity and flexibility in raising revenues, this trend seems especially unfair to most local government officials, since it obviously exacerbates the fiscal difficulties they face. In 1995, Congress passed a law restricting the use of unfunded mandates, but the issue is by no means dead.

The Budgetary Process

Although states and localities have responded to fiscal crises with massive cutbacks in the goods and services they provide, there are certain inherent limits to the process of budget-cutting, at least in the short run. The nature of the budget-making process tends to impede any effort at comprehensive reassessment of state and local expenditures. First of all, unlike the federal government, almost every state requires a balanced budget; localities are mandated by the states to do the same. Moreover, "current" expenses, such as employees' salaries, maintenance costs, and benefits to individuals, must be paid for out of taxes and fees. "Capital" expenses—investment in physical improvements—are to be funded through borrowing. In theory, at least, the two types of expenditure are to be budgeted separately in terms of the source of their funds.

By and large, all states follow similar procedures in planning their annual or, in a number of states, biennial budgets. No sooner does a fiscal year begin (usually on July 1) than state agencies formulate their requests for the next fiscal year's appropriations. These are filtered upward through the bureaucracy, in most states to be ultimately reviewed by a state budget agency working with the governor. The fall season is devoted to putting together an "executive budget": the governor's spending proposals for the next fiscal year. This document is generally presented to the state legislature around January; the legislature then works on it until the beginning of the fiscal year. Once the budget is approved by both the legislature and the governor, it takes effect, and the process begins again. A roughly parallel process goes on in local governments, varying with the particular structure.

Throughout this procedure the budget requests of each agency are scrutinized, evaluated, and increased or cut back as the case may be. Under normal circumstances, year-to-year changes are generally piecemeal, and rarely are whole agencies eliminated or massively expanded all at once. This practice of budget-making is referred to as "incrementalism." The sheer complexity of the process, especially in the larger states, makes such an approach almost inevitable. Most budgets are constructed in terms of line-item requests—dollar figures for salaries, maintenance, supplies, and the like—rather than in terms of specific programs or objectives. This means that there is usually no way to evaluate an agency's budget in terms of what the agency actually produces. Waste and fraud, to whatever extent they may exist, are thus hard to root out. Although attempts (mostly unsuccessful) have been made to change these practices, their continuation renders almost impossible any attempt to construct an entirely new budget in one or two fiscal years. The politics of the budgetary process thus consists of negotiations and bargaining among agencies, budget officials, the governor's office, and the legislature, especially the committees most directly involved, over particular dollar amounts. The outcome determines who gains and who loses within the limits of the state's overall financial position.

What is more, a good portion of state and local expenditures simply cannot be legally or practically reduced in any large measure. Categorical grant programs, such as welfare (until 1996) or Medicaid, impose hundreds or thousands of regulations, which states must observe to receive federal money. Any changes at the state level require federal approval, which may take a long time. In addition, expenses such as interest on debt or employees' pensions cannot be cut without risking legal repercussions. The aforementioned state and local mandates also limit the extent of budget cutting. State aid to local schools is often accompanied by numerous requirements concerning levels of local spending on education; any change risks cuts in state money. To a considerable extent, then, states and localities are locked into the continuance of certain expenditures.

Given all this, if a solution to fiscal crises requires further cuts in expenditures, they are not going to be easy to make, given the need for services, a stagnant national economy with periodic recessions, political pressures, and the intricacies of the budget process. Politicians who claim that they can solve financial problems in a short time with extensive but "painless" cuts in spending are fooling themselves or trying to fool the voters.

Fiscal Crises: Causes and Cures

How, then, is the problem to be solved? Ideological perspectives on the answer start with assumptions about the ultimate responsibility for fiscal crises.

Conservatives believe that the causes and cures lie with the governments most directly affected. First of all, they feel that state and local governments have no business providing an array of social services that might better be handled by the private sector. This point of view is taken by scholars in politics and economics known as public choice theorists, who apply the tenets of market economics to public finance. They argue that governments should provide only what was referred to in Chapter 9 as "public goods," that is, goods which cannot be individually priced because they are unlimited in supply (as clean air is) or because it would be inefficient to price them in this way (city streets are an example). If a good or service can be priced and marketed, the private sector should assume that responsibility. Such an arrangement would be economically "rational" because consumers would then know the real prices of what they are demanding and would individually decide in the open market whether they would pay that price. The market, and not government, would then determine what goods and services would be provided and how much they would cost. If the government gets involved, politics becomes the determinant of what is to be provided, and consumers end up subsidizing the preferences of others—a result that is both inefficient and unfair.

If state and local governments must provide services, then they should pay as they go out of their own resources, employing flat-rate consumption taxes and user fees as the primary revenue sources. To achieve the goal of letting the market decide, conservatives favor contracting out services, or, ultimately, complete privatization. Conservatives believe that there could be many applications of this principle.

The conservative solution to fiscal crises, then, is a combination of limited government, fiscal self-reliance, "pay as you go," and the discipline of the laws of supply and demand. Government on all levels must do less—indeed, as little as possible.

Liberals believe that this is a formula for disaster. Most of the services provided by state and local government simply are not profitable for the private sector; privatization thus might mean elimination. This is especially true for those services that benefit the poor. From the liberal point of view, solutions rely on new sources of revenue and government attempts to stimulate economic expansion to broaden the state and local tax base.

Many liberals favor a more progressive tax system, featuring a moderately graduated income tax. They also tend to favor a greater assumption by the state governments and the federal government of the costs of education, and they feel that the federal government should take some of the burden off states and localities by assuming the costs of welfare and establishing national health insurance to reduce the load of Medicaid in state budgets. If the huge federal deficit makes such actions difficult, perhaps money can be found by reducing the military budget.

Liberals also seek to put urban revitalization on the agenda. In fact, that was the goal of the massive federal programs of the 1960s, which poured money into the inner cities. Successive Republican administrations have destroyed those programs; but increased urban unrest in the 1990s brought some attention back to the need to deal with decaying cities. So-called "neoliberals" have proposed a federal agency which would have sufficient power, independence, and financial resources to influence private investment decisions through tax breaks or loans; this could be applied to economic redevelopment of states and localities. As a part of this effort, the federal government should invest in the nation's infrastructure of roads, water and sewer systems, schools, and energy resources.

Socialists start from an entirely different standpoint. They believe that fiscal crises are rooted in the structure of capitalism itself. According to James O'Connor (1973), expanded public spending is consistent with keeping the capitalist system going, at least in prosperous times. State-financed industrial development increases labor productivity; social insurance lowers labor costs; welfare keeps the peace. This means that government assumes many of the social costs of private enterprise, whereas corporations keep the profits. Ultimately, the need to increase profits conflicts with the need for higher taxes to keep services going (which is what happened in the late 1970s), and fiscal crises ensue. When the economy stagnates, profits decline and business demands reductions in the size of the state sector. In short, the private sector grows at the expense of the public sector; the winners are those who make profits, and the losers are those who work for the winners. The policies of the Reagan administration are the ultimate expression of this conflict, in its "class war" on working people on behalf of business.

According to Plotkin and Scheuerman (1994), the ideology of "balanced-budget conservatism" has been used by business and government to rationalize cutbacks in public services. Deficit reduction has been the highest priority of the federal government, and this has made funds unavailable to assist states and localities. Plotkin and Schuerman question, however, whether deficit reduction deserves this status, arguing that unbalanced budgets by themselves are not harmful unless the money is spent wastefully on military spending and tax breaks for the rich, which was the case in the 1980s. This of course benefits the Pentagon and the upper class, and hurts middle- and working-class people.

From the socialist point of view, citizens should be entitled to services such as high-quality public education, decent housing, jobs, health care, child care, and a clean environment. Socialists totally reject the idea that these are or ought to be market commodities or services provided only to the needy. The federal government ought to have a responsibility to provide these things and should fund them out of progressive taxes, reductions in the military budget, and a publicly owned financial system to break the hold of the private banks on economic development. The goal should be more or less equal levels of service across the country, with state and local governments largely responsible for administration rather than finance, which would be a federal responsibility. In the long run, of course, the goal would be a democratic socialist economic system that would eliminate the causes of fiscal crises.

Conclusion

State and local governments find themselves enmeshed in a deepening fiscal crisis as a result of a combination of factors: (1) a regressive and inequitable tax structure which is less and less capable of generating adequate revenues in a stagnant or declining economy; (2) the effects of the tax revolt, which has worsened the fiscal position of states and localities; (3) reductions in intergovernmental aid, on which states and localities had become highly dependent; (4) a squeeze on borrowing, as interest rates increased and banks tightened the terms on which they lend money; and (5) continued political and economic pressure on the expenditure side combined with structural difficulties in the budgetary process. Periodic recessions make the situation worse. The issue is, then, how states and localities are to deal with fiscal crises in that context.

Conservatives demand adaptation to scarcity of resources by applying the principles of the free market in allocating goods and services, thus permanently reducing the level of government responsibility. Liberals see a need for federal action to ease the financial burden on states and localities and to promote economic development. Socialists see fiscal crises as an outgrowth of the warped priorities of capitalism and argue that the profit system must be modified or abolished to facilitate guarantees of basic services to all citizens as a matter of right.

It is the conservative direction which, especially after the elections of 1994, is now being taken by all levels of government; the Clinton administration has gone along with that trend. There are, however, serious questions of how far governments can go in cutting back services without severely damaging society. The impulse of state and local politicians is to postpone hard choices for as long as possible. It is not in their interest to take drastic action for the sake of the long run. Given the nature of the problem, however, this kind of procrastination may ultimately prove to be self-defeating.

Chapter 11:
The Politics of Economic Development

The quality of life in our communities is often not perceived as a political issue. Access to decent jobs and housing is treated by most people as a personal concern to be dealt with through maximum individual effort rather than through political action. People who have such access often tend to take it for granted, whereas those who do not, often write off politics as a means of getting it. But, in fact, economic and community development is a product of politics. Within a particular community, questions about what kinds of jobs we will have, where we will live, and whether the community can support human habitation without destroying the environment are answered by the political process as different groups fight for their preferences. Everyone favors a strong local economy, the availability of suitable housing, efficient transportation, and environmental safeguards, but there is certainly no consensus on how to achieve all this. It is the job of state and local governments to resolve this conflict in order to promote stable communities, and this requires explicit policy decisions in all the above areas.

Patterns of Economic Development

There are obvious differences in the level and pace of economic development among regions of the country, and among urban, suburban, and rural areas. Within cities and towns, neighborhoods often differ sharply in terms of their relative prosperity. This disparity is known as "uneven development." These ever-changing patterns of variation reflect public and private investment decisions as they affect a particular area.

Regional Development

There is nothing new about uneven regional development or about changes in the pattern of unevenness. The Civil War put an end to the slave economy of the South. This left unchallenged the industrial expansion in northern cities, fueled by cheap immigrant labor, as the wave of the future. For generations the South as a whole remained an economic backwater. World War I and the growth of the automobile industry transformed the Great Lakes region into a major industrial area. By the end of World War II, and in part as a consequence of it, the dozen or so states stretching from southern New England to the upper Mississippi, especially their urban centers, were firmly established as the economic heartland of the nation. However, in the late 1960s manufacturing went into decline. Thus the "heartland" began to stagnate as parts of the South, the Southwest, and the mountain states experienced considerable growth. Northeastern and midwestern cities lost business and population, whereas many cities on the "southern rim" gained in part because of the boom in oil prices. In the 1970s it was commonplace to use the words "sunbelt" and "frostbelt" to characterize the pattern of regional development. The migration of industry from the latter to the former became a familiar theme in discussions of economic growth and decline.

Although the economy grew after the recession of 1982–1983, the benefits were distributed very unevenly. As a result of higher military spending, advances in high technology, and the development of financial and service industries, states in New England, the Southeast, and the Southwest experienced considerable growth. A continued stagnation in manufacturing and agriculture hurt the Midwest; and Texas, Louisiana, and Oklahoma were hit hard by the collapse of oil prices. After the recession of 1991–1992, the "heartland" rebounded and the mountain states prospered. In 1995, the *Boston Globe* reported that the Northeast, "after leading the nation's economic recovery in the 1980s [was] back to a more familiar spot: bringing up the rear. By nearly any economic measure, the nine states the U.S. Census calls the Northeast—the six New England states plus New York, New Jersey, and Pennsylvania—are lagging behind this year, as they have throughout the 1990s" (3 December 1995, p. 1).

In their pursuit of lower wage costs, American industries have been encouraged by the "global economy" to abandon the country entirely by exporting jobs abroad, using cheap labor to produce commodities, and then importing the finished products to be sold at regular prices. The victims of this "capital mobility" are the states and localities left with empty factories and offices. Bluestone and Harrison (1988) refer to this as a "hollowing out" of America's productive capacity. The free-trade

policies favored by the Clinton administration are viewed by many as exacerbating that problem; the North American Free Trade Agreement (NAFTA), which was ratified in 1994, was opposed by those who feared it would encourage manufacturers to move to Mexico.

Metropolitan Development: Cities and Suburbs

The United States began as a primarily rural and agricultural nation, but this changed rapidly during the nineteenth century as urbanization and industrialization took hold. Cities grew in size, population, and wealth, although the benefits of growth were not shared evenly, as most large American cities were highly stratified socially and economically. A middle-class out-migration to the suburbs began early in the twentieth century, and suburbs grew quickly in the 1920s, but until the 1940s the central city remained the focal point of business and industry. The surrounding suburbs were primarily commuter villages (Congressional Quarterly 1978, 7).

That out-migration was hastened after World War II by favorable government policies: highway construction, subsidized home mortgages, and encouragement of suburban locations for commerce and industry. Working-class people, especially minorities, were left behind in the declining central cities of the Northeast and Midwest. In the 1970s and 1980s, the same process came to affect some southern and western cities as well: "Atlanta has become a black majority city of declining population, collared by a burgeoning and all too familiar white suburban ring. The prized location for new industry has shifted to the countryside 50 to 100 miles out of town. The city has been struggling with a flood of new hotel space, vacant offices, condominiums, and apartments" (Breckenfeld 1977, 87). By the 1990s, "edge cities" in the suburbs were becoming centers of economic development independent of the central city. These economic and demographic changes have had serious consequences for the relative prosperity of different locations and populations within metropolitan areas.

Most people are familiar with the stark contrasts between wealth and poverty within metropolitan areas. Most urban centers are sharply divided in terms of race, class, and economic development. The "inner city," whose residents are primarily low-income African-Americans and Hispanics, coexists uneasily with white middle-class neighborhoods. In "world cities" like New York or Los Angeles, it adjoins centers of immense wealth that stand in stark contrast to its poverty.

Massey and Denton argue that the existence of the "black ghetto" and the concentration of poverty within it are not arbitrary or accidental phenomena:

> This extreme racial isolation did not just happen; it was manufactured by whites through a series of self-conscious actions and purposeful institutional arrangements that continue today. . . . It shows little sign of change with the passage of time or improvements in socioeconomic status. . . . Residential segregation is not a neutral fact; it systematically undermines the social and economic well-being of blacks in the United States. (1993, 2)

Using Chicago as a typical example of older urban centers, Morenoff and Tienda (1997, 71) state that since the 1970s there has been "a dramatic spread of ghetto underclass neighborhoods," which is part of a larger "spatial concentration of affluence, exemplified by the spread of gentrifying yuppie neighborhoods during the 1980s." This kind of segregation "is fairly complete and systematic. It has a basis in the attitudes of whites who largely prefer not to live with blacks, and it is perpetuated by a social system that protects the interests of those who hold these attitudes" (Bashi and Hughes 1997, 120).

Urban-suburban economic differences are equally evident and have become more so in recent years. A survey conducted in 1991 found that America's fifty "hottest" counties in terms of growth in population and per capita income were largely in southern suburban areas; the "coldest" twenty counties encompassed major urban centers in the North and West. The growth pattern around Atlanta by this time consisted of eight of the "hot" counties arranged in a horseshoe shape around the declining central city. San Francisco, Denver, Saint Louis, Washington D.C., and New York City showed a similar, if less dramatic, pattern of development (Thomas 1991, 34 ff). In fact, "horseshoe" and "doughnut" are increasingly used as metaphors to describe that pattern. This is evident in examining the much-discussed "Massachusetts miracle" of the 1980s, which increased wealth and employment in the communities along Route 128 around Boston but did little for impoverished sections of the city itself, or for rural areas farther west. The trend has continued in the 1990s, as businesses relocate even farther from cities, into the fringes of metropolitan areas. The residential patterns that accompany this are similar to those existing in the central city, reinforced by a new division of labor imposed by a global economy:

On top of an already immense and calcified pattern of segregation, the major

beneficiaries of globalization—corporate managers and executives—continue to live in, and reinforce the exclusivity of posh suburban areas and gentrified enclaves. . . . Lesser beneficiaries of globalization—service workers and laborers—continue to live in lesser urban neighborhoods. At the lowest end of the continuum, low-wage and chronically unemployed workers (sometimes called the urban underclass) often live within eyeshot of gleaming office towers or spectacular homes but are miles from these worlds materially. (Wilson 1997, 10)

Rural Development

Rural America has historically been perceived as lagging behind metropolitan areas in economic growth. This has not always been the actual case, however, especially as manufacturing and service industries have begun to replace farming, mining, and fishing as the economic mainstays of rural areas. In the Northeast, New Hampshire and Vermont have experienced the fastest economic growth. Some areas, such as central Florida, have grown so fast that state governments have had to respond somewhat radically to control and even limit growth. Many rural areas, however, have no such problems, particularly those 200 or more rural counties with nearly half their population in poverty. The stagnation in agriculture has left such areas as rural South Dakota and Nebraska far behind others in economic growth. Many city and suburban residents are unaware of the extent to which poverty is a rural phenomenon. The disparities in rural development reflect again the relative levels of public and private investment. Rural areas that promise a profitable return attract private development as well as public funding for roads, housing, and schools to back it up. This, in turn, draws in new residents. Thus as the rural Midwest declined along with its farms, western rural areas brought in both new businesses and new residents in the 1980s and 1990s.

Perspectives on Uneven Economic Development

Economic analysts have a variety of perspectives on uneven development. Conservatives tend to view these changes and inequities as a natural outgrowth of the market economy, reflecting the ability of different areas to attract investment. If regions and states are forced to innovate and compete for this investment to stimulate economic growth, so much the better; government should not interfere by imposing excessive regulations or by attempting to equalize conditions.

Conservatives also emphasize the importance of individual responsibility for choices in the economic market, and they therefore argue that conditions in poor areas, especially the inner city, have a great deal to do with the antisocial or dysfunctional behavior of those who live there. In 1969, Edward Banfield wrote a book entitled *The Unheavenly City*, in which he asserted that slums were largely the result of "lower-class" values and attitudes, which he described as excessively "present-oriented." In other words, the poverty and decay of the inner city reflected the inability and unwillingness of its residents to plan ahead, sacrifice for the future benefit of the community, and adopt socially acceptable norms of behavior. With the spread of conservative ideas in the 1980s, the notion of an "underclass" as the source of urban problems has become widely accepted, even among many liberals.

Liberals in general, however, tend to focus on structural and institutional failures that lead to uneven development. The disparities in economic development, they claim, are a consequence of a transition to a postindustrial society. The old manufacturing industries are giving way to high-technology and service industries, thereby creating structural unemployment, that is, a gap between workers' present skills and existing jobs, which needs to be reduced by government action. Although "underclass" values may exacerbate the problem, urban decay and increasing economic inequality result primarily from the often arbitrary and unfair outcomes of our economic system, which the government has a responsibility to rectify.

Socialists emphasize the inherent inequities of the capitalist system, which regularly and consistently rewards profitable but socially destructive investment decisions. The decline of the cities "was the result of conscious choices by powerful actors with a predictably unequal distribution of costs and benefits [leading to] waves of disinvestment, demolition, and speculative reinvestment—at various rates and in various forms" (Stone and Hartman 1997, 138). Many liberals, along with socialists, blame what has been called deindustrialization: a widespread, systematic disinvestment in the nation's basic productive capacity. According to Bluestone and Harrison (1982, 6), "Capital has been diverted from productive investment in our basic national industry into unproductive speculation, mergers, and acquisitions, and foreign investment. Left behind are shuttered factories, displaced workers, and a newly emergent group of ghost towns." These trends were exacerbated by the policies of the Reagan administration, which used fiscal and regulatory policy to encourage and subsidize these activities in the name of the free market (Bluestone and Harrison 1988).

The significance and permanence of economic change and uneven development are therefore a matter of hot debate as policy makers consider the proper response by government. State and local governments face an immense policy problem in promoting economic development and they have come up with a variety of responses.

State and Local Economic Development Policy

Repeated fiscal crises, periodic recessions followed by weak recoveries, and cutbacks in federal funds have combined to intensify state and local competition for private investment to strengthen the tax base. To that end, state and local governments have offered financial incentives, modified regulations, and adopted fiscal policies consistent with business priorities.

It has become of the utmost importance to stand high in assessments of "business climate." State and local governments take a considerable risk in pursuing policies that have even the appearance of hostility to business. As one analyst describes it, "The vocabulary of business is pervasive among the states. A popular metaphor in governors' conclaves even likens state chief executives to CEOs. . . . As Illinois four-term governor James Thompson notes, 'The centerpiece of almost every governor's activity these days . . . is to serve the cause of economic development" (Simon 1989, 11). Thus in 1992 Intel Corporation was able to attract at least two states, Arizona and New Mexico, to grant most of the 104 items on an "ideal incentive matrix" (more simply, "wish list") in exchange for two new computer chip factories (Mahtesian 1994, 37).

This of course enhances the political power and influence of business interests in all areas of state and local government. The issue is whether it serves the public interest as well. In any case, there appears to be no magic formula for success, and conservatives, liberals, and socialists differ sharply on the issue of which policies are most effective.

The Federal Role
Part of the agenda of President Lyndon Johnson's "Great Society" was urban redevelopment. For the first time, the federal government launched extensive programs to eradicate the problems of the inner cities through grants-in-aid. The Demonstration Cities and Metropolitan Redevelopment Act of 1966 (known as "Model Cities") stated that "im-

proving the quality of urban life is the most critical domestic problem facing the United States." This priority was reflected by an increase in federal outlays for community development and housing from $200 million in 1961 to $3.3 billion in 1972 (Judd 1984, 329–330). An attempt was made to build a relationship between the federal government and neighborhood organizations in planning development projects in declining urban areas, which resulted in considerable opposition from state and local politicians.

This emphasis began to shift when Richard Nixon took office in 1969 and showed favoritism to the suburban and rural areas, which provided his Republican constituency. Nixon's "New Federalism" moved away from grants-in-aid targeted to urban areas to a strategy of revenue-sharing and block grants. Revenue-sharing was embodied in the State and Local Fiscal Assistance Act of 1972, which returned a relatively small amount of federal revenue to state and local governments with a minimum of restrictions on its use. Block grants were the basis of the Housing and Community Development Act of 1974, which consolidated a variety of categorical grants to cities into a single Community Development Block Grant (CDBG) program. Despite some attempts during the Carter administration to steer CDBG money to poor areas, it was largely used by localities to leverage private investment in downtown business expansion. The 1977 Urban Development Action Grant (UDAG) program similarly subsidized the construction of convention centers, malls, and private projects, rather than low-income housing or inner-city renovations.

The Reagan administration effectively ended even these limited subsidies. Consistent with its conservative principles of reliance on the free market and devolution of responsibility to lower levels of government, funding for community development was cut throughout the 1980s. The UDAG program was ended in 1989, and only limited funding was made available for the CDBG program. Although the Los Angeles riots of 1992 brought national attention back to the problems of the cities, there was little response from the Bush administration. The Clinton administration also has produced no new initiatives. States and localities have been forced to rely almost entirely on their own resources to promote economic development. What now remains of all these government efforts is about 2,000 community development corporations (CDCs), which rely on a combination of private and public money to stimulate economic development in poor (but not necessarily the poorest) neighborhoods. Despite their energy and creativity the CDCs are, in the words of Robert Halpern (1995, 145–146), fragile, marginal institutions that have "not been able to reverse the basic process of economic decline in the most isolated and disadvantaged inner-city communities. . . . [They] remain an inadequately supported and underutilized community development resource."

A more promising approach is represented by the so-called "neighborhood initiatives" that began in the 1980s. An example is the Dudley Street Neighborhood Initiative in Boston. Started with financing from a private foundation, it established a collaborative effort among residents and local institutions to clean up the area, acquire land to construct low-rent housing, and improve public services. Similar programs have begun in inner-city neighborhoods in Los Angeles, New York, Baltimore, Atlanta, and several other cities. Yet these, too, remain isolated efforts, vulnerable to financial difficulties and political obstruction.

Policies Toward Labor

One of the most important cost items for business is wages. Thus, corporations seek out locations where labor costs are minimal. Insofar as unions apply pressure on management to grant higher wages, their weakness is a benefit to business. Since union organizing is subject to a variety of federal and state regulations, an antilabor bias on the part of government is a desirable feature for investors. On a national level, the Reagan administration used its regulatory power to severely diminish the capacity of unions to organize workers. On a state level, the existence of so-called "right to work" laws is an indicator of probusiness policies.

In 1947, Congress passed the Taft-Hartley Act over the veto of President Harry Truman. One of its provisions permitted states to outlaw the "closed shop," that is, agreements between labor and management that required union membership as a condition of employment. Almost half the states, mostly in the South and West, now have "right to work" laws, which allow individuals to make a choice about union membership whether or not they are covered by a union contract. Thus unions are impelled to persuade each employee individually to join and are saddled with a "free rider" problem in shops that they have organized—that is, nonmembers are entitled to the same union wages and fringe benefits as members.

Weak unions are correlated with low wage levels, and this combination initially attracted industries to sunbelt states. As a consequence of antilabor public policies and poor leadership, by the 1990s unions had fewer members and less political clout than at any time since the 1920s. This overall national weakness has lessened the distinction among states. The increasing international mobility of capital, however, brings in competition from countries in Asia and Latin America, where wage levels are far below those of the United States, and where, in some cases, labor unions are officially discouraged or even illegal. Thus, few states or localities are willing to take any political position that might indicate a leaning toward organized labor or that might have the effect of raising wage levels.

Financial Incentives

As economic stagnation and fiscal crises became more apparent in the mid-1970s, state and local governments began to offer prospective business investors an incredible array of financial incentives to promote economic development. These included short- and long-term exemptions from property taxes, lower income taxes, loans to new businesses, investment tax credits, and industrial revenue bonds (financing private industrial expansion by lending money raised through the sale of state bonds). "Smokestack chasing" became the goal of fifty state and hundreds of local economic development agencies, each extolling its own particular economic virtues and financial incentives. The result was bidding wars, which threatened to cost more than they gained. For example, a multistate competition in 1976 to attract a new Volkswagen plant was won by Pennsylvania at a cost of $25 million in rail and highway improvements, a 1.75 percent loan of $40 million, a 95 percent property tax abatement for two years, and a below-scale wage for workers at the plant (Goodman 1979, 2–3). Springfield, Massachusetts, became something of a model for its economic development program in the late 1970s, but the program required a massive combination of government loans and subsidies amounting to an expenditure of $200 million over five years (Kantor 1988, 228). In 1993, thirty-five states competed over the location of a Mercedes-Benz sports-utility vehicle plant. Alabama won with a $300 million incentive package, about $200,000 for each of the expected 1,500 jobs (Mahtesian 1994, 38).

As the *Wall Street Journal* reported, companies have taken further advantage of this situation by using threats of relocation to demand financial concessions from state and local governments:

After years of losing big employers to the South and West, states in the Northeast and industrial Midwest are now holding on to many potential defectors, but only after giving in to what some critics consider blackmail. Thanks to $90 million in subsidies and tax breaks offered by the city of Toledo and the state of Ohio, Owens-Corning Fiberglas Corp. decided to stay put in its hometown of more than 57 years. . . . The company said tax breaks from Toledo beat out "feelers" from Dallas, St. Louis, and Monroe, Mich. . . . Bic Corp. and the Pratt & Whitney division of United Technologies Corp. withdrew their threats to move in 1993 after [Connecticut] came up with tax and other incentives to stay. The one for Pratt was worth $32 million. (8 March 1995, 8)

In 1994, IPSCO Steel, which had been negotiating with several states over the location of a new mill, accepted a $75.6 million incentive package from the Iowa state government, including exemptions from local property taxes and sales taxes; an investment tax credit; and several million dollars in grants, loans, and subsidies. In addition, the county in which the mill was to be located offered $1.5 million to cover infrastructure costs, all for the 300 jobs that IPSCO promised to provide (Fisher and Peters 1997, 109).

Yet many of these incentive programs have failed. By 1983, the Volkswagen plant had laid off half its workers; in 1987 it was closed. In 1992, Minnesota offered Northwest airlines an $840 million loan and tax break package to locate two repair facilities in the state's depressed northern region. After accepting $270 million, the financially troubled airline indefinitely postponed its construction plans. Similar stories of failure are common throughout the United States. Even after receiving its tax breaks, Pratt & Whitney continued to cut thousands of jobs.

Some researchers have concluded that the effects of state and local economic development policies in general are no more than modest at best:

Evidence is inconclusive about which policies exert the greatest effects and under what circumstances. The conditions under which state policies can significantly influence business location and economic growth are limited, mainly because the most important determinants of a jurisdiction's relative rate of economic growth are largely beyond the control of state and local governments—for example, labor costs, the availability of appropriately skilled labor, energy costs, climate, and the availability of natural resources. . . . Competitive forces have narrowed differences among states in both business tax burdens and business incentives, dampening the effectiveness of any new measures. (Bradbury et al. 1997, 1)

To a considerable extent, then, the economic fate of American states and localities is an arbitrary outcome of international economic trends.

In a global economy, states and localities can do little more than position themselves to take advantage of economic forces over which they have little or no control, and which offer no guarantee of lasting growth or prosperity. Cleveland, for example, has been able to recover from its decline in the 1970s owing to "serendipity and aggressive promotional efforts." Its ultimate fate rests on its "competitive position with the national and, increasingly, global division of labor. . . . Given the instability of capitalism, in which the only constant is change, the only certainty is that the current renaissance will not last indefinitely" (Warf and Holly 1997, 221).

These unstable conditions and the uneven track record of financial incentives has led some state officials to question the value of interstate competition. In 1993, Governor Jim Edgar of Illinois attempted to put together a truce at the National Governors' Conference under which states would end these bidding wars. But this has proved easier said than done; a similar compact among New York, New Jersey, and Connecticut in 1991 collapsed within months. The dynamics of economic competition are something like those of the international arms race during the cold war—the stakes are too high, and the temptation to stay one step ahead of the opposition is too great.

Some states, however, are seeking alternatives. Legislation granting tax breaks to businesses now often includes "clawback" provisions, which link the incentives to specific economic goals. In 1996, Massachusetts granted a $40 million tax reduction to its mutual fund industry in exchange for a promise to increase employment by 5 percent annually, unless specific adverse economic conditions prevailed. Despite such changes, however, business continues to have the better bargaining position, and the bidding wars are likely to continue.

High Technology and Economic Development

The economic promise of high technology loomed large in the 1980s and inspired some state governments to go beyond tax incentives and industrial revenue bonds. They began to expand high technology research in various universities and to grant financial aid to specific companies. By the mid-1980s, the growth of high-technology centers in eastern Massachusetts, the Research Triangle Park in North Carolina, and the so-called "Silicon Valley" in California were cited as models for other states. Yet even in the early 1980s, there were warnings that high technology would not be the wave of the future. In 1983, a study by economists in the U.S. Bureau of Labor Statistics correctly predicted that high technology was expected to provide a relatively small proportion of employment (Riche et al. 1983, 58).

A good deal of high technology research and development has been financed by military spending. The Reagan administration launched a major expansion of military spending in the 1980s, justifying it as a response to a perceived Soviet threat. This benefited states with military installations. A large amount was also spent on research and development of weapons systems, which meant significant amounts of money for those with the appropriate research facilities.

The economic boom known as the "Massachusetts miracle" was largely created by increased production and employment in high technology, which in turn depended to a considerable extent on military spending. Cutbacks in that spending in the late 1980s, along with inadequate consumer demand and corporate errors in assessing the market for high technology, helped put an end to it. By 1992, the recession had taken a heavy toll of high-technology jobs. In July of that year, the Digital Corporation, once a national success story, declared a loss of almost $2 billion and announced 15,000 additional layoffs—in a company that once prided itself on its no-layoff policy.

Public-Private Partnerships

Partnerships between government and business to encourage downtown revitalization became the primary strategy for economic development in the cities during the 1970s. The goal was to bring business enterprise and middle-class consumers and residents back into downtown areas. The resulting economic benefits were then expected to spread into surrounding neighborhoods.

The process would start with the organization of a formal or informal leadership group composed of government officials, planners, and local businesspeople and bankers. Together, they would establish priorities for redevelopment, with particular emphasis on the commercial potential of the downtown area of the city. Financing was to be arranged by using federal and state grants, along with local financial incentives, to leverage private investment. A result in many cities was the reconstruction of downtown areas—including shopping malls, hotels, convention centers, office buildings, and cultural facilities—under the coordination of a relatively small number of politicians and businesspeople using public and private money. If housing was to be part of the plan, it would involve either the construction of market-rate (unsubsidized) rental housing or the rehabilitation of old buildings inhabited by working-class people, who were eased out in favor of middle-class people who could pay the new, higher rents or afford outright purchase. This process is known as "gentrification."

Although such partnerships still exist and are active, the increasing scarcity of public funds slowed the pace of redevelopment. Many states and communities turned to planning and public relations rather than construction. Texas established a state-level partnership known as the Strategic Economic Policy Commission to draw up a long-range plan to pull the state out of the economic doldrums created by the collapse of oil prices (Cadenhead and Farley 1989, 15–18). On the local level, the Houston Economic Development Commission, consisting largely of top businesspeople but subsidized by the city government, spent most of its money on communications, public relations, and marketing to make the city more attractive for specific kinds of investment. It is too early to judge the impact of the new emphasis, but the effects of public-private partnerships on downtown redevelopment are apparent everywhere and have had at best mixed success. Some examples are worth noting.

Detroit, dependent almost entirely on the stagnating automobile industry, was by the late 1970s in a severe crisis. The solution was the formation of local economic development corporations with power to combine public and private money for redevelopment. The goal was to change from an industrial city to a financial and administrative services center. The means was the massive reconstruction of the entire downtown area. The centerpiece was to be the "Renaissance Center," a corporate, commercial, and residential complex on the riverfront. The entire project came close to bankruptcy in 1983, and by the mid-1980s one analyst concluded that "the Renaissance of the urban core is fragile. The central-place activities . . . are tied to the economic well-being of the region as a whole. And the economic vitality of the region remains tied to manufacturing. Continued industrial disinvestment threatens to undermine the whole Renaissance effort" (R. Hill 1986, 116).

In Denver in the late 1970s, public-private efforts culminated in the construction of the "Skyline Project": twenty-seven acres of land covered with new high-rise banks and hotels, public buildings, and a performing arts center, financed by over $2 billion in mostly out-of-state private capital leveraged by $200 million in public money (Judd 1984). But the declining economy burst the speculative bubble; by the late 1980s office space in Denver was being auctioned for prices as low as fifty cents a square foot, down from $20 or more a few years earlier (Bluestone and Harrison 1988, 67).

Whatever the merits of public-private partnerships as a whole, regional and national economic trends are clearly the most powerful influence on state and local economic development. The extent to which such partnerships succeed depends on whether the surrounding region is doing well and the local industries are sound nationally. The inability of most of these experiments to thrive or even survive during economic downturns is sufficient evidence to cast doubt on such planning strategies.

In the 1950s and 1960s the strength of the national economy was enough to pull most regions of the country ahead, even if at different paces. This has all changed. Declining regions, states, and localities have redoubled their efforts to maintain an economic base. With the federal government offering little help, state and local governments have tried a variety of means to attract their share of a decreasing stock of investment. The results are at best inconsistent and at worst ineffective, exacerbating the problem of uneven development to the disadvantage of urban centers. It is thus appropriate for students of economic and community development to ask whether there might not be alternatives. Before dealing with this, however, we need to look at several other factors in economic development, notably housing, infrastructure, and the quality of the environment.

Other Factors in Economic Development

Housing

In his second inaugural address in 1937, President Franklin D. Roosevelt referred to the United States as a nation that was one-third ill-fed, ill-clad, and ill-sheltered. At the time, and for the next twenty or thirty years, America was indeed beset by dilapidated and overcrowded housing. The massive post–World War II housing boom, especially in the suburbs, alleviated the crisis, and a growing economy provided buying power for the middle class. But by the late 1970s, decent housing was increasingly priced out of reach of even the middle class, not to mention lower-income people. Throughout the following decade, homeless people became an ever more common sight on the streets of the nation's cities. The immediate causes were higher interest rates for mortgages, real estate speculation driving up the costs of land, and the apparent inability of the housing market to provide affordable shelter for middle- and lower-income families.

The government first became involved in alleviating housing problems in 1937—the year Roosevelt made the statement cited above—when Congress passed the Housing Act, which established the federal public housing program. The law provided for the establishment of local housing authorities to plan, construct, and administer low-rent housing. An annual federal payment was to cover the mortgage costs of site clearance and construction, and the low rents paid for maintenance.

The initial purpose of public housing was to revive the construction industry and provide transitional shelter for working- and middle-class people saving money for the down payment on a home. Instead, it became a system of warehouses for the elderly and the poor. In 1949 and 1954, the federal government established urban renewal, which subsidized local purchase and clearance of land for private redevelopment. The ostensible purpose was slum clearance, to make room for new housing and other development. The actual result was the elimination of existing low-income housing on a grand scale, to be replaced either by high-rise projects or by residential and commercial facilities for business and upper-income people. Thus all the social ills of a poor neighborhood became concentrated in towering apartment complexes, which then became a natural target for budget cuts in maintenance and services. In many cases, the projects became literally uninhabitable, some to the extent that they had to be demolished. By the 1970s, public housing had as a result become politically unpopular, and construction of new federally subsidized units was virtually halted. The federal government has gradually shifted away from pushing states and localities into the development of low-rent housing and toward programs based on subsidizing individual tenants or homeowners.

That shift actually began after World War II with federal mortgage subsidy programs that enabled the white middle class to leave the cities for private homes in the suburbs. In 1968, this approach was applied to public housing programs in the Housing and Urban Development Act, which provided subsidies to low- and moderate-income individuals and families and to nonprofit groups seeking to construct housing for them. The Section 8 program of the Housing Act of 1974 provides for paying landlords a subsidy for the rent of eligible low-income tenants, and for offering rent vouchers to those tenants. However, federal assistance for low-income housing was cut 70 percent between 1981 and 1986 (Nenno 1987, 122). In 1986, nearly 400,000 households were on waiting lists for public housing, and another 400,000 on lists for Section 8 assistance (Edgar and Matulef 1987, 139). In the late 1980s, the federal government developed Project HOPE, which was designed to sell public housing units to their residents. This has not been successful owing to lack of money and lack of interest on the part of potential buyers.

State and local governments have tried to fill the gap with programs of their own modeled on the federal example, including financial aid for construction of low-income housing, rehabilitation loans, and housing vouchers. But fiscal crises created funding difficulties for these programs as well, particularly given their political vulnerability. A case in point is New York City, which constructed the very first housing project in the nation in 1934, and over the next fifty years developed 275 more, housing at one time or another 1.25 million people. In 1984, the *New York Times* reported that the city was resorting to a $300,000 program to paste vinyl decals picturing curtains, shades, shutters, and flowerpots over the empty windows of abandoned tenements in the devastated South Bronx section of the city (25 June 1984, B3; 7 November 1983, A1). More recently, however, the city has undertaken a relatively successful publicly funded renovation of thousands of slum buildings.

Infrastructure and Environment

References have been made earlier in this book to a growing concern with the deteriorating condition of America's infrastructure, that is, the public works facilities that are a part of economic and community development. These include roads and highways, mass transit, public buildings, water supply, and sewerage. According to many observers, there is a need for extensive reconstruction or rehabilitation of many of these facilities:

> The problems of developing, maintaining, and rehabilitating the infrastructure are staggering—41 percent of the nation's bridges are deficient and more than one million miles of highway will need to be resurfaced by 2000. Half of the country's communities cannot accept more industrial or residential development because their wastewater facilities are operating at or near capacity. Existing landfills are approaching capacity and siting considerations are forcing new facilities to be located farther out, thus increasing per unit disposal costs. Leaking water supply lines are causing some major cities to lose up to 30 percent of their drinking water daily. Against this backdrop of needs, the United States has been reducing spending on infrastructure relative to GNP for the past

several decades. (Whitman 1992, 27–28)

This is largely a consequence of fiscal problems, as the need to cut budgets has taken its toll on expenditures for maintenance and new construction. The largest component of infrastructure is related to transportation, and although roads, highways, and mass transit are primarily state and local responsibilities, the federal government has had enormous influence over the years.

Transportation. States and localities build streets, roads, and highways by floating bond issues as part of their capital budgets. Maintenance of these facilities is paid for out of current revenues. In 1988, about one-quarter of the funding for state and local highways came from motor fuel taxes, another one-quarter from federal grants, and 20 percent from user fees and tolls. Spending on highways has generally lagged behind the costs of construction and maintenance; after accounting for inflation, expenditures declined in the late 1970s and early 1980s and have only recently begun to match the level spent in 1975 (Snell 1991a, 40 ff.).

The federal role in state highway construction remained minor until 1956, when the National Defense Highway Act established a federal trust fund based on fuel taxes to pay for a network of interstate highways, whose cost was to be shared on a 90-10 basis with the states. By the mid-1980s, more than a decade after the targeted date, the system was 95 percent completed, at which point the need to repair the sections built two or three decades earlier became an issue. At the same time, revenues from fuel taxes have declined owing to more fuel-efficient automobiles; the result is likely to be even higher taxes and user fees to finance the necessary maintenance.

An alternative to dependence on the automobile is mass transit, including railways, streetcars, buses, and subways. In the late nineteenth and early twentieth centuries electric streetcars were the mainstay of urban mass transit, providing cheap and efficient, if slow, service. A few cities, such as New York, had well-developed subway systems. These lines were mostly privately owned and only marginally profitable; and as the age of the automobile dawned, a combination of public demand, corporate pressure, and government policy favored the development of streets and highways for use by automobiles, trucks, and buses. The energy crisis of the early 1970s led to a re-examination of mass transit alternatives, and some financial aid for the decaying subway systems came from the federal government. But the Reagan administration ended most of these subsidies in the 1980s.

Within metropolitan areas in the last ten years, more new jobs have been created in the suburbs rather than the central cities. This has created a need for "reverse commuting" transit services, especially if unemployed inner-city residents without cars are to have access to those jobs. Aside from a few experimental programs, there has been little effort to provide them (Stanfield 1996, 2546). This is not surprising, since there has often been resistance from white middle-class suburbanites against the extension of mass transit into their communities.

The conclusion appears to be that federal, state, and local governments have spent a good deal of money developing a transportation system which is not especially clean, efficient, or economical, which depends on a constant supply of oil, and which is prone to increasing obsolescence. The devolution of financial and administrative responsibility to state and local governments in a time of fiscal austerity may make matters worse, at least in the short run.

Water Supply and Waste Disposal. The most critical natural resource for economic and community development, which in many regions of the country is usually taken for granted, is water. In the southwestern United States, the issue is who will have access to the limited supplies that are available; in most of the rest of the country, especially in urban areas, the issue is how to keep the supply clean. The political conflict in areas of scarcity is a relatively straightforward battle among different interests seeking their share of a precious commodity. Where there is usually ample water, the politics of pollution presents more difficult problems.

Until the 1970s, the solution to water shortages in the Southwest was massive federally subsidized construction of dams and reservoirs, with little or no concern for the ecological damage that resulted. Ultimately, the environmental movement succeeded in forcing a halt to the construction and pressuring state and local governments to emphasize water conservation as a priority.

Also as a result of environmentalist organizing, since 1970 federal and state governments have developed an extensive body of regulation to deal with pollution of all kinds. Many localities, however, have found it increasingly difficult to deal with a complex and highly fragmented regulatory system and have complained of the excessive red tape and the excessive expense involved in attempting to comply with the rules.

There is also some question whether all this regulation has actually had the intended effect of protecting the environment. According to the environmentalist Barry Commoner, although $100 billion has been spent to deal with water pollution since the passage of the Clean Water Act in the early 1970s, "the campaign to reduce river pollution has stalled, after reaching only a very modest level of success" (1990, 26). He attributes this to an emphasis on cleaning up pollution rather than preventing it; that is, as long as our economic base depends on industries that produce pollutants, we cannot hope to keep up with the stream of toxic chemicals that foul the water supply. It is far more expensive in the long run to develop cleansing technologies than to find new and less polluting methods of production. But the problem is that our economic system is not designed for the kind of planning that would lead to preventing pollution, and those who own and run it are not inclined to make such investments.

An inevitable product of economic and community development is, of course, waste of all kinds. As pointed out earlier, disposal of that waste has become a tremendous problem as land grows scarcer and more expensive. As landfills can no longer accommodate the increasing volume of waste, they must be "capped," and the waste must be transported to dumps farther away. At the same time, the old landfills become environmental hazards themselves. This imposes a huge financial burden on state and local governments as the volume of waste increases but available disposal sites become fewer and fewer. This is especially true for the disposal of hazardous materials. The response to this problem has, again, been increased federal and state regulation, but without the necessary funding to finance the extra efforts required. Thus in the last decade, suburban and rural communities have encountered environmental problems which used to concern only major cities.

The downside of economic and community development is therefore the cost attached to developing the necessary physical infrastructure to promote that development, and the need to protect the environment at the same time. In the rush to develop during the 1950s and 1960s, these costs were ignored or mortgaged to the future. Unfortunately, now that the bill is due, state and local governments lack the funds to pay it.

Policy Alternatives

Conservative Approach
Except for the most extreme advocates of government noninterfer-

ence with the free market, conservatives favor most of the prevailing policies in economic development. Competition for private investment among states and localities is considered healthy. Public-private partnerships are a constructive activity for government. Using the tax system to provide incentives for business is good fiscal policy. The alleged antisocial behavior of the "underclass" is to be discouraged by cutting welfare programs and providing incentives for seeking employment.

For those conservatives who would take another stab at reviving the cities, however, the "enterprise zone" is the policy of choice. Developed by British politicians and economists in the 1970s, the idea is to designate limited areas in declining cities which would be subject to special incentives for private industry in the form of extensive deregulation and huge tax breaks. The initial proposals included elimination of minimum wages, along with exemption from most taxes, labor legislation, and economic regulation—in short, an economic "free port," similar to what conservatives saw in Hong Kong at the time. Obviously, this had to be modified for use in the United States.

The Reagan and Bush administrations tried numerous times, unsuccessfully, to enact federal legislation for enterprise zones. In any case, by 1992, thirty-six states had already created 600 such zones, ranging in size from a few city blocks to entire counties. A typical program was that of Maryland, which provided subsidies for infrastructure as well as property tax abatements and income tax credits for job creation. However, the U.S. General Accounting Office concluded in 1989 that "the Maryland experience does not show that enterprise zones are effective. . . . Employment increases . . . could not be attributed to the enterprise zone program" (*Boston Globe* 6 July 1992, 4). Bill Clinton succeeded where his predecessors had failed, and in 1993 the Empowerment Zone and Enterprise Community Act, a mixture of liberal and conservative approaches, became law. Under its provisions, by late 1994 eleven zones in eight cities and three multicounty rural zones were eligible for substantial federal aid; ninety-nine smaller cities and rural areas became eligible for lesser amounts. The jury is still out on the effects of such programs. A study by the Federal Reserve Bank of Boston in 1997 found that most of the research on the benefits of empowerment or enterprise zones "is merely suggestive and rather contradictory" because of difficulties in measurement (Fisher and Peters 1997, 128).

From the conservative point of view, the development of housing and transportation is best left to the free market. If assistance must be given to the poor for housing, it should be in the form of rental vouchers, similar to the Section 8 program. The housing shortage as a whole, conservatives argue, can be solved by constructing market-rate housing which ultimately should "trickle down" to low- and moderate-income consumers.

Overall, conservatives favor user fees for publicly owned services, accompanied by greater privatization of public facilities that could be turned over to private corporations for profitable and therefore more efficient operation:

> Private firms provide a means to escape the excessive rigidities of overly-bureaucratized public agencies and public labor-management problems. Private firms can sometimes be more efficient and operate at less cost than public agencies because of their ability to swiftly introduce new technology; their greater flexibility in the use of worker incentives; their ability to reduce or eliminate an unneeded service by simply not continuing a contract; and their often superior understanding of economies of scale and specialization. (Choate and Walter 1983, 1–2)

On the issue of pollution, conservatives agree that a certain amount of government regulation might be necessary, at least in the form of tax incentives for companies choosing to invest in the appropriate technology. But even here the market may have an application. After all, a community could choose, as some communities have done, to market itself as a site for waste disposal. Given the difficulties of finding such sites, the financial benefits could be substantial, thus solving two problems at once: waste disposal and, for the town itself, economic underdevelopment. On a broader level, conservatives have proposed a system of "pollution credits": setting an overall limit on pollution and allowing industries falling below that limit to sell their unused credits to industries that exceed it.

Liberal Approach

Liberals reject the notion that the free market alone should shape the direction of community development. Government should have a responsibility to mitigate the most inegalitarian side effects of capitalism by regulating market forces. Many so-called "neoliberals" look to the federal government to do the job through the formulation of a national "industrial policy," which would use federal money to promote, in a consistent, planned way, the expansion of growth industries, the rehabilitation of infrastructure, and the redevelopment of declining areas. Specific policies would be determined by a newly established national agency representing business, labor, and government. Liberals who favor this approach often cite Japan, which has such a policy, as a model for the United States in this regard. More recently, Singapore, South Korea, and Taiwan—the "Asian tigers"—have provided examples of dramatic economic growth stimulated by government direction and guidance in the context of a capitalist economy. Paul Tsongas, a candidate for the Democratic presidential nomination in 1992, was a leading advocate of this policy. Recent economic difficulties in many of these countries have perhaps made the industrial policy model less attractive, however.

A prototype of this approach was developed in Rhode Island in 1982. The so-called "greenhouse compact" would have involved a seven-year investment of $750 million, one-third of it from public funds. It would have established a Strategic Development Commission, a quasi-public agency with the authority to target potential growth industries and make the necessary investments to enhance their possibilities for expansion. The plan required a statewide referendum to approve bond financing. In June 1984, the voters rejected it by a margin of four to one, because of their perception of the compact as elitist and unfair (Silver and Burton 1986, 277–288).

Less comprehensive versions of industrial policy have been attempted with some success in other states. The Massachusetts Community Development Finance Corporation was begun in 1978; its purpose was to finance small community-based enterprises with funds raised from the sale of bonds. The Connecticut Development Authority finances loans to small high-risk firms through similar methods. Most of these experiments, however, have been limited, cautious, and underfunded.

Liberals have also proposed what is known as "linked development" in areas experiencing considerable growth. During the construction boom in Boston in the early 1980s, Mayor Ray Flynn implemented such a policy. Developers had to pay an "impact fee" of $5 per square foot for projects exceeding 100,000 square feet. The money raised was sent to a Neighborhood Housing Trust Fund. Alternatively, developers could produce an equivalent amount of low- and moderate-income housing. Whatever the merits of the idea, its effects were minimal, and once the boom ended the program was essentially obsolete (M. Smith 1989, 85 ff).

Some local governments have gone even farther. Edward Goetz

(1994) identifies a "new paradigm" of "progressive municipal [development] policy": expanded public regulation of private property, promotion of alternatives to the private market, public ownership and planning, identification of specific groups who are to benefit from development, and increased participation of citizens and community-based interests. Chicago under Mayor Harold Washington implemented many of these ideas, including the incorporation of more than 100 neighborhood groups into the economic development policy-making process.

Liberals generally believe that private industry should assume greater responsibility for the community, particularly for the effects of plant closings. To that end, liberals support stronger state and federal laws, providing advance notice to workers if a company intends to shut down or move. A number of states have weak versions of such laws, and the federal government enacted similarly toothless legislation in 1986.

As far as housing, infrastructure, and environmental policy are concerned, most liberals believe that state and local governments are financially and administratively incapable of implementing effective and comprehensive programs without substantial federal assistance. Any progress in those areas would have to come as part of a national industrial policy to provide the proper planning and coordination. President Clinton seemed to favor this policy when he first took office in 1993, but even his limited proposals for public investment in infrastructure were rejected by a conservative Congress.

Socialist Approach

Many socialists endorse the kind of economic planning proposed by liberals but criticize its undemocratic aspects. An industrial policy makes sense, but only if the community as a whole, rather than a small expert elite, is involved in formulating it. Socialists believe in democratic control of economic development, under the assumption that

> The most important sources of private capital investment in this country are commercial banks, the life insurance industry, and the retained earnings of the corporations themselves. That is where the money comes from. To a substantial extent this is our money. . . . Capital is a social resource. We created it collectively by our labor, savings, and our presence in a community which creates markets. It is absurd to say that, once this money moves into the hands of some financial intermediary, it ceases to be ours and is no longer accountable to public concerns. (D. Smith 1979, 8)

Socialists are careful to distinguish their version of economic planning from the centralized, bureaucratic planning of the former Soviet Union. Democratic planning involves public participation in establishing long-range priorities for the use of the nation's resources. Overall planning in key industries could be the responsibility of the federal government, perhaps based on what the urban planner Robert Goodman calls "regional socialism": a bottom-up cooperative structure which would develop a national economic plan out of state proposals maximizing the use of the states' own resources (1979, 177). Without using the word "socialism," Bluestone and Harrison (1988, 181 ff) call for an industrial policy combined with workplace democracy, stronger labor unions, and a right to social services. Sidney Plotkin advocates a process

> organized from the bottom up, with local citizens and their representatives making the key decisions about economic directions. . . . Community planning would be established in the context of national economic and environmental policies that stress security as the basis of economic growth. National programs would aim at establishing a protective framework within which citizens could work to shape the substance of their local economies without abusing their land and without fear of sudden economic or social dislocation. Community production and consumption would be consciously joined and harmonized. (1987, 240)

This kind of planning necessitates a certain amount of direct public ownership. In particular, state governments could establish and finance publicly owned banks and utility companies to provide the necessary financial and energy infrastructure. Some local governments have in fact pursued or at least considered such alternatives, including the for-profit leasing of public property to private entrepreneurs, gaining public equity holdings in private enterprises, and directly entering the local real estate market (Imbroscio 1995).

Ecological concerns are paramount in any socialist program of economic development. Barry Commoner (1990, chap. 10) argues that a certain amount of "social governance of production" is necessary to protect the environment. Housing and infrastructure would be part of the planning process. Instead of financing and subsidizing private developers, some socialists have advocated programs such as direct grants or low-interest loans to nonprofit developers such as labor unions to build tenant-owned and managed housing. Land costs could be controlled by local "land banks" held for future public development. Stone and Hartman (1997) argue for implementing a "right to housing" through expansion of "nonspeculative social housing," that is, outside the private market and socially owned and controlled. In the long run a more progressive tax system along with public pension funds could provide the necessary financial resources.

The prerequisite for such a drastic program of change would be political movements committed to it. More modest programs consistent with the whole might, however, be politically possible in the short run. To put it simply, given sufficient political organization, at least parts of the socialist program might be achievable.

Conclusion

Increasing economic distress in many states and localities has led their governments to experiment with a variety of mostly conservative programs to encourage development. These have had, at best, mixed results and have definitely not resolved the problems arising from economic stagnation, fiscal crises, and abandonment of federal responsibility. Conservatives propose going even further in letting the market, rather than the government, make the necessary decisions as to which communities grow or decline. Liberals want to see a national industrial policy designed to target aid to growth industries and urban areas. Socialists advocate a program of democratic planning in which the public, working through the institutions of government, takes the overall responsibility in determining the direction of community development. In perhaps no other policy area on the state and local levels are the choices so critical; the path of economic development affects the quality of our lives most directly, in terms of how we earn our living and where and in what conditions we will live.

Chapter 12: The Politics of Welfare

In August 1996, President Bill Clinton signed the "Personal Responsibility and Work Opportunity Reconciliation Act." This terminated the nation's most important cash welfare program, Aid to Families with Dependent Children (AFDC), which through categorical grants-in-aid to the states had established a federal guarantee of benefits for poor families. It was replaced with a block grant program called Temporary Assistance to Needy Families (TANF), which, unlike AFDC, gives to the states most of the responsibility for financing and administering public welfare. This effectively ended a federal commitment to aiding the poor dating back to the New Deal.

However, the often expressed claim by lawmakers that this change would "end welfare as we know it" is open to challenge. High expectations accompanying earlier reforms have not been fulfilled. Although the federal commitment to assist the poor has been significantly reduced, the structure and approach of that assistance remain largely intact. Welfare policy is thus likely to continue to be a contentious political issue and may well present even more problems for states and localities in the future.

For most people, the word "welfare" brings to mind all kinds of negative associations: idleness, illegitimacy, waste, fraud, and the like. No other issue on the state and local levels seems to kindle such strong feelings and at the same time to be so obscured by prejudice and misinformation. There are legitimate ideological differences on welfare policy, but they are often hard to separate from myths and stereotypes.

Welfare programs are a very costly burden for state and local governments. They are generally recognized as having failed both at supporting poor families and at encouraging employment as an alternative. A serious discussion of welfare as a policy problem requires an examination of the structure of the labor force and the issues of poverty and unemployment.

Low Income as a Policy Problem

Poverty

In 1994, 38 million Americans—15 percent of the population—were on any given day living on incomes below the officially established poverty line: $15,141 for a family of four per year (or more or less depending on family size). The rate of poverty has remained essentially unchanged since the late 1960s. The government calculates the poverty line as a figure three times the cost of what the Department of Agriculture deems an "economy" food budget; the figure is revised upward annually to account for inflation. This is a rather arbitrary calculation, and as such has come under attack from all sides.

Liberals consider the figure too low. They argue that poverty is a relative rather than absolute condition; that is, poverty is deprivation in relation to what is recognized as a decent standard of living. Thus the poverty line ought to be figured as a percentage of median income. At 50 percent of median household income—equivalent to $16,132 in 1994—the poverty rate would be closer to 20 percent. From a liberal perspective, it is noteworthy that many families are poor for only part of the year, which implies that an even larger number of people are constantly "at risk" of poverty.

From the conservative standpoint, even the government's figures are too high. This argument is based on the fact that only cash income (including welfare) is calculated in the poverty line. The "in-kind" (noncash) benefits received by many poor people are not counted. Some economists have argued that if food stamps, housing subsidies, and medical care, among other services, were included, the real poverty rate might be as low as half of what the government estimates (Paglin 1980). There is, then, strong ideological disagreement as to whether much of a poverty problem actually exists in the United States.

Who Is Poor and Why?

Using the official poverty figures, we note that two groups stand out as disproportionately poor: female-headed families and minorities. Well over one-third of the former fall below the official poverty line, as do one-quarter to one-third of all black and Hispanic families. Blacks and Hispanics make up about 25 percent of the population, but more than 40 percent of the poor.

Why are these groups disproportionately poor? Why is anyone poor

Table 12.1: Poverty Rate by Race and Ethnicity, 1960-1995 (Percent)

Year	All Races	White	Black	Hispanic
1960	22.2	17.8	55.0	NA
1970	12.8	9.9	33.5	NA
1975	12.3	9.7	31.1	23.0
1980	13.0	10.2	32.5	21.8
1985	14.0	11.4	31.3	28.
1990	13.5	10.7	31.9	26.2
1995	13.8	11.2	29.3	30.3

Source: U.S. Department of Commerce, *Statistical Abstract of the U.S., 1997,* p. 475.

at all? A full discussion of the various reasons offered by adherents of the different ideologies could, and does, fill volumes. At the risk of oversimplification, the crucial ideological issue appears to be the extent to which the poor themselves are responsible for their own poverty, if at all, and to what extent the economic system works to impoverish certain kinds of people, or whether poverty is a combination of both effects.

Conservatives emphasize individual responsibility. Whatever the economic conditions, the logic of competition under capitalism demands that people exert maximum effort to advance themselves. If a person has a particular disadvantage or disability, it must be up to that individual to make the most of the situation. To put it simply, those who are poor may not be trying hard enough, perhaps because their motivation has been diminished by overly generous government programs, in particular welfare.

Liberals do not reject the idea of individual responsibility. Indeed, in recent years many liberals have moved closer to conservatives on the issue of family structure and its impact on poverty. However, liberals place more emphasis on the inequities of the economic system and on a history of racial and sexual discrimination that has heaped those inequities on minorities and women. Liberals accept a certain measure of inequality as a necessary part of the system, but excessive and persistent inequality, especially when concentrated among certain groups, represents a flaw in the system. It follows that government must bear responsibility for alleviating poverty.

Socialists go much further. Increasing poverty is an inevitable consequence of capitalism. The capitalist system must constantly expand to

Table 12.2: Poverty Rate by Race and Family Status, 1996 (Percent)

Race	Total Population	Female-Headed Families	Married-Couple Families
White	11.2	27.3	5.1
Black	28.4	43.7	9.1
Hispanic	29.4	50.9	18.0

Source: U.S. Census Bureau: www.census.gov/ftp/pub/hhes/www/poverty.html

survive, and that expansion is fueled by ever-increasing amounts of capital accumulation for investment. That capital has to come from somewhere, and it comes from the worker, who is pushed to produce more at lower pay, to increase the profits which provide investment capital. Ultimately, this means an increasing maldistribution of wealth, creating mass poverty. This is most visible on an international scale and worsens during a time of economic stagnation. Thus the prerequisite to abolition of poverty is abolition of the capitalist system.

Unemployment

Ideological differences over the extent and sources of unemployment fall into a similar pattern.

Calculating the unemployment rate is the responsibility of the U.S. Bureau of Labor Statistics (BLS), which conducts a monthly poll of 60,000 households. Individuals over age sixteen who did any work during the survey week are counted as employed (including vacationers, strikers, absentees, and unpaid workers in family businesses working more than fifteen hours). Employment for less than thirty-five hours weekly is included as part-time. Those who did not work but actively looked for a job in the previous four weeks are counted as unemployed. All others are considered as not in the labor force. Thus in an average month in 1995 there were almost 200 million citizens over sixteen, but only 132 million were counted in the labor force. Of these, 7.4 million were unemployed, and therefore the unemployment rate was 5.6 percent.

Depending on our ideological perspective, the official unemployment rate is either an underestimate or an overestimate. The BLS in fact calculates at least seven different unemployment rates. For example, if only persons unemployed for fifteen weeks or longer were counted, the unemployment rate in 1995 would have been 1.9%. If the calculation included a proportion of those who work part-time because they cannot find full-time jobs ("part-time for economic reasons") and a proportion of those who have stopped looking for work ("discouraged workers"), the rate would have been 12.7 percent. From the conservative point of view, the lower percentage is the most accurate measure of unemployment, since it counts only those who have actively sought a job for a considerable length of time, and who therefore are most likely to really need and want work. Liberals prefer to use a higher estimate, believing that involuntary part-timers and at least some discouraged workers should be included in the tally of the unemployed. Socialists would agree and would also point out that millions of people—the "working poor"—are employed at full-time year-round jobs and still cannot earn enough to break through the poverty line. According to the Census Bureau, in 1992, 18 percent of Americans with such jobs had earnings of less than $13,091, which was $1,500 below the poverty line (U.S. Department of Commerce 1993). Over 1.3 million full-time year-round workers earned no more than the minimum wage of $4.25 in 1995. From this perspective, perhaps as many as 20 million people might be considered "underemployed," even in times of economic growth.

As is the case with the extent of poverty, this statistical debate on unemployment represents ideological differences on the question of who is responsible. The implication of conservative arguments on unemployment rates is that competition for jobs is not so great as it seems, and therefore individual efforts to find work should suffice given the appropriate motivation. If less than 2 percent of the labor force is suffering from long-term unemployment, that hardly warrants massive government efforts to intervene in the job market.

As liberals and socialists interpret them, the figures indicate a serious economic problem that prevents workers from finding jobs, although socialists, unlike liberals, feel that mass unemployment is a necessary and inevitable outcome of capitalism. Of particular concern from either point of view is the severe impact of unemployment on specific groups: African-Americans and Hispanics have consistently higher rates of unemployment than whites. Joblessness is therefore a legitimate object of governmental action.

Inequity in Gender Pay

Perhaps the most significant but least acknowledged issue in relation

Table 12.3: Inequity in Gender Pay

A. Mean Earnings of Year-Round Full-Time Workers, Age 15+, 1996

Race	Male	Female
White	$43,118	$28,596
Black	31,126	25,576
Hispanic	26,790	22,523

B. Mean Earnings of Year-Round Full-Time Workers, Age 18+ , By Education, 1996

Education	Male	Female
All workers	$ 42,077	$28,355
Professional degree	112,873	90,711
College graduate	52,354	36,555
High School graduate	35,521	21,893
Less than 9th grade	20,153	15,150

Sources (A and B): U.S. Census Bureau
(http://www.census.gov/hhes/income/histinc., p.27, 29).

C. Median Usual Weekly Earnings of Full-Time Workers by Occupation, 1996

Occupation	Male	Female
Managerial and professional specialty	$ 908	$ 644
Technical, sales, admin. support	595	408
Service occupations	381	286
Precision production, craft, repair	562	389
Operators, fabricators, laborers	447	313
Farming, forestry, fishing	296	271

Source: U.S. Bureau of Labor Statistics (http://stats.bls.gov/news.release/wkyeng.to3).

to the labor force and welfare is unequal pay for men and women. Notwithstanding widespread public opinion to the contrary, the gap between men and women in the wage structure has changed very little over the last forty years. A slight decline in the average wage for men narrowed the gap somewhat beginning in the 1980s; but the fact remains that in 1994 women made up 42.8 percent of all full-time workers in major occupations and earned an average of 76.4 percent of the median weekly earnings of men. A similar income inequity holds true in each major occupational category. In fact, in only a handful of occupations do women earn 90 percent or more of men's average wage. Moreover, the higher the percentage of women in a particular job, the lower the wage. For example, men dominate higher-paid occupations such as engineering, medicine, law, construction, and skilled trades, while women are concentrated in low-paying positions in sales, clerical work, food service, clothing manufacture, and child care (U.S. Department of Labor 1990, 194–198).

As Table 12.3 indicates, women are consistently paid less than men even when they are in the same job and have the same educational background. Unless we are prepared to conclude, as perhaps a few conservatives do, that the market provides an accurate assessment of the value of women's work, these figures must reflect the effects of discrimination against women in the labor force.

Implications for Welfare

Until the changes of 1996, the liberal interpretation of all these problems guided the basic structure of the welfare system. On this interpretation, the extent of the problems is seen as indicating that lack of individual effort cannot be the primary explanation, as conservatives generally argue. A capitalist economy creates inequality, but liberals (unlike socialists) believe that large-scale poverty and unemployment is *not* an inevitable result. Rather, for historical and political reasons, certain groups of citizens suffer from personal or social disadvantages that make them less likely to find decent jobs. Minority groups suffer discrimination and have been exploited as low-wage labor. Women do not get equal pay for equal work. As Sar Levitan (1982, 11) summarizes it, "Despite canards about the link between laziness and poverty, most of the unemployed working-age poor are simply not employable either because of personal handicaps or because not enough jobs are available for them."

Liberals believe that the cause of poverty is no jobs and no money but feel that the needs of the poor differ as their individual situations differ. Thus they believe it is necessary for the government to establish a network of "categorical" programs, for which individuals qualify depending on the particular category of need they fall into. Overall, the welfare system still reflects this perspective.

This does not mean that liberals are satisfied with the welfare system. They are highly critical of its escalating costs, its inequities, and its inefficiencies, and they recognize that it may no longer serve the purposes that were intended when the programs were originally introduced. Nor do they necessarily reject the idea that welfare recipients must assume greater responsibility for improving their situation. Indeed, as mentioned earlier, many liberals have moved closer to conservatives on this issue. Nonetheless, liberals recognize a need for extensive government action to reduce levels of poverty and unemployment, including at least some kind of welfare system; and most liberals oppose TANF, which is based solidly on conservative assumptions about poverty and unemployment.

The Welfare System

The basic distinction among government aid programs is between what is called social insurance and what is called welfare. The former—Social Security, Medicare, and unemployment insurance—is funded through special payroll taxes. Age and payment of the tax for a specified period are the sole qualifications for Social Security and Medicare, which are administered by the federal government. Unemployed workers, if their former employer is covered, receive unemployment insurance regardless of their financial situation. Administration is shared by federal and state governments, the latter determining eligibility and benefit levels.

Welfare differs in two respects from social insurance. First, payments come out of general revenues. Second, individual eligibility depends on need and other criteria as defined by the government. Whether or not the perception is correct, it therefore has the connotation of a gift rather than a return on a paid premium, as is supposedly the case with social insurance.

There are five important welfare programs in the United States. Two of them, Medicaid and food stamps, offer "in-kind" benefits. The former, administered and financed by federal and state governments, pays medical bills for those poor enough to qualify; the latter, a federal program, provides recipients with a limited amount of vouchers to pay for food. A third program, Supplemental Security Income (SSI), is a cash program financed and administered by state and local governments, as was AFDC, which in some cases was administered by county governments as well. Fourth, TANF, which replaces AFDC, is a state-run program subsidized by federal block grants. Fifth, General Assistance is a program run and financed by the state governments. Although the housing programs discussed in Chapter 11 may be considered welfare, it should be noted that most welfare recipients do not receive housing aid of any kind.

Supplemental Security Income (SSI) was developed in 1974 by combining the separate welfare programs for the aged, blind, and disabled. A basic payment is made to qualifying individuals by the federal government to supplement payments under Social Security disability programs if those are inadequate. Federal SSI payments are in most cases further supplemented by the states. SSI has not created very much controversy because the aged, blind, and disabled are regarded by many as more deserving. The basic disability program under Social Security, however, was a target of tightened eligibility rules under the Reagan administration.

The programs known as welfare distributed over $225 billion in benefits in 1994, almost two-thirds of it for Medicaid. Although this figure represents no more than 7 percent of all governmental expenses nationwide, it often consumes a much larger proportion of the budget in particular states. Also, the figure does not include the cost of administering the programs.

Sixty Years of AFDC

Evaluating the reasoning behind the termination of Aid to Families with Dependent Children requires an understanding of how it worked. Designed in 1935 as part of the Social Security Act, AFDC was originally a small aid program for dependent children in female-headed families lacking alternative means of support. It was supposed to disappear as Social Security survivors' benefits and other welfare programs took hold. Instead, it became the biggest cash program; by the 1960s it had become by default a wage supplement program for working-poor single

Table 12.4: Welfare Recipients and Benefit Costs, 1994

	Average Number of Monthly Recipients (Millions)	Federal Funds (Billions)	State and Local Funds (Billions)
Medicaid	34.0	$ 82.1	$ 61.4
Food Stamps	28.9	25.6	1.8
AFDC	14.2	14.1	11.8
SSI	6.4	23.5	3.8
GA	1.1	--	3.3
TOTAL		145.3	82.1

Source: U.S. Dept. of Commerce, *Statistical Abstract of the U.S., 1997*, p. 375.

single parents.

Aid to Families with Dependent Children was a categorical grant-in-aid program. This means that the federal government committed itself to share its costs with any state choosing to implement the program, subject to federal regulations, which established certain ground rules concerning administration, benefits, and eligibility. States would have to operate their programs within those parameters in order to qualify for federal money.

In all states a lone parent with one or more dependent children and with income and property below a certain level qualified for AFDC. The Family Support Act of 1988 made short-term benefits available to two-parent families as well, but 85 percent of all recipients were divorced, deserted, or single mothers and their children. Each state set a "need standard," the amount required by a family to fulfill its needs of food, clothing, and shelter. That standard has been set rather arbitrarily: in 1993 in Virginia, for example, a family of three "needed" $393 monthly, while in Vermont such a family "needed" $1122 (DeNitto 1995, 189–190). The changes in welfare introduced in 1981 by the Reagan administration tightened eligibility by limiting it to families whose "countable" monthly income (after fixed deductions for child care and work expenses) did not exceed 150 percent of the need standard. This was later raised to 185 percent. Property ownership was generally limited to a house, a cheap car, personal effects, and a small amount of other personal property. Specifics varied from state to state.

Among the fifty states, there have been literally a dozen or more different methods of computing benefits, all of them variations on this formula: monthly AFDC benefit equals all or part of need standard *less* countable income. Thus in Massachusetts in 1993, a mother with two children earning up to $997 monthly would be eligible to apply. However, unless her net income was less than the need standard, she would receive no benefits. In fact, she would receive the maximum payment of $539 per month only if she had no countable earned income at all. Nowhere in the United States could she have received an AFDC check larger than $923, and for that she would have had to move to Alaska. Benefits were particularly low in the South: for instance, the maximum grant was $120 in Mississippi, $190 in Louisiana, and $204 in Arkansas (DeNitto 1995, 189–190).

Before 1981, the woman in this example could have kept part of her welfare check even if her earnings increased. As a result of changes that year, her check was decreased dollar for dollar if she earned a wage. The point of this change was to force welfare mothers to choose between work and AFDC. Most chose work, even though it hurt them economically.

In recent years, even under AFDC, states began to apply stronger restrictions and limitations on eligibility and benefits. They moved toward increasing economic pressure on welfare recipients by imposing time limits on welfare benefits, refusing to increase benefits for illegitimate children born to a welfare mother (the "family cap"), cutting off benefits for children not attending school, and tightening work requirements. Although such measures are politically popular, they are based on negative stereotypes of an "irresponsible" welfare population that may not in fact be accurate.

Work and Welfare
Ideology can become mythology when it is based on beliefs regarding welfare that are demonstrably untrue. This is particularly so in relation to welfare. Among the myths regarding are the following: (1) that most welfare recipients do not or cannot work; (2) that most recipients are dependent on welfare for a long time; and (3) that the working and the welfare poor are two different groups.

Over the last decade volumes of research have been published showing conclusively that (in the words of one book's title) "work and welfare go together." Most welfare recipients work at least intermittently, since welfare benefits alone cannot support a family. Indeed, many work "off the books" so that their benefits will not be reduced; this is the most common form of welfare fraud. The average duration on welfare at any one time is about two years; only a small proportion of recipients remain on welfare for an uninterrupted period of five years or more. The *Boston Globe* (1 May 1989) reported a study by the Census Bureau in 1989, which showed that nearly one-fifth of all Americans, including one-fourth of all children, received welfare at some point during the period 1983–1986 (1 May 1989). Thus, there is no sizable "underclass" of welfare recipients. Rather, large numbers of women working in the low-wage labor market use welfare as a stopgap during times of crisis.

The central issue for AFDC, then, may be what some researchers have called the "feminization of poverty": women's wages are lower than men's, and poor women heading families thus often find it necessary to resort to welfare to support themselves and their children.

This discussion should make one point clear: welfare has not been a generous handout to the idle poor. It is to a considerable extent a subsidy for female heads of families in low-wage jobs. Nor are there any "welfare Cadillacs," at least not on public funds. Even with food stamps (which generally add around $200 to $250 monthly) and Medicaid, almost no family can raise itself above the poverty level on welfare. Moreover, under AFDC, when earned income went beyond a certain amount, a family might find itself with not only less cash, but a total loss of Medicaid, which is not prorated. Thus AFDC families were in the tricky position of calculating just how much they would keep from each additional dollar earned on the job. In the language analysis of welfare policy, this is called the "notch problem": at a certain point a welfare family hits a notch where an additional dollar of income may actually cost several hundreds of dollars in welfare.

Changing the Welfare System

As stated earlier, the welfare reform law of 1996 ended AFDC and thus also ended the commitment of the federal government to aid low-income families. The federal government will now provide block grants to the states, which will determine their own eligibility requirements and benefit levels. But it also imposes several new mandates. Each state must put half of all its adult recipients to work by 2002, or else its block grant will be reduced. Welfare assistance funded with federal money will be limited to a maximum of five years in a lifetime (subject to a limited number of exemptions), and able-bodied adults will have to work after two years (although this is subject to waiver for mothers of young children). Aside from these limitations, state governments are thus free to invent their own welfare programs, but they cannot count on any consistent, specific amount of federal funding to assist them, since block grants change from year to year. Initially, certain states, including those in New England, are expected to benefit because of the way the grants are being calculated. The new welfare law also has some limited provision for additional contingency funding if the economy declines. Ultimately, however, TANF will most likely provide less money than categorical grants under AFDC. Thus the new state welfare programs are most likely to be less generous and more restrictive. Indeed, as of early 1997, about half the states submitting TANF plans to the federal government had more stringent time limits and work requirements than those required by the new law (Springfield, Massachusetts *Sunday Republican*, 23 February 1997).

Given the complexity, inequity, and irrationality of AFDC, it is small wonder that the program had few defenders. The real question is whether TANF is an acceptable replacement. An evaluation requires a review of the ideological perspectives on welfare.

Conservative Approach

Conservatives feel that official statistics on poverty and unemployment are overestimates, and that in any case these conditions are primarily caused by individual lack of motivation and effort or by insufficient incentives for self-improvement. Therefore, the ultimate goal is the elimination of the welfare system. Economic growth is seen as the ultimate solution to poverty; attempts by the government to alleviate poverty are said to have made it worse. On the basis of his analysis of the trend lines of different measures of poverty, Charles Murray concludes:

> Changes in gross national product have a very strong inverse relation to changes in poverty. As GNP increases, poverty decreases. . . . The effects of economic growth [in the 1960s and 1970s] did indeed trickle down to the lowest economic levels of society. But the flip side of this finding is that social welfare expenditures did not have an effect on poverty. . . . The Great Society reforms exacerbated many of the conditions they sought to alleviate. (1982, 11–12)

Until a growing market economy makes welfare unnecessary, some conservatives, such as Milton Friedman, have proposed a negative income tax (NIT) as a transitional program. The NIT would cash out all existing social insurance and welfare programs and replace them with a single program of outright cash grants, varying inversely with earned income and administered by the Internal Revenue Service. This was to some extent the basis of President Nixon's proposal of 1969 known as the Family Assistance Plan, which failed to pass Congress.

In the short run, conservatives believe that whatever welfare system exists ought to be strictly limited to those who cannot work in the regular job market, and that it should be structured to provide incentives for work and disincentives for continued dependence on welfare. The program most consistent with this is "workfare," an essential element of TANF, which requires recipients of welfare either to work off all or part of their benefits at public jobs paying at or near the minimum wage, or to participate in a variety of job training programs. A number of states began to apply this program during the 1970s and 1980s, usually limiting it to recipients of General Assistance. Ronald Reagan put workfare on the federal agenda in 1981, when he unsuccessfully proposed mandatory state workfare programs. In 1988, however, the Family Support Act was signed into law. It required states to implement "job opportunities and basic skills training" programs (JOBS) for most welfare recipients, including mothers of children over the age of three. These JOBS programs were to include two of the following: job search activities, on-the-job training, wage-subsidized private sector work, or working off benefits at minimum wage rates in the public sector. Workfare became at least nominally the law of the land. The states, however, were somewhat lax in developing fully funded individual programs consistent with the federal mandate. This has not been the case with TANF, since for TANF, unlike AFDC, federal block grants depend on compliance.

The welfare law of 1996 is essentially a conservative proposal, emphasizing state rather than federal responsibility and imposing work requirements as a means of encouraging and even forcing individuals to support themselves and take responsibility for their families.

In the long run, free-market conservatives feel that less government involvement in the economy will help produce economic growth, which should ultimately cure poverty and unemployment. This will provide opportunities for those who prefer work to welfare, and make it possible to impose work requirements on those who supposedly prefer welfare.

Liberal Approach

Liberals believe that poverty and unemployment are perhaps even more extensive than official figures estimate, and they recognize that women do not receive equal pay for equal work. These inequalities are generated by flaws in the economic system which can be rectified at least to some extent by government action. Liberals acknowledge the inadequacies of the welfare system but are divided on how to proceed. All share the view that the primary initiatives have to come from the federal government. Many would agree with the economist Henry J. Aaron (1973, 69): "The reason [it is] difficult to find a plan that provides universal benefits at a level regarded as reasonable that preserves work incentives and that is not vastly more expensive . . . is that no such plan exists or can be devised. These objectives are mutually inconsistent." Thus perhaps only incremental reform is possible.

This was the goal of the Manpower Development and Training Act of 1962, which helped states and localities administer and pay for programs of job training and placement. The work incentive program (WIN) of 1967 attempted to do this on a larger scale, with a particular focus on welfare recipients. The Comprehensive Employment and Training Act (CETA), enacted in 1974, provided federal grants to state and local governments for training people without jobs or on welfare and then employing them in public service positions. None of these programs realized its goals, largely because the private sector jobs for which people were being trained simply did not materialize. Ultimately, all of them were terminated. Massachusetts attempted its own experiment in training programs, known as "ET" (Employment and Training), which offered a variety of choices and subsidies to welfare mothers. It became something of a national model and a point of pride for Governor Michael Dukakis, who cited its ostensible successes in his presidential campaign in 1988. Yet it was not clear whether ET deserved credit or whether it belonged to the so-called "Massachusetts miracle" of the 1980s.

In the past, liberals have advocated more comprehensive approaches, such as setting federal standards for welfare benefits and perhaps placing welfare fully under federal control. In 1977, President Jimmy Carter's "Program for Better Jobs and Income" moved in this direction, providing for a combination of the separate welfare programs and an expanded public service employment and training program, but Congress refused to pass it into law. Basically, comprehensive welfare reform raised too many difficult political and ideological issues all at once. Further liberal attempts in that direction were in any case effectively stopped with the election of Ronald Reagan in 1980.

Most but by no means all liberals opposed TANF because they felt that the federal government should have the responsibility to guarantee assistance for the poor, and that the states either could not afford or would not be willing to fulfill that responsibility to the same extent. The result would thus be further impoverishment of children in low-income families. On the other hand, for a variety of political reasons many liberals have abandoned their usual proposals and moved closer to the conservative point of view on welfare. This appears to have been President Clinton's motivation in signing the legislation.

Socialist Approach

Socialist proposals have something in common with the ideas of those liberals who prefer a total restructuring of the welfare system. If huge welfare caseloads are seen as an outgrowth of systemic unemployment and poverty, and the private sector is incapable of providing enough jobs no matter how much economic growth there is, then one solution is a government guarantee of employment to anyone who wants to work and cannot find a job. Modest and only partly successful efforts to accomplish this have been made. The Employment Act of 1946 and the Full Employment and Balanced Growth Act of 1978 are federal laws. The former was originally introduced with a declaration that "all Americans able to work and seeking work have the right to useful, remunerative, regular, and full-time employment." The latter started out in much the same way. As a result, they both came under attack from conservatives and the business community and ended up as vaguely worded commitments to expanded job opportunities.

Advocates of "full employment" define it as a regular job at a decent wage for every adult who wants one. Both socialists and liberals who favor this envision a need for government action to accomplish it, but they differ on the means. Liberals favor reliance on the private sector, with transitional albeit useful and well-paid jobs in the public sector as a last resort. The CETA program and perhaps the emergency employment programs of the New Deal are their models. Socialists go much further. As economists Paul Sweezy and Harry Magdoff put it (1983, 7), "The capitalist system is sick, and persistence of mass unemployment is a chief symptom of this sickness. Put simply, private enterprise has not been able to provide enough jobs to keep pace with the growth in the population, and government has been unwilling to do so."

A socialist program to transform the welfare system could take two approaches. One might be to recognize rearing one's own children as a type of employment and subsidize single parents who choose to do so. Another might be an expanded public sector providing permanent and socially useful jobs, focusing on goods and services that are not adequately provided by the private sector. This would have to include a revision of the wage structure to guarantee equal pay for equal work for both sexes, complemented with the necessary supportive services, such as health insurance and child care, to enable women to seek paid employment. With all this in place, welfare would then become a residual program for those actually unable to work. Needless to say, this would obviously require much more government involvement in the economy and would certainly create competition for private industry, which could be expected to fight any such program bitterly.

The Future of Welfare Policy

The welfare system has been a patchwork of categorical programs which act as temporary wage subsidies for the working poor, even if they are not recognized as such by the general public. Work and welfare go together because it is difficult for the poor, especially female family heads, to live off either one alone. The jobs programs favored by liberals have a poor track record. The massive cutbacks introduced in 1981 have apparently only forced more people to work for less. Socialist alternatives would require a fundamental reordering of societal priorities.

Temporary Assistance to Needy Families will drastically alter the welfare system by converting it from a categorical grant program to a block grant program, although its patchwork pattern of coverage remains. States will now have the freedom to design their own welfare programs with less federal regulation, though also with less financial assistance. Many governors, especially Republicans, have welcomed this trade-off, but advocates for the poor have criticized the proposal, arguing that the states have even less incentive than the federal government to provide adequately for low-income families. It is, of course, too early to predict what kind of welfare programs this reform will produce in the states. Also, there appears to have been a significant reduction in the welfare rolls in many states as the new programs have developed, but analysts have not yet been able to explain it.

Beyond this, comprehensive overhaul of the system may still be needed, but conservatives, liberals, and socialists are far apart on alternatives. For now, the various conservative options have center stage. But they do not provide a full solution, not least because they do not deal with the issue of health care, which is another major complication in developing a solution to the "welfare mess."

The Health Care System

The health care system in the United States embodies several striking contradictions. It is a highly fragmented private industry, yet it operates like a monopoly in pricing its services. Power in this industry is increasingly concentrated, even without any central planning body or multinational corporations. The system is able to provide high-quality care but distributes it unevenly and inequitably. The results are skyrocketing costs, little public accountability, and inadequate health care for millions of people. The role of state and local governments now is to regulate the industry, provide supplemental and quite limited public health services, and partly finance the system through Medicaid. The contradictions and the ensuing problems make this role difficult and expensive to handle.

Cost and Accountability

Over $950 billion was spent on health care in 1994, more than double the amount spent ten years earlier. In fact, health care costs have gone up faster than almost any other component in the Consumer Price Index. The main reason for this up to now has been the absence of any requirement or incentive to hold costs down, and the presence of numerous incentives to allow costs to increase. Health care providers decide on their own what services to deliver and what to charge for them. There is no real competition to keep prices down and no consistent or comprehensive control by public and private insurers over prices. Thus the more services doctors and hospitals provide, the more income they receive; and few questions are asked by the patients being charged. Medical care has also become capital intensive—that is, dependent on technology to do its work. Hospitals vie with each other to buy the latest high priced machinery, doctors are financially rewarded for conducting expensive medical tests, and pharmaceutical companies enjoy huge profits on new drugs. Society pays the bill, but without having much to say about where the money goes. The cost of health care is therefore to a considerable extent out of control by the public.

Hospitals and insurance companies, not physicians, now dominate the medical industry. Institutional power determines health care policy in America. In the 1970s, one highly critical analysis described these dominant institutions as "medical empires," whose main motivation is increasing power and prestige, not to mention professional salaries (Kotelchuk 1976). The expansion of what is known as "managed care" in the 1990s is leading to a further consolidation of the health care industry, with an emphasis on cost-cutting. That task has fallen primarily to insurance companies, which increasingly determine the type and extent of health care to be offered by providers. The major nongovernmental source of health care financing is the private insurance company known as Blue Cross-Blue Shield, whose history and administrative structure is closely tied in with the larger hospitals.

Although there is considerable state and local regulation of health care, it is usually executed by boards whose members have strong connections to the industry they are supposed to regulate. Individual physicians are accountable to patients only through inefficient, expensive malpractice suits. Physicians do compete for patients, but usually not by cutting prices. Overall it can be said that the health care system is relatively well insulated from accountability to the community.

Distribution of Health Care

Low-income individuals, residents of rural areas, members of minority groups, and many young people are at a disadvantage in terms of access to good-quality medical care. Although Medicare and Medicaid have improved conditions overall, poor people still suffer disproportionately from chronic health problems. Rural residents have a hard time finding and getting to physicians, who have no financial or professional incentives to locate in rural areas. Much the same can be said about inner-city areas. Infant mortality rates are a commonly used indicator of health care standards. The high U.S. rate has been falling steadily, but that of other nations has been falling faster; the rate is considerably higher for blacks than whites.

Many people who are neither rural, poor, nor black lose access to health care because of unemployment, since most people in the United States receive insurance coverage through their jobs. Those employed part-time or in small businesses often have no health benefits. Thus over 40 million people have no medical insurance of any kind. Young people in particular, no longer covered by family plans and unable to find jobs which provide health benefits, are especially at risk in that regard. Local public hospitals, which have historically dealt with this problem, are under tremendous pressure from the fiscal crisis, and many have closed or been sold; this is especially true in urban areas.

Health care in America is rationed by the market. Those who have the means to pay the price receive care, to the exclusion of those who do not. As a result, there is a strong correlation between economic status and health in the United States.

Medicaid

The United States is just about alone among industrialized nations in lacking some kind of national health insurance program. Instead, it has two categorical programs, Medicare and Medicaid. The former covers the elderly under Social Security; the latter is a grant-in-aid welfare program financed from general revenues.

The battle over health insurance had continued for decades when Medicare and Medicaid were signed into law by President Lyndon Johnson in 1965. Previous efforts on the state or federal level had been defeated by the powerful medical lobbies as well as by conservative opponents. Medicaid was designed as a categorical grant-in-aid program providing federal grants to states that set up a medical assistance program consistent with federal guidelines.

States seeking federal grants for Medicaid are required to offer coverage to those receiving AFDC or SSI. States may also receive federal grants for Medicaid services to other low income individuals and families within the categories covered by TANF and SSI, and for services to the "medically needy," those who are not low-income but who have incurred large medical expenses and who meet certain state-established standards. All fifty states have Medicaid programs; most offer aid to the medically needy (U.S. Department of Health and Human Services 1990, 61–69). The greatest change in Medicaid over the last twenty-five years has been in whom it covers:

> Medicaid was originally intended to provide medical services to low income women and children, the disabled and the impoverished elderly, in contrast to the federal Medicare program, designed as a health insurance plan for the elderly. But the Medicaid program has evolved, and is continuing to evolve, into a program of much greater scope than originally envisioned. Since its inception in the mid-1960s, Medicaid has developed into the largest third-party payer of long-term care (primarily a service provided to the elderly) in the

United States. (Hutchison 1990, 16–17)

This change has had a major impact on how much and for what purpose money is spent for Medicaid. Although in 1994 almost two-thirds of all Medicaid recipients were families on welfare, they incurred less than one-third of the total cost of $108 billion. The 11 percent of recipients who were elderly and generally in nursing homes incurred the same proportion. Low income disabled clients amounted to 15 percent of the caseload but nearly 40 percent of the cost (U.S. Department of Commerce 1996).

The Cost of Medicaid. The same forces that have escalated the costs of medical care have pushed Medicaid costs ever higher. Until 1981, states were required to pay after the fact whatever "reasonable" costs were incurred by health care providers. Even with greater cost controls since that time, the fiscal crisis has made the financial commitment related to Medicaid especially painful. Medicaid expenditures grew from $1.3 billion in 1966 to almost $145 billion in 1994, outpacing enrollment growth and inflation. Medicaid's share of state budgets went up from less than 3 percent in 1966 to 15 percent in 1990, varying from 4 percent in Alaska to 19 percent in Rhode Island. Annual per capita Medicaid costs for the elderly and disabled averaged $6,700 in 1990, more than six times the average cost for AFDC families (Dubin 1992, 5 ff).

Medicaid has therefore become a "budget-buster" for many states, although the increases began to level off in the mid-1990s. The combination of higher medical costs, an aging population, and federal mandates has made Medicaid a major and highly uncontrollable factor in worsening fiscal crises.

Medicaid: The State Response. During the first round of fiscal problems encountered by the states in the mid-1970s, they began to cut back on Medicaid by tightening eligibility or trimming benefits. In 1981, cutbacks in social services by the Reagan administration included reductions in federal reimbursements for Medicaid but also allowed states a freer hand in determining how Medicaid dollars would be spent.

State governments have made numerous attempts to control Medicaid costs since that time. "Fixed price contracting" is one alternative: states contract with health care providers, sometimes using competitive bidding, to serve Medicaid patients at an agree-upon annual cost. Other methods have involved experiments with managed care programs such as health maintenance organizations (HMOs), taxing hospitals to fund un-compensated health care pools (funds for indigent patients), mandates for expanded employer health insurance coverage, and various state-sponsored health insurance projects. But according to one analyst of these reforms, "Despite the states' best efforts, even the most innovative programs have not contained health care costs. . . . In fact, isolated efforts to control costs may even exacerbate the problem. Most 'solutions' involve shifting costs to another payer elsewhere in the system" (Hutchison 1991, 14).

Alternatives to Medicaid

The states are restricted by the federal structure of the Medicaid program and their own limited resources from doing anything more than tinkering with reforms in providing health care. Comprehensive change requires federal initiatives, although a few states, such as Vermont, Minnesota, and Oregon, have been experimenting with full-scale state health insurance programs. Although there is considerable support for such changes, no consensus exists on what ought to be done.

Conservative Approach. Conservatives see the problem of health care as a result of "market failure": insufficient competition among providers, which breeds inefficiency and exorbitant prices. The culprit is the system of financing, which generally reimburses physicians, hospitals, and nursing homes for whatever they decide to charge. Medicaid and Medicare are part of this, as is the Blue Cross–Blue Shield insurance monopoly. More government control would only make matters worse by hindering competition even more. The solution lies in government policies that would encourage the operation of a competitive market in health care by creating incentives for cost cutting. Deregulation of the health care industry to promote competition would be a first step. Changes in the tax laws to encourage employers to offer workers a menu of health care insurance policies would facilitate choice and reduce costs. Health care vouchers could replace Medicaid and Medicare, offering the poor and elderly similar choices.

The results, conservatives believe, would be a proliferation of diverse insurance plans along with the growth of physicians' group practices, HMOs, and competitive for-profit hospitals, all of which would increase incentives for a more rational and efficient allocation of health care without government interference. The ultimate prescription to cure the inefficiency of government-protected private monopolies is a stiff dose of the free market.

Liberal Approach. Liberals do not see health care as purely a market commodity and thus believe that market principles do not apply. They do not, however, generally propose that health should be a public service like education. They recognize that the present system does not work well, and many have proposed some form of mandatory national health insurance as an alternative to current categorical programs.

The first such proposals arose during the New Deal and, except for strong opposition from the medical profession, might have been part of Social Security when it was enacted in 1935. President Harry Truman tried several times to gain passage of such a plan but failed. In 1993, President Bill Clinton once again revived the issue, but a consensus was hard to achieve, and his plan failed. Even among liberals there are differences on how such a plan should be structured, especially whether employers should be mandated to provide insurance along with a supplementary government program for all noninsured citizens, or whether the federal government should itself become the insurer in a "single-payer" plan.

Socialist Approach.

> National health insurance will fail because it fails to face the fundamental questions about our health system--control, accountability, accessibility, priorities, responsibility to the community. . . . The only way to fundamentally change the health system . . . is to take power over health care away from people who now control it. Not merely the funding of the health system, but the system itself must be made public. (Kotelchuk 1976, 448)

Socialists, like liberals, reject a market approach to health care, but they go further, advocating that health care be organized as a government-run public service, not unlike the National Health Service in Britain. This alternative envisions health care as a right, guaranteed by government, whose organization and allocation is planned by the community. It would essentially nationalize the health care industry as well as abolish present government categorical health programs. If that is not politically achievable, socialists would favor a "single-payer" national health insurance plan.

Conclusion

Choosing a direction for welfare policy requires, first of all, a choice among analyses of the extent and causes of poverty, unemployment, and wage inequality, and second, a decision as to whether health care ought to be a commodity or a human right. In addition, one must determine whether the free market, the government, or some combination of the two offers the best mechanism for developing a new approach to welfare policy.

Conservatives believe that free-market capitalism can provide the economic growth that will reduce poverty and unemployment and can stimulate the competition that will reduce the costs of health care and improve individual access to medical services. In the meantime, they argue for strict limitations on who may receive welfare and under what conditions. Liberals see a need for federal action to improve the chances for welfare recipients to find private sector jobs, and to guarantee directly by one means or another that everyone has some kind of health insurance. Socialists and some liberals advocate a full-employment economy and government action to ensure that women earn equal pay with men for equal work; unlike liberals, they advocate a system of socialized medicine to rationalize the health care system.

In the late 1990s, welfare reform on the state level was being oriented toward the conservative program of a highly restrictive—liberals would say punitive—approach in defining eligibility and calculating benefits. In 1996, by implementing TANF, the federal government abandoned the commitment to welfare programs that it had begun during the New Deal.

The fiscal crisis and uncertain economic conditions guarantee that these issues will not be resolved without further government action; but given the ideological differences, consensus will be very difficult to achieve.

Chapter 13: The Politics of Education

Public education is one of the most vital of all governmental services, and it is primarily the responsibility of state and local governments, which administer and finance public schools, colleges, and universities. The importance of this responsibility creates controversy as to how it should be implemented. With tremendous disagreements concerning the effectiveness of the educational system, there is consequently a great deal of conflict over what policy directions state and local governments should take.

Issues in Public Education

Public education is the function of state and local government that entails the greatest expense and has the greatest impact on people. In 1993 it cost $240 billion to send over 40 million young people to public schools. Nearly 10 million more attended public colleges and universities at a cost to states and localities of $80 billion (US Dept. of Commerce 1997). As indicated in Chapter 7, 40 percent of state employees work in public higher education, and half of all local employees work in the elementary and secondary school system.

Conflict and controversy have always raged over the schools. Three issues have been especially contentious: (1) financing and administering the schools, (2) determining the purpose of public education, and (3) dealing with racial, gender, religious, and ethnic differences. Although these are political issues, in the public mind education and politics are not supposed to mix. Somehow the schools are supposed to remain above partisan and ideological conflict. In actuality, they cannot and do not. The development of public education has been shaped by politics, and its future direction is a political issue. Conflicts have arisen among different groups with different points of view which, although varying in relative intensity over time, have shaped the history of public education in the United States.

The Governance and Finance of Public Education

In theory, the structural decentralization and fragmentation that characterize the governance of American public schools should provide maximum access for participation by citizens. Yet by and large, power over the schools is increasingly concentrated in the hands of state government with relatively little direct input locally and decreasing levels of local control. In addition, the system of school finance creates serious inequities among states, communities, and even neighborhoods in terms of their ability to provide a high-quality education for all young people.

School Boards. Although state governments can and do in varying degrees direct overall state education policy, local boards of education run the schools on a day-to-day level. In the fall of 1789 Boston acted under a newly passed state law to establish the first popularly elected school committee. This was to become the pattern for the states, and ultimately for the nation. Most of America's 16,000 school districts have an elected or appointed board of education with financial and administrative responsibility for the district's public schools. In practice this means formulating a school budget and appointing a superintendent of schools. About half the states have some kind of intermediate governing board between the school district and the state, usually on the county level.

No nationwide generalization can be made about the actual power of the local boards. In some states they are relatively constrained by state laws; in others they have considerable discretionary power. Boards vary in their independence from local budgetary decisions. Some boards are connected at least implicitly to one or the other political party or to particular local interest groups. Board members may be inclined to defer to professionals' judgment or may assert their own authority. Particular decisions by school boards often depend on the state's laws and the particular constellation of political power in the community. Generally speaking, however, by virtue of their usual middle-class makeup and middle-of-the-road ideology, boards are not inclined to go too far outside what they interpret as the community consensus. If decentralization is supposed to encourage innovation and experimentation, the local school boards do not serve as good examples. In the 1990s, however, the so-called "Christian right" often ran candidates for school boards as a means of imposing its conservative educational agenda on the public schools.

State Government and Education. Local boards operate within the framework of state laws, and the execution of those laws is the responsibility of the state educational administrative apparatus: the chief state school officer (CSSO), the state board of education, and its staff. The CSSO, known by a variety of titles such as commissioner or state superintendent, is responsible for the formulation and implementation of state educational policy within the limits of his or her delegated authority. This officer works with the state board of education. In a majority of the states the board is appointed by the governor, and about half these boards select the CSSO. In most other states the board is elected, and the CSSO is either elected or appointed by the governor. Usually, as is the case on the local level, the CSSO is expected to assume policy leadership with the cooperation and under the supervision of the board. The administrative details are attended to by the staff of the state department of education.

State officials must guarantee that local officials operate within the limits of state law. States vary in the degree of centralized control. Hawaii, for example, is a unitary system. The entire state is financially and administratively one school district. In matters such as teacher certification, school accreditation, and special and vocational education, most states exercise a great deal of control. Indeed, state mandates have become especially significant in the education of special needs students. In other concerns, such as curriculum, teacher employment, and school construction, there is considerable variation. For example, most southern states apply statewide courses of study and limit textbook selection, whereas in the Northeast and Midwest these issues are in good measure local options.

The school reforms of the last fifteen years have strengthened the trend toward centralization, especially in curriculum and course requirements. Evaluation of this trend is not possible outside a context of educational goals and values. It is the preferred alternative of those who feel that only the state can guarantee uniform high standards, as well as a certain degree of educational equality. Advocates of the educational rights of minorities, including handicapped students, see state intervention as the means of achieving their goals. Proponents of decentralization feel that it enables the community to control its schools more directly and thus serve its own particular needs; they are particularly concerned about the increasing use of "unfunded mandates," state requirements, especially in the area of special education, that cost localities money they are unable to raise. To a considerable extent, the dispute over which level of government should control the schools is intertwined with the issue of who should pay for them.

School Finance. In 1979, for the first time, state governments surpassed local governments as the prime source of revenue for the nation's public schools. Since that time, the proportion of state and local funding has remained roughly even. In 1996, states paid 45 percent of the costs, local governments paid 48 percent and the federal government a mere 7 percent (U.S. Department of Education 1996). This was the culmination of a trend that had begun in the 1930s.

The discussion of the property tax in Chapter 10 noted its inconsistencies and inequities. Since it is the mainstay of local funds for public schools, this has meant tremendous disparities in the ability of communities to pay for education. Localities with low property values either have to charge exorbitant property taxes or provide inadequate schooling; wealthy towns and cities need not exert themselves. Jonathan Kozol condemns what he calls "savage inequalities" in school systems, resulting in large part from an inequitable funding system. Describing the appalling conditions of public schools in poor and minority communities such as East Saint Louis, Illinois, he asks,

> Why not spend on children here at least what we would be investing in their education if they lived within a wealthy district? . . . Wouldn't this be natural behavior in an affluent society that seems to value fairness in so many other areas of life: Is fairness less important to Americans today than in some earlier times? Is it viewed as slightly tiresome and incompatible with hard-nosed values? What do Americans believe about equality? (1991, 41)

State governments do make efforts to equalize the burden through aid to school districts, although these efforts are modest and inconsistent and their extent varies from state to state. Certain states depend less on local taxes than do others: as of 1996, the school systems of Washington, North Carolina, Alabama, New Mexico, and Michigan, among others, were mostly funded with state aid. Illinois, Massachusetts, Connecticut, and New York school systems were heavily dependent on local funding. Hawaii's system is almost entirely state-funded, whereas 90 percent of New Hampshire's school money has up to now come from local taxes(U. S. Department of Commerce 1997, 170). This does not necessarily correlate with the quality of schools statewide, nor with per capita

Fig. 13.1: Inequality of School Funding in Metropolitan Areas, 1992–1993

New York City

Jericho	$15,453
Bronxville	$13,559
Levittown	$ 9,792
Mount Vernon	$ 9,075
New York City	$ 7,313

Chicago

New Trier High School	$12,590
Niles North High School	$10,858
Winnetka K-8	$ 7,436
Wilmette K-8	$ 6,074
Chicago K-12	$ 5,568

Source: Stan Karp, et al., eds. *Funding for Justice,* Milwaukee: Rethinking Schools, 1997, pp. 26–27

spending for education overall. Rather, it is an indication of how far state governments will go to ensure some measure of equity in school finance.

Each state has its own particular way of distributing the aid. The oldest and most widely used formula is the "foundation plan," which sets a statewide per pupil minimum expenditure and also sets a minimum standard for local property tax rates or school expenditures. The state then compensates localities whose assessed valuation is too low to generate the revenue to meet the per pupil amount by itself. Other methods are even more complex, but all aim to one extent or another to shift state aid to poorer communities. Short of the full state funding which exists in Hawaii, a real effort at equity would mean high per capita expenditures, heavy reliance on state funds, and a highly redistributive aid formula. Possibly no state meets all those criteria. As a result, there is still significant fiscal inequality among the nation's school districts, which does tend to lead to unequal levels of educational effectiveness.

Over the last fifteen years, courts in many states have stepped in to redress the balance. One of the first instances, in 1971, was in California, where the state supreme court ruled that the system of school finance inherently violated state and federal constitutional guarantees. The state was thus forced by the ruling, and by the impact of Proposition 13, to increase its share of the budget for public education. The fiscal crisis of the 1990s, however, has pushed California in the opposite direction, leading to a severe deterioration in the quality of its schools. The U.S. Supreme Court, on the other hand, has refused to intervene. In a 5-to-4 decision in 1973 (*Rodriguez v. San Antonio, Texas*), the court rejected the contention that a system of school finance based on property taxes violated the Constitution. In effect, it concluded that there was no national right to an equal education, financially speaking. Ultimately the Texas courts stepped in and forced the state legislature to make amends. Indeed, a number of legislatures have reformed their state school systems in anticipation of such court rulings. Perhaps the most radical of such initiatives—indeed, some called it socialist—was "Act 60," passed in Vermont in 1997. This law abolished local property taxes and implemented a uniform statewide property tax to fund public schools on an even per-student basis. This meant that property taxes increased in the wealthy communities, but the resulting revenue was redistributed to poorer communities.

Federal Aid. In 1965, the Elementary and Secondary Education Act (ESEA) became law, climaxing more than a century of struggle over the issue of federal aid to education. Title I was its main component:

> The Congress hereby declares it to be the policy of the United States to provide financial assistance . . . to local educational agencies serving areas of concentrations of children from low-income families to expand and improve their educational programs by various means . . . which contribute particularly to meeting the special educational needs of educationally deprived children. (Van Geel 1976, 46)

In 1982 ESEA Title I became Chapter I of the Educational Consolidation and Improvement Act, which also combined twenty-eight other categorical aid to education programs into one block grant under Chapter II. Funding was also cut back to a significant degree. A new aid distribution formula shifted a good deal of money away from urban school districts. Thus the concept of federal involvement in public education to mitigate fiscal inequities was severely weakened. The federal government continues to play only a minimal role in public education.

The Purpose of Public Education

"For over 200 years [until 1865] Americans had looked to their schools and schoolmasters to solve their social, economic, and political problems. From the beginning the schools had been viewed as the panacea—first to preserve civilization, then to prepare for the unexpected, and finally to guarantee good government" (Perkinson 1968, 12). Americans still have high expectations of what their schools can accomplish to improve society but are sharply divided as to exactly what the specific goals ought to be.

Schools and Equality. There has always been disagreement about the role of public education in promoting social and political equality. On the one hand, some early proponents showed "a tendency to stress the conservative role of educational institutions in overcoming an excess of public liberty. . . . An informed obedience on the part of the people was at least as important as their particular freedoms" (Welter 1962, 27–28). On the other hand, Thomas Jefferson, who unsuccessfully struggled all his adult life for a comprehensive public education system in Virginia, saw the schools as a means of protecting the people from a potentially tyrannical government. An even more radical view was expressed by the Workingmen's Party of Philadelphia in the 1830s:

> The original element of despotism is a monopoly of talent which consigns the multitude to comparative ignorance, and secures the balance of knowledge on the side of the rich and the rulers. If then the healthy existence of a free government be . . . rooted in the will of the American people, it follows as a necessary consequence of a government based upon that will that this monopoly should be broken up and that the means of equal knowledge—the only security for equal liberty—should be rendered by legal provision the common property of all classes. . . . Until the means of equal instruction be equally secured to all, liberty is but an unmeaning word and equality an empty shadow. (Carnegie Commission 1973, 28)

To some extent the intensity of this conflict at first kept states from taking decisive steps to establish public schools. In 1784 the University of the State of New York was set up as the control agency for a unified school system. Five years later Massachusetts passed a law requiring towns to set up public elementary schools. Yet it took forty or fifty years until there was any real development of a public education system on the local level in either state.

A particularly intense partisan conflict over the schools arose in

Massachusetts between Whigs and Democrats. The Whigs in general favored education as a means of social control; the Democrats followed the more egalitarian Jeffersonian tradition. Horace Mann, a Whig who was the founder of the state's public school system, started off by fighting for schools as a means of ending "the mobs, the riots, the burnings, the lynchings perpetrated by the men of the present day . . . because of their vicious or defective education." To accommodate the Democrats, however, he ultimately changed his tune, describing public schools as "the great equalizer of the conditions of men—the balance wheel of the social machinery" (Perkinson 1976, 63, 86). Similar conflicts and compromises were played out in other states, and gradually public education expanded, although largely in the Northeast. The southern states instituted only "pauper schools" before the Civil War. The establishment of public high schools did not become widespread until late in the nineteenth century.

The struggle between elitists and democrats in public education has marked its whole history. In the early twentieth century, adherents of the social and educational philosophy of John Dewey contended, with mixed success, for their ideas of a more democratic "progressive" education. Advocates of a "tracked" system fought for the separation of vocational and academic schools rather than a common education for everyone. The 1950s saw a greater concern for gifted students, the 1960s for disadvantaged students, and the 1970s for disabled students. During the 1980s, and continuing into the 1990s, the banner of "excellence" was raised in the battle for school reform. The question of whether the public schools can or should promote greater social and political equality is still at the core of the politics of education.

Education and the Economy. A major impetus for change in the school system has come from the demands of a changing economy. Economic development is seen by many people as directly related to the quality of education.

A good deal of legislation in aid of education has been in response to the perceived need to catch up technologically and economically with our competitors abroad. The National Defense Education Act (NDEA) of 1958, providing aid to schools for improvements in science, mathematics, and languages, and offering loans to college students, was passed largely in reaction to the Soviet Union's launching of the first space satellite the previous year. In the 1960s economists began to develop arguments for education as an investment in "human capital," giving part of the rationale for the passage of the ESEA in 1965 and the Basic Educational Opportunity Grant (BEOG) program in 1972; the latter awarded grants to college students.

In the 1980s, the United States began to fall behind other nations such as Japan and Germany in economic growth and technological development, the need to keep up with international competition became a major impetus for school reform. In a wave of critical reports issued early in the decade, schools were urged to promote "excellence" to prepare students as a high-quality labor force capable of adjusting to the demands of a postindustrial society. Heavy emphasis was placed on improvement in basic skills along with the development of computer literacy. The use of standardized achievement tests to measure both teachers' and students' proficiency became even more widespread than it had always been.

Not everyone has accepted the linkage between education and economics. First of all, no concrete evidence exists that investment in schooling is actually repaid by economic expansion. Second, high technology seems to have lost its promise as a mainstay of continued economic prosperity in the United States. Finally, many educators object to the idea of connecting the direction of public education to that of the market economy, fearing excessive control of the schools by business and excessive vocationalization of the curriculum.

Race and Gender in Public Education

The United States is, of course, a heterogeneous society. Inevitably, the schools have to confront the issue of how to develop educational programs that serve the needs of a diverse population, and how to resolve the conflicts arising over that issue.

Segregation and Integration. In 1842 the New York State legislature established a publicly funded, publicly controlled school system in New York City and rejected a demand from the Roman Catholic church that its separate schools receive a share of state money. Catholics had separated themselves educationally in reaction to the implicit Protestantism of the quasi-public nonsectarian schools then in existence. The state's response was a system of public education genuinely free of any religious ties. This was one of the first attempts to deal with the issue of public education in a multicultural, multiracial society. That issue has gained in importance and contentiousness ever since. Race, of course, has been at the center of the greatest controversy.

Slaves received no formal education; in fact, most slave states made it a crime to teach them to read. Free blacks in the North and South attended segregated schools. After the Civil War, despite efforts at integration, the southern states ultimately imposed racial segregation by law in all public facilities, including schools. In 1896, the U.S. Supreme Court, ruling on the constitutionality of laws segregating railroad cars in Louisiana, determined that "separate but equal" arrangements in public facilities were consistent with the Constitution, even though in fact segregated facilities were far from "equal." This case, *Plessy v. Ferguson*, allowed states and localities to enact "Jim Crow" laws segregating all public facilities.

All this started to change in 1954, when the Supreme Court, using psychological evidence as its rationale, unanimously reversed itself in the decision known as *Brown v. Board of Education of Topeka, Kansas*. The court declared that separate was inherently unequal, and one year later called for "all deliberate speed" in implementing desegregation. This was followed by rulings requiring busing of students, in the North and South, in all cities with school systems which were segregated, even if not by law. Most cities integrated peacefully, though with notable exceptions such as Boston in 1974.

The struggle for integration is far from over. During the 1980s and 1990s a more conservative Supreme Court reduced pressure on localities to pursue school integration. Southern schools have become more integrated, but schools in the northeastern and north central states are now more segregated than ever. This appears to be largely a consequence of "white flight" from urban public schools. The question still remains whether the schools can be used as a means of dealing with racial conflict.

As a result of the civil rights movement in the 1960s, African-Americans and Hispanics developed a stronger awareness of their history and culture, which had previously been ignored or suppressed by the white majority. Similarly, the feminist movement created a consciousness among women that their position and choices in life were severely limited by a male-dominated society. Insofar as the schools were an instrument of socializing children and shaping their economic future, it was argued that they reflected the goals and values of the dominant groups and ignored those of minorities and women. As a result, there has been increasing pressure on the schools to eliminate what is seen as sexism and racism from the curriculum. One of the demands has been for a "multicultural" approach to education, which recognizes that American society is a combination of diverse racial and ethnic cultural components and therefore structures the curriculum in that spirit. This has met with strong resistance from most conservatives, who see the schools as a means of establishing a common set of "American" values, and who attack multiculturalism as divisive and academically substandard.

There has been a similarly long conflict over issues of gender equality in the public schools. Not until early in the twentieth century were young women present in any numbers in the public high schools. Until the 1970s, it was a common practice to "track" them into particular vocational paths, such as clerical work or home economics. Numerous studies have indicated discriminatory and unequal treatment in the classroom based on gender. Such issues have by no means been resolved, and the struggle to guarantee equal educational opportunities for both sexes has continued until the present day.

In dealing with educational policy, then, states and localities handle intense conflicts over basic social and economic values. Given the fragmented structure of educational decision-making in the United States, this is a particularly serious problem. It is made no easier by the fact that there are widely different perspectives among Americans on the nature of proper solutions. An examination and evaluation of those perspectives is therefore critical.

Public Higher Education

Higher education presents a somewhat similar set of issues. State colleges and universities depend largely on the state government budget. They are supported by general revenues paid to the state, along with various federal grants. Tuition is merely a user fee that generally goes into the state's general fund and is not usually applied to the maintenance of a particular campus. Thus state legislatures directly shape public higher education by exerting financial control, and in recent years this has meant trouble for public colleges and universities in many states.

Historical Development. The first American public institution of higher education in the modern sense was the University of Virginia, founded in 1825 as the result of a long struggle led by Thomas Jefferson. The real growth of public higher education came after the Civil War; it was shaped largely by what were perceived to be the needs of economic growth. The Morrill Act of 1862 granted federal lands to states for the financing of colleges and universities, primarily to promote teaching in "agriculture and the mechanic arts." Eastern states used the money to subsidize private colleges such as Cornell, Brown, and Dartmouth; in the South and West, the public institutions were the beneficiaries.

The massive expansion of public higher education after the Second World War was paid for by educational benefits to veterans and prompted by the need for more skilled professionals in an expanding job market. The NDEA, providing loans for college students, aimed specifically at improvements in science, math, foreign languages, and other areas related to economic and military needs. In the 1980s the ostensible need for development of skills in high technology has often been cited as the rationale for the survival of public higher education in a time of fiscal stringency. This direction, of course, comes into conflict with the idea that higher education should primarily promote individual intellectual development rather than simply vocational skills.

Financial Prospects for Higher Education. The ideology of growth, combined with a prosperous economy and public demand, led states to increase their funding for public higher education from $600 million in 1950 to over $12 billion in 1975. Enrollment doubled and redoubled during that period. After 1975, however, economic stagnation and the accompanying fiscal crisis, as well as a decreasingly activist student population, led to budget cuts in public higher education, especially in the Northeast and Midwest. The political strength of private colleges and universities in those areas, however, has resulted in continued state support for their survival. Budgetary support for public higher education is therefore weakest in the northeastern states, and considerably stronger in the South, Midwest, and West. Further reductions in support in the late 1980s have of course shifted the cost to the students. Average tuition in four-year public colleges increased from $1,935 in 1976 to almost $5,000 in 1989 (U.S. Department of Education 1991, 296).

The federal government has reduced its role in higher education, as it has in elementary and secondary education. In 1972, in addition to the NDEA loan program, the federal government began aiding college students directly under the BEOG program (later known as Pell grants) and with the guaranteed student loan program, which subsidized interest costs on private bank loans to college students. By 1981, 2.6 million students shared $2.4 billion in grants, and 3.5 million students had borrowed nearly $8 billion (U.S. Department of Commerce 1984, 166). However, both programs came in for tighter regulations, restricted eligibility, higher interest rates, and funding cutbacks under the Reagan administration, along with a greater reliance on loans rather than grants.

It should be added that the issue of multicultural education has created even fiercer conflicts on college campuses than it has in elementary and high schools, as traditionalists defend the European-oriented "canon" of knowledge they feel all students should master against demands from multiculturalists for heterogeneity and diversity. Thus, the questions that have been raised about elementary and secondary education apply, in a somewhat different form, to higher education as well.

Ideology and Educational Policy

In the spring of 1983, nationwide media attention was given to a report by the National Commission on Excellence in Education. Entitled *A Nation at Risk*, it concluded that "the educational foundations of our society are presently being eroded by a rising tide of mediocrity that threatens our very future as a nation and a people. . . . If an unfriendly foreign power had attempted to impose on America the mediocre educational performance that exists today, we might well have viewed it as an act of war."

The report struck a chord with state and local officials who shared these sentiments, and who were already formulating agendas to improve the educational system. For the next three years, a tidal wave of reform swept over the public schools. By the end of 1983, over 100 formal state commissions had been established to develop programs for improving the schools. By 1986, forty-three states had raised graduation requirements, thirty-seven had instituted statewide assessment testing of students, twenty-nine had imposed mandatory competency tests for teachers, and eighteen states had increased teachers' salaries (Hill 1989, 50–55). In contrast to the emphasis on equal opportunity in the 1960s, which had been a response to political pressure from below, reform in the 1980s was a top-down process, often initiated by state governors, which stressed standards and "excellence." This has continued at a somewhat slower pace in the 1990s.

The question is, however, whether this flurry of activity had any real meaning. Movements for school reform had surged and ebbed many times before, usually having only limited effects on the schools. The educational system seemed to frustrate efforts at comprehensive change, and by the end of the decade many observers were drawing the same conclusion in regard to the ambitious goals of the newest generation of reformers. In 1990, a Gallup poll indicated that 51 percent of all parents of children attending public school graded their local schools "C" or below; 36 percent saw no improvement since 1985, and 30 percent felt the schools had gotten worse (Elam 1990, 41–55).

If the schools are really such failures, the problem may lie in the whole structure of the system, which none of the recent reforms addressed. Conservatives and socialists are particularly emphatic on this point. Conservatives see widespread mediocrity and stagnation, blaming the government's monopoly of educational services for stifling incentive and competition. They propose to apply market principles of consumer choice to the educational system. Socialists accuse the schools of deliberately perpetuating social and economic inequality and advocate, among other things, fiscal equalization, greater public control, and an end to tracking. Liberals tend to be less critical, calling for more federal action to maintain what they see as the balance between two conflicting educational goals: equality and efficiency.

Conservative Approach

Support for policies that expand freedom of choice in the school system comes from several different camps, not all of which consider themselves conservative in all respects. This confusing situation requires some explanation.

Conservatives usually criticize public education for its inefficiency in terms of productivity. Supposedly, the measurable economic benefits produced by the schools are not sufficient to justify the cost to the taxpayer. This kind of analysis, often quantified in terms of national economic growth, leads to a focus on how well the schools provide an incentive for educational excellence. Conservatives point out that students are assigned to schools owned and controlled by the government, which receive no reward for spending less than their allotted annual budget, whose teachers are tenured and paid according to seniority, and whose curriculum is prescribed by the bureaucracy. Under such circumstances, there is simply no reason for administrators, teachers, or students to excel. Mediocrity is the natural product of an environment where there is no competition or incentive for merit. This is, as conservatives emphasize, what can be expected of a public bureaucracy.

A different but related kind of argument came from a group of educational historians known as "revisionists," who, writing mostly during the 1970s, applied elite theory to the politics of education: "The educational state that emerged in twentieth century America did so ultimately as an instrument of those political and economic elites who managed the American corporate state" (Karier 1973, 6). The schools are "sorting machines" that create a smooth-running labor market and repress social conflict. The culprit is government control of the schools; the result is, again, mediocrity, stagnation, waste, and repression of individual freedom. Although revisionists do not always refer to themselves as conservatives, their arguments converge with those of conservatives in laying the blame on government and seeing the solution in freedom of choice.

More recently, some of the strongest advocates of using computers in the schools have taken the position that conventional public schools are technologically obsolete. Seymour Papert, for example, compares American public schools with the highly bureaucratized and inflexible economic system of the former Soviet Union and calls for a radical transformation along the lines proposed by conservatives (1993, chap. 10).

The most thorough change advanced for the public schools by conservatives is the voucher system. Milton Friedman's plan, proposed in the 1960s, is the original. To put it simply, each family would receive a voucher for an amount of money from the state, financed by tax revenue, which it could take to the school of its choice to pay for its children's education. Public schools would have to finance themselves on this basis in competition with each other and with private schools that chose to accept vouchers. The ultimate result would be a free market in education. Schools would survive only if they could attract enough vouchers. They would thus be forced to satisfy educational consumers at the lowest possible cost. Friedman argues this would make the schools more responsive, more efficient, and probably more integrated than they are now, and competition would enhance academic excellence. The possibility of making choices would stimulate greater interest in the schools (Friedman and Friedman 1980, chap. 6). Several variations of this proposal exist. Friedman would allow schools to charge more than the vouchers; other advocates of vouchers have proposed limiting or prohibiting additional charges, or even different voucher amounts for different kinds of families.

In the short run, conservatives favor quantitative and monetary ways of measuring and enforcing higher standards in the public schools, not unlike the reforms of the early 1980s. Tuition tax credits, which would reduce the tax bill of people who are paying tuition to a private school, have been strongly promoted by conservatives, particularly for higher education. In 1997, Congress passed and President Clinton signed tax reform legislation that provided credits up to $1,500 annually for families with children attending college.

No state or locality has imposed a full-fledged voucher plan or even tax credits. Minnesota, however, has a statewide "open enrollment" program, and Massachusetts has adopted programs allowing limited choice by families among schools in their own or neighboring communities. Many states have passed laws permitting the establishment of "charter schools," which, as the name implies, are privately run schools that receive public funds in exchange for an agreement with the state or local government—the "charter"—that defines the school's structure and purposes. A few communities, such as Baltimore and Hartford, have attempted full-scale privatization of their schools by hiring an outside firm to run them. These experiments have quickly failed, although Chelsea, Massachusetts, has had its schools under the control of Boston University since 1990. If fiscal crises continue and schools do not improve significantly, we can expect to see an expansion of such programs to relieve states and localities of the burden of educational finance.

Liberal Approach

Liberals reject the conservatives' assumptions about the purpose and outcome of public education. In the first place, according to liberals, schools have not done such a bad job:

> Despite its flaws and setbacks, American education has been remarkably successful in giving a high measure of social and political cohesion to a diverse population without any common ethnic or historic heritage. If schools have failed to wipe out poverty and eliminate conflicts of wealth and status, they nevertheless prevented those social and economic strata from becoming frozen. Education may not have emerged as the "great equalizer" envisioned by Horace Mann, but American education, more than any other force, has kept society fluid and upwardly mobile. (Hechinger and Hechinger 1975, 408–409)

Furthermore, the schools have no single elite-determined function, as the revisionists assert. According to educational historian Diane Ravitch, the schools reflect liberal ideas:

> Liberal democracy, in the modern era, has been posited on the belief that equality must be balanced with liberty and efficiency, and that none of these values should be jeopardized by the others. . . . Education in a liberal society must sustain and hold in balance ideals that coexist in tension: equality and excellence. (1977, 99, 173)

The free market cannot possibly achieve this balance, so education must be a responsibility of government. Problems and conflicts lie in the difficulty of maintaining it, that is, constructing a public school system that rewards ability without promoting elitism. This calls for action on three fronts: greater equality in school finance, racial integration, and special emphasis on helping educationally deprived groups. Generally, this means more state and, especially, federal involvement. The Elementary and Secondary Education Act and the various compensatory programs of the 1960s such as Head Start are good examples of the liberal agenda for the federal government. Liberals do not advocate a federal takeover of education but rather encourage categorical aid programs targeted at needy populations. Together with greater equalization aid from state governments, this would go a long way toward promoting equity in school finance.

School integration has a variety of rationales. Liberals have focused largely on economic opportunity. Schools with predominantly minority populations, so runs the argument, are not likely to receive necessary funding and staffing from states or localities, whose governments are more responsive to the white middle class. Integration, by involuntary busing if necessary, will guarantee minorities access to the same education offered to whites.

Of course, liberals support integration as a matter of principle as well. A pluralistic society cannot flourish with extensive racial separation. In addition, most liberals support a multicultural curriculum. All this ties into the liberal belief that public schools can act as instruments of social change. In fact, since liberal ideas have been the most influential in the development of public education, schools have always been looked to as a means of solving a tremendous variety of social problems. Of course, they will not always succeed, but from a liberal perspective that is no reason to stop trying.

In a way, much of the current concern with education as a factor contributing to economic growth emerges from the liberal perspective. The concept that schooling develops "human capital" was largely a creation of liberal economists in the 1960s; the economic stagnation of the 1980s and 1990s has revived that argument in the form of advocating greater emphasis on high technology in the curriculum, among other things. Educational reform legislation in the states is thus a somewhat peculiar mixture of these liberal concerns with many conservative proposals.

Socialist Approach

Socialists do not measure the success of a social service in terms of economic productivity; nor do they accept the view of equality and efficiency as goals that need to be balanced. From a socialist point of view, if efficiency means the smooth functioning of capitalism, then efficiency is undesirable. Socialists do not accept the revisionist idea that the schools are merely instruments of the elite. However, they do agree that schools try to classify people into occupational slots, not on the basis of ability but by race, class, and gender and on the basis of inherent biases of most middle-class professionals and the standardized examinations they favor. Socialists are particularly critical of the reforms of the 1980s, arguing that these have sacrificed even the pretense of equality in favor of serving the needs of corporate capitalism for a docile labor force.

John Dewey (1859–1952), perhaps the most important American educational theorist, was a self-described socialist. He argued for a system of education that would promote democratic citizenship and social improvement. In his view, the curriculum should be "student-centered," directly related to community life, and explicitly designed to enable young people to participate in building a political and economic democracy in the United States. His followers attempted to implement his ideas, however imperfectly, in what were known as "progressive education" programs. These were quite popular in the 1930s and 1940s, but died out in the following decades partly as a result of conservatives' attacks on what they considered communist ideas. In recent years, Dewey's educational theories, updated to include multiculturalism and democratic governance of the schools, have attracted many new followers. Although most would not call themselves socialist—preferring the label "progressive"—their ideas are consistent with socialist ideology.

As described in *Rethinking Schools,* a journal whose goals are "to promote educational equity [and] support progressive educational values," a modern version of progressive education would include a "multicultural, antiracist, projustice" curriculum "grounded in the lives of our students" which would "equip students to 'talk back' to the world." Traditional classroom practice should be "rethought" to "provoke students to develop their democratic capacities . . . to see themselves as truth-tellers and change-makers." The goal is to create a "hopeful, joyful, kind, visionary" school system that is both academically rigorous and culturally sensitive (Bigelow et al. 1994, 4–5).

A primary target of change in the curriculum would be the tracking system, that is, the involuntary assignment of students to particular educational programs on the basis of standardized tests and professional assessments. Socialists assert that this system is not for the benefit of the student, as often claimed, but for the convenience of an economic system that profits by keeping people in their place. They support their case by pointing to statistics indicating that racial minorities are overrepresented in vocational and other nonacademic tracks, and that white males and students from wealthier families score higher on SATs. Socialists therefore call for an abolition of the tracking system and for changes in curriculum and teaching to develop the ability for independent, critical thinking toward the end of democratic participation in society.

A socialist, or progressive, program for education would therefore promote social equality and democratic participation at the expense of capitalist efficiency. This is possible, to some extent, within the limits of the existing system. Socialists would thus support the liberal goals of financial equalization and racial integration, but they would also stress thorough changes in school governance and curriculum. In terms of the former, greater community involvement with the schools is needed to break up the monopoly of power held by bureaucrats, professionals, and unrepresentative school boards.

Undoubtedly, there would have to be some kind of national coordination of state and local school systems to reach these egalitarian goals. This would require a delicate balance between centralization and decentralization; community involvement would have to go on within the context of a general set of nationwide goals that reflected the public interest rather than corporate interests. Perhaps the socialist program for education can thus be summed up as calling the system's bluff: making it do what liberals say it can do (and indeed what Thomas Jefferson and John Dewey wanted it to do) but what, because of its promotion of capitalist inequality, it has been unable to achieve.

Conclusion

Deteriorating economic conditions appear to have revived government and public concern with the performance of the school system. The focus is on the ability of the schools to develop the skills needed for competition on the world market. High technology has received considerable attention in this regard. Yet clearly, the politics of education runs deeper than that. Conflicts over purpose and direction, governing structure, and finance go back two centuries or more. The central issue is the role of government. Conservatives see government itself as the problem and advocate an educational system based on the model of a market economy. Liberals believe that only governments, especially federal and state governments, can promote equal opportunity in education. Socialists want to change the whole direction of government in its conduct of the school system. The conflicts continue and are not likely to abate.

Bibliography

Aaron, Henry. 1973. *Why Is Welfare So Hard to Reform?* Washington, DC: Brookings.

Adamany, David. 1984. Political Parties in the 1980s. In *Money and Politics in the United States,* ed. Michael Malbin. Chatham, NJ: Chatham House.

Adrian, Charles, and Charles Press. 1977. *Governing Urban America.* New York: Mc-Graw Hill.

Advisory Commission on Intergovernmental Relations. 1981. *Changing Public Attitudes on Government and Taxes.* Washington, DC: ACIR.

————. 1982. *State and Local Roles in the Federal System.* Washington, DC: ACIR.

Alexander, Herbert E. 1992. *Financing Politics.* Washington, DC: Congressional Quarterly.

Alinsky, Saul. 1971. *Rules for Radicals.* New York: Random House.

Ambrosius, Margery M., and Susan Welch. 1988. "State Legislators' Perceptions of Business and Labor Interests." *Legislative Studies Quarterly* 13:199–207.

Aronson, J. Richard, and John Hilley. 1986. *Financing State and Local Governments.* Washington, DC: Brookings.

Banfield, Edward. 1970. *The Unheavenly City.* Boston: Little, Brown.

Barlett, Donald, and James Steele. 1994. *America: Who Really Pays the Taxes?* New York: Simon and Schuster.

Bashi, Vilna I., and Mark A. Hughes. 1997. "Globalization and Residential Segregation by Race." *Annals of the American Academy of Political and Social Science* 551:105–120.

Bell, Charles G. 1986. "Legislatures, Interest Groups, and Lobbyists." *Journal of State Government* 59:12–17.

Bennett, S. E., and David Resnick. 1990. "The Implications of Nonvoting for Democracy in the United States." *American Journal of Political Science* 34:771–807.

Berman, David R. 1992. "State-Local Relations: Mandates, Money, and Partnership." *Municipal Yearbook.* Washington, DC: International City Management Association.

Bernstein, Barton. 1969. The New Deal: The Conservative Achievements of Liberal Reform. In *Towards a New Past,* ed. Barton Bernstein. New York: Vintage.

Beyle, Thad. 1992. *Governors and Hard Times.* Washington, DC: Congressional Quarterly.

———. 1993. "Being Governor." In *The State of the States 1992–1993,* ed. Carl Van Horn. Washington DC: Congressional Quarterly.

———. 1996. "The Cost of Winning." *State Government News,* April.

———. 1997. Introduction. In *State Government: CQ's Guide to Current Issues and Activities 1997–1998.* Washington, DC: Congressional Quarterly.

Biemesderfer, Susan. 1990. "Campaigning Ad Nauseum." *State Legislatures,* September.

Bigelow, Bill, et al. 1994. Creating Classrooms for Equity and Social Justice. In *Rethinking Schools,* ed. Bill Bigelow, et al. Milwaukee: Rethinking Schools.

Bluestone, Barry, and Bennett Harrison. 1982. *The Deindustrialization of America.* New York: Basic.

_____. 1988. *The Great U-Turn.* New York: Basic.

Bradbury, Katherine, et al. 1997. "The Effects of State and Local Public Policies on Economic Development: An Overview." *New England Economic Review,* March–April.

Breckenfeld, Gurney. 1977. "Business Loves the Sunbelt and Vice Versa." *Fortune,* June.

Bryan, Frank, and John McClaughry. 1989. *The Vermont Papers.* Post Mills, VT: Chelsea Green.

Burnham, Walter D. 1982. *The Current Crisis in American Politics.* New York: Oxford.

Busch, Andrew E. 1997. Early Voting: Convenient, But ...? In *State Government: CQ's Guide to Current Issues and Activities 1997–1998,* ed. Thad Beyle. Washington, DC: Congressional Quarterly.

Cadenhead, Gary M., and Robert Farley. 1989. "The Texas Two-Step." *State Legislatures,* March.

Carnegie Commission. 1973. *Higher Education: Who Pays? Who Benefits? Who Should Pay?* New York: McGraw-Hill

Caro, Robert. 1974. *The Power Broker.* New York: Vintage.

Chisman, Forrest P. 1995. "Can the States Do Any Better?" *The Nation,* 1 May.

Choate, Pat, and Susan Walter. 1983. *America in Ruins.* Durham, NC: Duke University.

Citizens for Tax Justice. 1991. *A Far Cry from Fair.* Washington, DC: Citizens for Tax Justice.

Committee for Economic Development. 1976. *Improving Productivity in State and Local Government.* New York: CED.

———. 1979. *Redefining Government's Role in the Market System.* New York: CED.

Commoner, Barry. 1990. *Making Peace with the Planet.* New York: Pantheon.

Conant, James K. 1988. "In the Shadow of Wilson and Brownlow." *Public Administration Review* 48: 892–898.

Congressional Quarterly. 1978. *Urban America: Policies and Problems.* Washington, DC: Congressional Quarterly.

Cotter, Cornelius. 1991. State Party Committees. In *Political Parties and Elections in the United States: An Encyclopedia,* ed. L. S. Maisel. New York: Garland.

Council of State Governments. 1994. *Book of the States 1994–1995.* Lexington, KY: Council of State Governments.

———. 1996. *Book of the States 1996–1997.* Lexington, KY: Council of State Governments.

Dahl, Robert. 1961. *Who Governs?* New Haven, CT: Yale University.

———. 1981. *Democracy in the United States.* Boston: Houghton–Mifflin.

———. 1982. *Dilemmas of Pluralist Democracy.* New Haven, CT: Yale University.

Del Guidice, Michael. 1986. "Mario Cuomo as New York's CEO." *Journal of State Government,* July–August.

DeLuca, Tom. 1995. *The Two Faces of Political Apathy.* Philadelphia: Temple University.

DiNitto, Diana. 1995. *Social Welfare: Politics and Public Policy.* Boston: Allyn and Bacon.

Dolbeare, Kenneth. 1982. *American Public Policy: A Citizen's Guide.* New York: McGraw-Hill.

Domhoff, G. William. 1970. *The Higher Circles.* New York: Vintage.

————. 1978. *The Powers That Be.* New York: Vintage.

————. 1990. *The Power Elite and the State.* New York: Aldine De Gruyter.

Dubin, Elliott. 1992. "Medicaid Reform: Major Trends and Issues." *Intergovernmental Perspective* 18:5–9.

Dye, Thomas R. 1983. *Who's Running America: The Reagan Years.* Englewood Cliffs, NJ: Prentice-Hall.

————. 1990. *American Federalism: Competition Among Governments.* Lexington, MA: Heath.

Dye, Thomas R., and Harmon Zeigler. 1981. *The Irony of Democracy.* Monterey, CA: Duxbury.

Edgar, William J., and Mark Matulef. 1987. "Public Housing: Can We Keep Up What We Have?" *Journal of State Government,* May–June.

Edsall, Thomas B. 1984. *The New Politics of Inequality.* New York: Norton.

Ehrenhalt, Alan. 1992. *The United States of Ambition.* New York: Times Books.

Eichler, Michael. 1995. "Consensus Organizing: Sharing Power to Gain Power." *National Civic Review,* Summer–Fall.

Elam, Stanley. 1990. "The 22nd Annual Gallup Poll of the Public's Attitudes Toward the Public Schools." *Phi Delta Kappan,* September.

Elazar, Daniel. 1984. *American Federalism: A View From the States.* New York: Harper and Row.

―――. 1990. "Opening the Third Century of American Federalism: Issues and Prospects." *Annals of the American Academy of Political and Social Science* 509:1–15.

Entman, Robert. 1983. "The Impact of Ideology on Legislative Behavior and Public Policy in the States." *Journal of Politics* 45:175–190.

Fabricius, Martha. 1991. "More Dictates from the Feds." *State Legislatures,* February.

Fainstein, Norman and Judith. 1978. "National Politics and Urban Development." *Social Problems* 26:125–146.

Fainstein, Susan, et al., eds. 1986, *Restructuring the City.* White Plains, NY: Longman.

Fenton, John. 1966. *Midwest Politics.* New York: Holt.

Ferguson, Thomas, and Joel Rogers. 1986. *Right Turn.* New York: Hill and Wang.

Fisher, Peter S., and Alan H. Peters. 1997. "Tax and Spending Incentives and Enterprise Zones." *New England Economic Review,* March–April.

Fisher, Robert. 1984. *Let the People Decide.* Boston: Twayne.

―――. 1994. "Community Organizing in the Conservative 1980s and Beyond." *Social Policy,* Fall.

Flaningan, William J., and Nancy Zingale. 1979. *The Political Behavior of the American Electorate.* Boston: Allyn and Bacon.

Francis, Wayne L. 1985. "Leadership, Party, Caucuses, and Committees in U.S. State Legislatures." *Legislative Studies Quarterly.* 10:243–257.

Freely, Malcolm. 1983. *Court Reform on Trial.* New York: Basic.

Friedman, Milton and Rose Freidman. 1980. *Free to Choose.* New York: Avon.

Gaebler, Ted, and David Osborne. 1992. *Reinventing Government.* New York: Addison-Wesley.

Gaines, Larry K., Victor Kappeler, and Joseph Vaughn. 1997. *Policing in America.* Cincinnati, OH: Anderson.

Gallagher, Jay. 1989. "New York Leaders Loosen the Reins." *State Legislatures,* November–December.

Garson, G. David, and J. O. Williams. 1982. *Public Administration: Concepts, Readings, Skills.* Boston: Allyn and Bacon.

Gerston, Larry, and Terry Christensen. 1991. *California Politics and Government.* Pacific Grove, CA: Brooks–Cole.

Gerth, H. H., and C. Wright Mills. 1958. *From Max Weber.* New York: Oxford.

Gibson, James, et al. 1985. "Whither the Local Parties?" *American Journal of Political Science* 29:139–156.

Gibson, James, John Frendreis, and Laura Vertz. 1989. "Party Dynamics in the 1980s." *American Journal of Political Science* 33:66–89.

Gillam, Richard, ed. 1971. *Power in Postwar America.* Boston: Little, Brown.

Goetz, Edward. 1994. "Expanding Possibilities in Local Development Policy." *Political Research Quarterly* 27:85–105.

Gold, Steven D. 1991. "A New Twist for State Tax Policy in 1991." *State Legislatures,* December.

_____. 1994. "It's Not a Miracle, It's a Mirage." *State Legislatures,* February.

Goodman, Robert. 1979. *The Last Entrepreneurs.* New York: Simon and Schuster.

Gormley, William T., Jr. 1993. Accountability Battles in State Administration. In *The State of the States,* ed. Carl Van Horn. Washington, DC: Congressional Quarterly.

Gray, Virginia, Herbert Jacob, and Robert Albritton. 1990. *Politics in the American States.* Glenview, IL: Scott-Foresman .

Greenberg, Edward S. 1979. *Understanding Modern Government.* New York: Wiley.

Greer, Edward. 1979. *Big Steel.* New York: Monthly Review.

Greiner, John. 1979. "Motivating Improved Productivity: Three Promising Approaches." *Public Management,* October.

Gurwitt, Rob. 1992. "The Mirage of Campaign Reform." *Governing,* August.

Hale, George, and Marion Palley. 1981. *The Politics of Federal Grants.* Washington, DC: Congressional Quarterly.

Halpern, Robert. 1995. *Rebuilding the Inner City.* New York: Columbia University.

Hansen, Karen. 1997. "Term Limits for Better or Worse." *State Legislatures,* July–August.

Harrigan, John, 1981. *Political Change in the Metropolis.* Boston: Little, Brown.

Harrington, Michael. 1989. *Socialism: Past and Future.* New York: Plume.

Harris, James W. 1990. "Third Parties Out." *The Nation,* 12 November.

Hayes, Edward C. 1972. *Power Structure and Urban Policy.* New York: McGraw-Hill.

Hechinger, Fred and Grace Hechinger. 1975. *Growing Up in America.* New York: McGraw-Hill.

Herzberg, Donald G., and Jess Unruh. 1970. *Essays on the State Legislative Process.* New York: Holt, Rinehart, and Winston.

Hill, David. 1989. "Fixing the System from the Top Down." *Teacher Magazine,* September–October.

Hill, Richard C. 1986. "Crisis in the Motor City." In *Restructuring the City,* eds. Susan Fainstein et al. White Plains, NY: Longman.

Hosansky, David. 1995. "The Other War Over Mandates." *Governing,* April.

Hunter, Floyd. 1963. *Community Power Structure.* New York: Anchor.

Hunter, Kenneth, Laura Ann Wilson, and Gregory Brunk. 1991. "Societal Complexity and Interest Group Lobbying in the States." *Journal of Politics* 53:488–503.

Hutchinson, Tony. 1990. "The Medicaid Budget Tangle." *State Legislatures,* March.

_____. 1991. "The Medicaid Budget Bust." *State Legislatures,* June.

Imbroscio, David L. 1995. "Nontraditional Public Enterprise as Local Economic Development Policy." *Policy Studies Journal* 23:218–227.

International City Management Association. 1990. *Municipal Yearbook 1990.* Washington, DC: ICMA.

Jewell, Malcolm. 1982. *Representation in the State Legislatures.* Lexington, KY: University of Kentucky.

————. 1989 "The Durability of Leadership." *State Legislatures,* November-December.

Jewell, Malcolm, and Samuel C. Patterson. 1977. *The Legislative Process in the United States.* New York: Random House.

Jones, Rich. 1990. "The Legislature 2010: Which Direction?" *State Legislatures,* July.

Judd, Dennis. 1979, 1984. *The Politics of American Cities.* Boston: Little, Brown.

Kantor, Paul. 1988. *The Dependent City.* Glenview, IL: Scott-Foresman.

Karier, Clarence, ed. 1973. *The Roots of Crisis: American Education in the Twentieth Century.* Chicago: Rand McNally.

Key, V. O. 1956. *American State Politics.* New York: Knopf.

Kling, Joseph, and Prudence Posner. 1989. *Dilemmas of Activism.* Philadelphia: Temple University.

Kotelchuk, David, ed. 1976. *Prognosis Negative.* New York: Vintage.

Kozol, Jonathan. 1991. *Savage Inequalities.* New York: Crown.

Lamare, James W. 1981. *Texas Politics.* Saint Paul, MN: West.

Levitan, Donald, and E. E. Mariner. 1980 *Your Massachusetts Government.* Newton, MA: Government Research.

Levitan, Sar. 1982. *Programs in Aid of the Poor for the 1980s.* Baltimore, MD: Johns Hopkins University.

Lindblom, Charles. 1980. *The Policy-Making Process.* Englewood Cliffs, NJ: Prentice-Hall.

Lockard, Duane. 1966. The State Legislator. In *State Legislatures in American Politics,* ed. Alexander Heard. Englewood Cliffs, NJ: Prentice-Hall.

Mahtesian, Charles. 1994. "Romancing the Smokestack." *Governing,* November.

_____. 1997. "The Sick Legislature Syndrome and How to Avoid It." *Governing,* February.

Massey, Douglas S., and Nancy Denton. 1993. *American Apartheid.* Cambridge, MA: Harvard.

McNeely, Dave. 1989. "Last of the Good Old Boys." *State Legislatures,* November.

Michels, Robert. 1962. *Political Parties.* New York: Collier.

Mills, C. Wright. 1956. *The Power Elite.* New York: Oxford.

Moore, W. John. 1988. "Election Day Lawmaking." *National Journal,* 17 September.

Morenoff, Jeffrey D., and Marta Tienda. 1997. "Underclass Neighborhoods in Temporal and Ecological Perspectives." *Annals of the American Academy of Political and Social Science* 551: 59–72.

Morlan, Robert. 1984. "Municipal vs. National Election Voter Turnout: Europe and the U.S." *Political Science Quarterly* 99:457–470.

Murray, Charles A. 1982. "Two Wars Against Poverty: Economic Growth and the Great Society." *Public Interest,* Fall.

Nathan, Richard P., and Fred Doolittle. 1987. *Reagan and the States.* Princeton, NJ: Princeton.

Nathan, Richard P., and Mary M. Nathan. 1979. *America's Governments.* New York: Wiley.

Nenno, Mary K. 1987. "States Respond to Changing Housing Needs." *Journal of State Government,* May–June.

Neubauer, David. 1979. *America's Courts and the Criminal Justice System.* N. Scituate, MA: Duxbury.

Newfield, Jack, and Paul DuBrul. 1977. *The Abuse of Power.* New York: Penguin.

Nye, Russell. 1959. *Midwest Progressive Politics.* E. Lansing, MI: Michigan State.

O'Connor, James. 1972. *The Fiscal Crisis of the State.* New York: St. Martin's.

Okun, Arthur. 1977. Equality and Efficiency: The Big Tradeoff. In *Political Economy: An Urban Perspective,* ed. David M. Gordon. Lexington, MA: Heath.

Olson, Mancur, Jr. 1965. *The Logic of Collective Action.* New York: Schocken.

O'Neill, Tip. 1987. *Man of the House.* New York: Random House.

Ostrom, Vincent, Eleanor Ostrom, and Robert Bish. 1988. *Local Government in the United States.* San Francisco: Institute for Contemporary Studies.

Owens, John, Edward Constantin, and Louis Weschler. 1970. *California Politics and Parties.* New York: Macmillan.

Paddock, Richard C. 1989. "A Speaker of Prominence." *State Legislatures,* November–December.

Paglin, Morton. 1980. *Poverty and Transfers In-Kind.* Palo Alto, CA: Hoover Institution.

Papert, Seymour. 1993. *The Childrens' Machine.* New York: Basic.

Parenti, Michael. 1980, 1988. *Democracy for the Few.* New York: St. Martin's.

Paterson, Andrea. 1986, "Is the Citizen Legislator Becoming Extinct?" *State Legislatures,* July.

Patterson, Samuel C. 1993. The Persistence of State Parties. In *The State of the States,* ed. Carl Van Horn. Washington, DC: Congressional Quarterly.

Patterson, Samuel C., and Gregory A. Caldeira. 1983. "Getting Out the Vote: Participation in Gubernatorial Elections." *American Political Science Review* 77: 675–689.

Pechman, Joseph A. 1985. *Who Paid the Taxes 1966–1985?* Washington, DC: Brookings.

Perkinson, Henry J. 1968. *The Imperfect Panacea: American Faith in Education 1865-1965.* New York: Random House.

―――. 1976. *Two Hundred Years of American Educational Thought.* New York: McKay.

Perlman, Robert. 1984. Alinsky Starts a Fight. In *Community Organizers,* ed. Joan Ecklein. New York: Wiley.

Persico, Joseph E. 1982. *The Imperial Rockefeller.* New York: Simon and Schuster.

Persinos, John F. 1994. "Has the Christian Right Taken Over the Republican Party?" *Campaigns and Elections,* September.

Peterson, John E. 1996. "Municipal Bond Market: The Post-Orange County Era." *Governing,* November.

Peterson, Paul. 1981. *City Limits.* Chicago: University of Chicago.

Piven, Frances, and Richard Cloward. 1971. *Regulating the Poor.* New York: Vintage.

————. 1979. *Poor Peoples' Movements.* New York: Vintage.

————. 1988. *Why Americans Don't Vote.* New York: Pantheon.

Plotkin, Sidney. 1987. *Keep Out: The Struggle for Land Use Control.* Berkeley: University of California.

Plotkin, Sidney, and William Scheuerman. 1994. *Private Interest, Public Spending.* Boston: South End.

Raimondo, Henry J. 1993. *Economics of State and Local Government.* New York: Praeger.

Ravitch, Diane. 1977. *The Revisionists Revised.* New York: Basic.

Ray, David. 1982. "Sources of Voting in Three State Legislatures." *Journal of Politics* 44:1074–1087.

Reagan, Michael, and John Sanzone. 1981. *The New Federalism.* New York: Oxford.

Reid, Sue Titus. 1982. *Crime and Criminology.* New York: Harper and Row.

Reiman, Jeffrey. 1995. *And the Poor Get Prison.* Boston: Allyn and Bacon.

Reiter, Howard. 1984. *Parties and Elections in Corporate America.* New York: St. Martin's.

Riche, Richard W., et al. 1983. "High Technology Today and Tomorrow." *Monthly Labor Review,* November.

Robertson, David, and Dennis Judd. 1989. *The Development of American Public Policy.* Glenview, IL: Scott-Foresman.

Rosen, Corey. 1974. "Legislative Influence and Policy Orentation." *American Journal of Political Science* 18:685–695.

Rosenthal, Alan. 1981. *Legislative Life.* New York: Harper and Row.

———. 1986a. "The Consequences of Constituency Service." *Journal of State Government,* Spring.

———. 1986b. "The New Legislature: Better or Worse and For Whom?" *State Legislatures,* July.

———. 1991. *Governors and Legislators: Contending Powers.* Washington, DC: Congressional Quarterly.

———. 1993. *The Third House: Lobbyists and Lobbying in the States.* Washington, DC: Congressional Quarterly.

———. 1995. "Sloppy Democracy." *State Government News,* January.

Rusk, David. 1994. "Bend or Die." *State Government News,* February.

Sabato, Larry. 1983. *Goodbye to Goodtime Charlie.* Washington, DC: Congressional Quarterly.

Silver, Hilary, and Dudley Burton. 1986. "The Politics of State Level Industrial Policy." *Journal of the American Planning Association* 52:277–288.

Simon, Lucinda. 1986. "The Mighty Incumbent." *State Legislatures,* July.

———. 1989. "The Vocabulary of Business Speaks to Both Branches." *State Legislatures,* March.

Singer, Sandra. 1988. "The Arms Race of Campaign Financing." *State Legislatures,* July.

Smith, Donald. 1979. The Public Balance Sheet. In *Developing the Public Economy,* eds. Pat McGuigan and Bob Schaefer. Cambridge, MA: Policy Training Center.

Smith, Michael P. 1989. The Use of Linked-Development Policies in U.S. Cities. In *Regenerating the Cities,* eds. Michael Parkinson et al. Glenview, IL: Scott Foresman.

Snell, Ronald. 1991a. "Paying for Paving the Way." *State Legislatures,* June.

————. 1991b. "The Tax the Public Loves to Hate." *State Legislatures,* December.

Stanfield, Rochelle. 1996. "The Reverse Commute." *National Journal,* 23 November.

Stanley, Harold, and Richard Niemi. 1994. *Vital Statistics in American Politics.* Washington, DC: Congressional Quarterly.

Stone, Michael, and Chester Hartman. 1997. Housing: Reconstructing the Federal Government's Role and Responsibilities. In *The National Government and Social Welfare,* eds. John Hansan and Robert Morris. Westport, CT: Auburn House.

Stumpf, Harry P., and John Culver. 1992. *The Politics of State Courts.* New York: Longman.

Sweezy, Paul, and Harry Magdoff. 1983. *The Deepening Crisis of U.S. Capitalism.* New York: Monthly Review.

Teaford, Jon. 1979. *City and Suburb.* Baltimore: Johns Hopkins.

Teixeira, Ruy. 1992. *The Disappearing American Voter.* Washington, DC: Brookings.

Thomas, G. S. 1991. "America's Hottest Counties." *American Demographics,* September.

Tipps, Dean, and Lee Webb. 1980. Taxes: How They Were. In *State and Local Tax Revolt,* ed. Conference on Alternative State and Local Policies. Washington DC: CASLP.

U.S. Department of Commerce. 1984. *Statistical Abstract of the United States, 1984*. Washington, DC: U.S. Government Printing Office.

———. 1993. *Statistical Abstract of the United States, 1993*. Washington, DC: U.S. Government Printing Office.

———. 1997. *Statistical Abstract of the United States, 1997*. Washington, DC: U.S. Government Printing Office.

———. Bureau of the Census. 1993. *The Earnings Ladder*. Washington, DC: U.S. Government Printing Office.

U.S. Department of Education. 1991. *Digest of Education Statistics*. Washington, DC: U.S. Government Printing Office.

——— . National Commission on Education Statistics. 1996. *Statistics in Brief*. Washington, DC: U.S. Government Printing Office.

U.S. Department of Health and Human Services. 1990. *Health Care Financing: Program Statistics*. Washington, DC: U.S. Government Printing Office.

U.S. Department of Labor. 1990. *Handbook of Labor Statistics*. Washington, DC: U.S. Government Printing Office.

U.S. Federal Election Commission. 1995. *Ballot Access*. Washington, DC: U.S. Government Printing Office.

Uslaner, Eric, and Ronald Weber. 1979. "U.S. State Legislators' Opinions and Perceptions of Constituency Attitudes." *Legislative Studies Quarterly* 4:570–580.

Van Geel, Tyl. 1976, *Authority to Control the School Program*. Lexington, MA: Heath.

Walker, David. 1981. "American Federalisms: Past, Present, and Future." *Journal of State Government*, January–February.

_____. 1989. *Toward a Functioning Federalism.* Cambridge, MA: Winthrop.

Warf, Barney, and Brian Holly. 1997. "The Rise and Fall of Cleveland." *Annals of the American Academcy of Political and Social Science* 551:208–221.

Weberg, Brian. 1988. "The Coming of Age of Legislative Staffs." *State Legislatures,* August.

Weiher, Gregory. 1991. *The Fractured Metropolis.* Albany, NY: State University of New York.

Welch, David. 1989. "Lobbyists, Lobbyists, All Over the Lot." *State Legislatures,* February.

Wellstone, Paul. 1978. *How the Rural Poor Got Power.* Amherst: University of Massachusetts.

Welter, Rush. 1962. *Popular Education and Democratic Thought in America.* New York: Columbia University.

Whitman, Max. 1992. "Improving the Infrastructure and Protecting the Environment." *Intergovernmental Perspectives,* Summer.

Wikstrom, Nelson. 1978. "Metropolitan Government Consolidation." *Growth and Change,* January.

Wilson, David. 1997. "Preface: Globalization and the Changing City." *Annals of the American Academy of Political and Social Science* 551:8–16.

Wright, Deil S. et al. 1991. "The Evolving Profile of State Administrators." *Journal of State Government,* January–March.

Yates, Douglas. 1979. *The Ungovernable City.* Cambridge: Massachusetts Institute of Technology.

Index